CRISIS ON MOUNT HOOD

CRISIS ON MOUNT HOOD

STORIES FROM
100 YEARS OF
MOUNTAIN RESCUE

CHRISTOPHER VAN TILBURG

MOUNTAINEERS
BOOKS

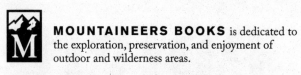

MOUNTAINEERS BOOKS is dedicated to the exploration, preservation, and enjoyment of outdoor and wilderness areas.

1001 SW Klickitat Way, Suite 201, Seattle, WA 98134
800-553-4453, www.mountaineersbooks.org

Printed in Canada

28 27 26 25   1 2 3 4 5

Design and layout: Jen Grable
Cartographer: Erin Greb Cartography

Front cover photographs: Top: *Aerial view of Mount Hood with snow in late winter* (Skyhobo/iStock); Bottom: *Crag Rats traversing a steep glacier using a hemp rope, circa 1930s* (Hood River Crag Rats Collection)
Back cover photograph: *The author training for mountain rescue on a cliff near Cloud Cap Inn* (Corey Arnold)

Library of Congress Cataloging-in-Publication data is on file for this title at https://lccn.loc.gov/2024049541

Mountaineers Books titles may be purchased for corporate, educational, or other promotional sales, and our authors are available for a wide range of events. For information on special discounts or booking an author, contact our customer service at 800-553-4453 or mbooks@mountaineersbooks.org.

Printed on FSC-certified and 100% recycled materials

ISBN (paperback): 978-1-68051-714-9
ISBN (ebook): 978-1-68051-715-6

MIX
Paper | Supporting responsible forestry
FSC
www.fsc.org
FSC® C016245

An independent nonprofit publisher since 1960

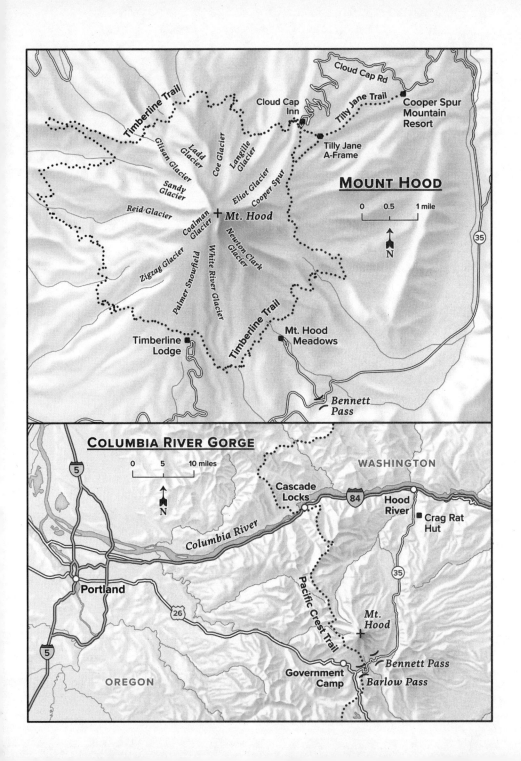

Cloud Cap Rd

Timberline Trail

Cloud Cap Inn

Tilly Jane Trail

Cooper Spur Mountain Resort

Glisan Glacier
Ladd Glacier
Coe Glacier
Langille Glacier
Sandy Glacier
Eliot Glacier
Cooper Spur

Tilly Jane A-Frame

MOUNT HOOD

0   0.5   1 mile

N

Reid Glacier

Coalman Glacier

+ Mt. Hood

Newton Clark Glacier

Zigzag Glacier

Palmer Snowfield

White River Glacier

35

Timberline Lodge

Mt. Hood Meadows

Timberline Trail

Bennett Pass

COLUMBIA RIVER GORGE

0   5   10 miles

N

5

WASHINGTON

Cascade Locks

84

Hood River

Crag Rat Hut

Columbia River

Portland

Pacific Crest Trail

35

26

Mt. Hood

+

5

Government Camp

Bennett Pass

Barlow Pass

OREGON

CONTENTS

PART I: WINTER
THE SAINT BERNARDS OF NORTH AMERICA, 1926 TO 1939

PART II: SPRING
MOUNTAIN CLIMBING EXPLODES, 1940 TO 1965

PART III: SUMMER
GROWING UP GEN X, 1966 TO 1999

PART IV: FALL
CONFEDERACY OF THE HIGH ALPINE, 2000 TO PRESENT

AUTHOR'S NOTE

The stories collected here are about real mountain rescue missions and real volunteer rescue mountaineers. However, these tales should not be construed as absolute fact. To protect the privacy of some individuals, identifying details such as gender, locations, dates, times, injuries, and other factors have been changed. In a few chapters, I created composites. The dialogue is not verbatim because it was not recorded and is dependent on my memory. I re-created typical banter to give you a flavor of how the Hood River Crag Rats interact. The history of the Crag Rats was compiled, as best I could, from sometimes detailed and other times patchy archives from the last hundred years—meeting minutes, logbooks, mission reports, scrapbooks of newspaper clips, and newsletters—and interviews with members. However, even reputable sources have conflicting, imprecise, and incomplete information. Additionally, I corroborated historical accounts with the few books that detail alpine rescues and climbing history in the Pacific Northwest.

Search and rescue missions are much more complicated than my singular involvement and perspective. I tried to give catholic representation to the history, the missions, and my friends and colleagues. But ultimately, these are my words only.

PROLOGUE:
CAMPOLONGO PASS, ITALY

E ven when I'm traveling abroad, I can't seem to get away from mountain rescue.

In the middle of September, a bright sunrise lights up the Dolomites in northern Italy. The sky is clear and the air crisp and cold. The smell of cappuccino and croissants greets me. Today I'm taking the day off from teaching a course in wilderness medicine to participate in Sella Day, when the Dolomite community shuts cars out of the famous mountain road around the Sella group, a tight collection of spires of sedimentary carbonate rock. The route, known as the Sellaronda, is utterly spectacular and challenging. In thirty miles, our group pedals five thousand feet up and spins five thousand feet down four passes—Gardena, Sella, Pordoi, and Campolongo—with, by my estimate, about five thousand cyclists from around the world. We can't go very fast because the uphills are steep, and the switchbacked downhills often don't have guardrails. Moreover, the scenery is so stunning that we have to stop often for the beautiful OMG views of the gigantic, jagged dolomite rock spires; the bucolic green valleys speckled with belled cows and iconic South Tyrolean cabins; the bubbling streams down low; and the misting, glacier-fed waterfalls.

We begin at nine o'clock in the morning from the hamlet of Corvara for the first climb, and by two in the afternoon—many laughs, pastries, cappuccinos, and burning legs later—we crest the final pass, where we wait to regroup with our crew. We have only a fifteen-minute downhill cruise back to our hotel.

Kristin, an ER nurse on our team, points to a huddle of spandex-clad riders alongside the road near a church. "Someone is having trouble over there."

"I'll check it out," I say and stride over, pushing my bike across the road. My instinct rarely lets me stand still. I'm an American physician with an eclectic career. Mostly I've focused on emergency and wilderness medicine, but I've worked as a public health officer, a medical examiner, a ski-resort clinic doctor, a medical-relief team leader, an occupational medicine clinician, and an expedition and cruise ship doctor. I've also been a volunteer with the Hood River Crag Rags, a mountain rescue group based at the bottom of Oregon's Mount Hood, for nearly twenty-five years.

Now, I find a man collapsed on the ground, where the bystanders are just starting CPR. A woman at the man's head must have some medical training because she shouts instructions in German and takes the lead with resuscitation. Two cyclists start chest compressions. A fourth gives mouth-to-mouth rescue breaths. Bedecked in my full spandex bike kit, bike shoes, and helmet, I jump into action. I yank off my gloves, check for a pulse, then do compressions for a cycle, pushing hard and fast on the man's chest while the sandpapery asphalt grinds against my knees.

I look at my watch to mark the time, knowing the duration of apnea (no breathing) and pulselessness (no heart function) could be critical for decision-making later.

"Did anyone call?" I ask the woman. This is another instinctive action: call for help.

"Yes, now." She points to another cyclist standing nearby, speaking into a phone.

In a few minutes, a motorcycle rider in a police uniform shows up and pulls an automatic external defibrillator (AED) out of a pannier. We hurriedly unzip the man's cycling jersey to expose his bare skin, slap the sticky pads on his chest, and turn on the machine, which spouts German. I struggle to pick out words familiar from a year of college Deutsch and watch for hand motions. The woman in charge signals for us to stop CPR so the AED can analyze the man's heart rate and rhythm. Everyone holds their hands up. We have a five-second pause, an eerie silence while the AED computes. Then the AED spits out more German, a button is pressed, the machine delivers a shock, and the body jerks on the pavement. We continue chest compressions, and someone continues mouth-to-mouth breathing.

I check for a pulse again—none detected. We stop CPR in a few minutes to let the AED reanalyze: "*Kein Schock,*" it says—no shock. The heart must be in asystole, which means not pumping and with no electrical activity, or pulseless electrical activity, which also means not pumping but with disorganized, ineffective nerve function. If the heart were in ventricular fibrillation, when the heart muscle twitches without pumping blood, or ventricular tachycardia, when the heart muscle contracts so rapidly that it can't pump blood, the AED would deliver a shock.

An ambulance shows up, and two crew members get out. One unzips a big medical kit and provides a breathing mask and bag so we can ventilate without mouth-to-mouth. The other starts assembling a suction device.

"Do we have a breathing tube?" I ask, pointing to the med kit. "I can put it in."

"No, we don't have," the woman in charge says, shaking her head. She compresses the one-liter bag to inflate the man's lungs while I hold the mask tightly to his face—to be most effective, this is a two-person job. Two others continue chest compressions, alternating every two minutes after counting loudly to *dreißig,* thirty. The AED again says, "*Kein Schock.*"

In about five minutes, the patient groans and tries to roll over. I check for a pulse. It's hard to locate, but I feel it weakly on his neck. I yell, "Pulse!" The man gasps for breath, and we stop CPR. I move from kneeling to a squat so I can jump out of the way if he vomits. He attempts to open his eyes, but they roll back underneath his upper eyelids. I watch his breathing, shallow and labored, and continue to monitor his pulse, which becomes increasingly difficult to find.

In less than a minute, I see him stop breathing. I check for a pulse again. "No pulse, not breathing," I say loudly, and everyone understands me.

"Restart CPR," the woman says. We roll him on his back and restart chest compressions and ventilation with the bag and mask.

A few more minutes pass, and he sucks in a breath again, this time more robustly. I feel for a pulse and find one, stronger now. "Pulse." He opens his eyes, then closes them and moans. "He's breathing." This time, the breathing and pulse might sustain life for more than a minute. I check my watch.

"Duration of CPR eighteen minutes," I say. A long time to be apneic and asystolic.

"Good for checking," the woman says, nodding.

The CPR rescuers disperse when they see a helicopter land in a nearby cow pasture. A man gets out and jogs up, carrying a comprehensive advanced life support kit. His red jumpsuit says *Notazrt*, rescue doctor, and I see the logo of Aiut Alpin Dolomites, a helicopter rescue service based in nearby Val Gardena. I tell him, "CPR for eighteen minutes, now ROSC" (return of spontaneous circulation).

The doctor points to the man's arm. "Help me hold," he says.

I pin the patient's arm against the asphalt because he's moaning and moving. The doctor expertly slides an IV catheter into an arm vein and injects propofol to sedate the man and then rocuronium to paralyze his muscles. This allows the doctor to pass the breathing tube into the man's trachea. The lever that moves the tongue and opens the throat is connected to a tiny camera and screen, to make it easier to see where to pass the tube. The sun glares into the screen, so I shield it with my hands.

"It won't go in," the doctor says.

I push down on the patient's neck at the Adam's apple to help open the airway. He has a two-centimeter horizontal scar on his neck, which I suspect is from prior surgery, likely a thyroidectomy. The tube slides past the vocal cords and into the trachea. I hold the tube while a helicopter medic secures it with tape and connects a breathing bag.

For five minutes, I ventilate the patient by squeezing the breathing bag while the doctor and the medic hook up a twelve-lead electrocardiogram machine. The heart tracing shows a fast rate at 120 beats per minute in a disorganized rhythm called atrial fibrillation, in which the top chamber of the heart is not functioning properly but the bottom chamber is still pumping, although not as efficiently as usual. The helicopter team puts on a LUCAS 3, an electronic mechanical CPR machine that looks like a movie prop from *Mad Max*. If the patient's heart stops again, the machine will pump the chest.

We wrap the patient in a vacuum mattress, a bright red vinyl bag filled with tiny polystyrene balls that, when deflated, becomes stiff like a board and lets us more easily transport him. The man is lifted onto a gurney and carried to the ambulance, which will drive him one hundred feet to the waiting helicopter.

"Scar on neck." I point. "Maybe that's why intubation was difficult—prior surgery?"

"I think so," the doctor says. "You have medical training?"

"I'm a mountain rescue doctor from the USA."

He smiles collegially. "Thank you for helping. I needed a ventilator." Then he points to the LUCAS. "How much do these cost back home?"

"About twenty thousand."

"Oh, cheaper in Italy." He smiles. "Thanks for your help."

We shake hands. And then, thirty minutes after the cardiac arrest, the helicopter lifts off and disappears over the Sella group. Just like that, it's over.

THAT EVENING, in my quaint hotel in Selva di Val Gardena, I call my daughters. Skylar, my oldest, and Avrie, who just finished college, thoroughly know my devotion to mountain rescue because they grew up with it: watching me leave our home in the small farming and recreation town of Hood River, Oregon, in the middle of dinner; seeing me come home filthy and exhausted; helping me sort and repack gear. Skylar is inquisitive about the fate of the man, and Avrie is fascinated by the day's events. Neither is surprised. I get comfort by telling them the story, then conscientiously pause on recounting my own adventures to catch up with theirs.

Afterward, I text my mountain rescue team, the Hood River Crag Rats, with a "You'll never guess what happened." My friend and colleague Lisa Rust texts back, "What an experience to add to an already rescue-packed life." She reminds me jokingly that on my last extended trip to Europe, the team had no missions while I was gone.

This time, I'll be away from home for seven weeks. I came to Europe to teach the wilderness medicine seminar in the Dolomites to doctors and nurses. We hike every day and learn patient packaging, assessment, splinting, and treatment for a variety of conditions like acute mountain sickness, hypothermia, frostbite, rabies, malaria, and dislocated shoulders. Next week, I will meet my daughters in the Canary Islands to kitesurf and hike. After that, I'm heading to a remote lagoon in Sicily to learn wing foiling, the latest sport descended from wind-surfing. Finally, I wrap up the adventure back in the Dolomites to attend the International Commission for Alpine Rescue conference as a delegate from America's Mountain Rescue Association. I'll also spend my trip working on this book, which focuses on a singular mountain peak and the extraordinary group of men and women who help guard it.

The inselberg would be Oregon's iconic, gigantic, formidable Mount Hood, the craggy, pointed 11,245-foot-high stratovolcano that sees an estimated ten thousand summit attempts a year—making it likely the most climbed glaciated peak in the world. And this group would be the Hood River Crag Rats, the oldest mountain rescue team in the nation, formed in 1926. After 2022, our busiest year yet, we have become closer, more skilled, and tighter than ever. But we're also *strained*; our all-volunteer crew of forty rescuers and another thirty was pushed to the limit by sixty days of rescues, nearly double our annual average over the past decade. All this, of course, on top of our busy lives and day jobs.

I've worked at Providence Hood River Memorial Hospital nearly my entire time living in Hood River, in various clinical capacities: emergency department, occupational and travel medicine clinic, and the Mountain Clinic at the Mt. Hood Meadows ski resort. Recently, I've begun migrating to medical director positions in a few aspects of the greater organization, Providence St. Joseph Health. And just before the pandemic, I accepted a part-time position for Hood River County as the public health officer and medical examiner.

Additionally, I've worked in a position that gets me exactly zero wages: a volunteer rescue mountaineer with the Crag Rats. A few years ago, I also agreed to serve as medical director for other regional teams: Pacific Northwest Search and Rescue, Clackamas County Search and Rescue, and Portland Mountain Rescue. While all these positions make me seem busy, I have enough time and balance in my life to attend two-thirds of the mountain rescue missions and spend twelve weeks a year abroad teaching, adventuring, guiding, and doctoring.

I grew up with parents who had a strong ethic of volunteering. They were involved in Friendship Force International, a person-to-person exchange program started by Jimmy and Rosalynn Carter. My dad was an orthodontist, and my mom was a nurse, so they also provided dental care on medical missions to underdeveloped countries. By the time I graduated from college, I'd traveled to four continents and realized I like helping people. But more importantly, I knew I was deeply passionate about the outdoors, and that I have to be outside in motion every day—climbing, trail running, cycling, skiing, kitesurfing. It's where I'm most comfortable in the world. It's not a choice but a primal need.

I started writing in high school, covering school sports for the local newspaper. After authoring several books on the outdoors, I penned two mountain rescue memoirs, both centered on Mount Hood. My first, *Mountain Rescue Doctor: Wilderness Medicine in the Extremes of Nature*, covered my early years with the Crag Rats and explained the wondrous, thrilling, burgeoning field of wilderness medicine, a microspeciality for which I was just developing expertise. My second memoir, *Search and Rescue: A Wilderness Doctor's Life-and-Death Tales of Risk and Reward*, was issued a decade later and explored topics that I became acutely cognizant of after becoming a leader in the Crag Rats.

In this, my third memoir, I initially set out to document the gripping, covert, and mysterious history of the Crag Rats. However, I realized—with the help of colleagues, my astute agent, and my sharp editor—that this is not just a story of the nation's oldest mountain rescue team. A deeper, newer, timelier story exists, one that has me troubled, one that supersedes the topics of wilderness medicine and individual risk. Like our team, Mount Hood—just a one-hour drive from the Portland and Vancouver, Washington, metro area, with about 2.5 million people as of 2020—is strained. Increasing crowds, rapidly advancing technology, and changing human interactions are impacting the seracs, crevasses, cliffs, glaciers, canyons, and pinnacles of this peak.

What is happening on our mountain?

We have perennial, omnipresent risks on this volcano. Falling, sharp, and speeding objects like ice daggers, rime rockets, and chunks of basalt and andesite peel off the Steel Cliff—the craggy, ice-clad rim of the summit crater—and pelt climbers, especially in warm conditions. Steep, icy slopes cause "slides for life," when someone slips, falls, is unable to stop, and careens down the mountain, an all-too-common occurrence that has accounted for several fatalities. "Chickenheads," surface globules of rock-hard blue ice shaped by wailing winds and ranging in size from golf balls to basketballs, make climbing and skiing deadly and have claimed several lives as well.

This mountain has holes, big ones: crevasses, bergschrunds, fumaroles, glide cracks—you should understand the difference if you plan to climb this peak. People fall in, and we yard them out. Usually alive and traumatically injured. Sometimes minimally injured. And once or twice a year, deceased.

Let's not forget about avalanches. I've witnessed skier-triggered slides on the Zigzag Glacier near Illumination Rock and the Coalman Glacier, both popular ski destinations on the most popular facet, the south face.

And if that's not enough, one more gargantuan dragon lurks: weather. Unlike continental ranges, Mount Hood is a solo stratovolcano that collects weather like a magnet when marine air blows in from the Pacific Ocean, just over one hundred miles away, and ramps into a storm as quickly as a flash flood. In a whiteout above timberline, no trees exist to provide guidance, so climbers get stuck in the Mount Hood Triangle, a phenomenon in which climbers descending the standard south-side route erroneously downclimb the fall line, which leads them down Zigzag Glacier to Mississippi Head, a sheer andesite cliff at 7,159 feet. Instead, climbers need to follow magnetic south on a compass, a subtle and awkward sidehill that takes them back to the trailhead at 6,000 feet at Timberline Lodge.

But these omnipresent objective hazards don't solely account for the recent uptick in rescues. Why? I believe it's a combination of crowds, modern technology, and modern human behavior.

First, unprecedented numbers of people are climbing, skiing, snowshoeing, and even snow running Mount Hood and exploring the Columbia River Gorge National Scenic Area, an eighty-mile stretch of foothills straddling the river between Oregon and Washington. This surge can be attributed partly to the mountain's proximity to Portland and its accessibility: you can drive on snowplowed pavement to historic Timberline Lodge and to one of the many trailheads in the gorge. We saw an increase in mountain sports over the last decade, but when the COVID-19 pandemic hit, people began flocking to the outdoors in droves—we have no accurate records as to exactly how many, but at least anecdotally, this uptick in usage is apparent. Meanwhile, backcountry skiing and ski mountaineering are two of the fastest-growing segments of the $1-trillion-per-year outdoor-recreation industry, helping fuel the increase in rescues. We've got more people, and more people means more accidents.

A second issue: people flock to the outdoors year-round now, likely a combination of better equipment, better information about climbing conditions, and warmer, clearer weather. Mount Hood is no longer only a spring or summer volcano climb, and the nearby trails in the lowlands of the Columbia River Gorge National Scenic Area are no longer a three-season playground. It's full on, all year long. Even in midwinter on Mount Hood, we see several hundred people on sunny weekend days either climbing to the summit or skiing to ten thousand feet.

A third problem: people adventure into the forest, canyons, and mountains unprepared and ill-equipped. Although this is not necessarily a new problem, it's one that has become more pronounced with the greater numbers of people. I summited Mount Hood six times during the pandemic, and one day in the parking lot I spied a man wearing tights, running shoes with traction spikes, and a ten-liter running vest. He held a tiny aluminum ice axe. Yes, you read that correctly: traction spikes and running shoes! Most mountaineers would agree that this footwear is not adequate for climbing a giant, glaciated volcano.

"Going for the summit?" I asked quizzically.

"Yes," he said, eyeing my jacket bedecked with mountain rescue patches, "but I'll turn around at the Pearly Gates"—a steep, icy couloir guarding the final approach to the summit—"if it looks bad." A cerulean sky and stable snow made it a good summit: I topped out and skied down the Old Chute, a gully adjacent to the Pearly Gates. I later connected with the runner, who'd turned around shy of the Pearly Gates.

Similarly, the technology has changed exponentially, both in terms of recreational outdoor gear and technical rescue equipment. The gear we have now— polyester and nylon clothing, high-tech boots, specialized mountaineering skis, carbon-fiber climbing tools—allows us to get into the backcountry much more quickly and with much less effort than in years past. We can climb higher and faster, using more weatherproof, lighter, and stronger equipment and clothing. Not only do we have phone service in much of the wilderness, but navigation apps that use satellite global positioning make routefinding easier and render obsolete the old-school, more difficult technique of map-and-compass navigation.

Finally, the internet has made the outdoors both safer and more dangerous. A plethora of information exists for trip planning, including real-time telemetry for precipitation, temperature, and wind. I love being able to get firsthand, up-to-date information on route conditions from someone who climbed the mountain that day. When I first climbed Mount Hood in 1995, I had to call the ranger station, where I would maybe or maybe not reach the climbing ranger, who had maybe or maybe not been on the mountain recently. Route conditions were an educated guess based on whatever information we could get. But the internet and social media have downsides. Trip reports on social media may be inaccurate, misrepresentative, or inconsistent. For example, posts describing the Pearly Gates from one of Facebook's mountaineering groups downplayed the technical aspects by saying, "Fun menageries of ice" and "Did my first climb in running shoes and microspikes." Plus, it's no secret that modern media can push risk tolerance. Instant, positive reinforcement comes from the glamor and glory of social media likes.

But we have a deeper issue. One that reveals itself more stealthily than the crowds we can see on sunny spring days, the beeping and buzzing technological devices in our pockets, or the constant bombardment of social media. The mountain itself is changing, albeit gradually, perhaps due in part to the planet's natural rhythms but certainly also because of one all-encompassing factor: humans. We have melting and even disappearing glaciers, clear-cut forests that have been replanted with monoculture, construction of roads and buildings, dammed and otherwise altered streams, and depleting aquifers and reservoirs. Because of the slow and cumulative effects of human impact—namely, climate change—Mount Hood, like the world, is in crisis.

Thus begins this ruminative screed about my beloved Mount Hood and my beloved mountain rescue team, the Crag Rats.

It's true that I'm fascinated with Crag Rats' history and culture. In writing this book, I want to see where we came from, understand the deep-seated passion for volunteer rescue mountaineering, and learn from stalwart leaders of the past, the titans of the craft. But I'm a participant in the present, and I want to document this fantastic and unique group that I am fortunate to call friends and trusted colleagues. I want to capture the esprit de corps, the camaraderie, the friendships, the trials, the risks, the rewards, and the successes in this time of exploding technology, exploding crowds, and exploding new sports. And finally, I'm a prognosticator. I'm curious about the future of the Crag Rats and Mount Hood as we charge forward into the next one hundred years.

AFTER THE CARDIOPULMONARY resuscitation in the Dolomites and a good night's sleep, I have a cappuccino and croissant with my group at our inn in Selva di Val Gardena. After breakfast, I ask our guide to make a few calls on my behalf. She learns that the stricken cyclist was flown to Bolzano and had a procedure, which I surmise was an angiocatheterization to open a blocked cardiac artery. The next morning, he woke up. This one goes in the win column for all of us— the concerned bystanders, the police, the ground ambulance, the flight team, and the hospital crew all worked together to save a life.

I have a brief hour in the morning to reflect on the lifesaving teamwork, then we need to finish our class before I catch a car, train, and flight to meet my daughters. Amid the beautiful yet dangerous crags of the Dolomites, I realize that I will never leave mountain rescue—or Mount Hood. But as I reach sixty years of age the same year the Crag Rats reach one hundred, I understand things will change—the mountain, the Crag Rats, the recreationalists we rescue, and me. Like the team who saved the downed cyclist on Campolongo Pass, I hope we can all work together to save Mount Hood—a peak possibly soon in need of resuscitation—and our ailing world.

PART I
WINTER

THE SAINT BERNARDS OF NORTH AMERICA, 1926 TO 1939

CHAPTER 1

JANUARY: CRISIS ON THE SUMMIT

In the high alpine, the air is clear, cold, and clean—it's invigorating and eye-opening. Because of the frigid air, my lungs fight to inhale the deep breath that my muscles demand. Air—or oxygen, more properly—is, after all, life's most essential necessity, one that without, we can't live for more than four minutes. The crystalline, cloudless, cobalt sky showcases the stark beauty and rugged peacefulness of this mountain. The bright white snow is firm, not too icy to be slippery and not so soft that our skis sink. The sun peeks over the horizon at seven o'clock this winter morning and warms the air in spirit but not in Fahrenheit. This doesn't seem like January, but more like April. But then, nothing seems quite the same anymore on Mount Hood.

We are mountain climbing—or more properly, ski mountaineering— during the middle of a six-week stretch of midwinter high pressure over the Pacific Northwest and Rocky Mountain West. This makes for excellent climbing conditions on the glaciers. But this same long stretch of sun means we have a dearth of snow, a worrisome indication of the changing ecosystem and a sign of the cumulative effects of human impact. The frozen glaciers, bubbling streams, rocky cliffs, and dense forests have indelibly changed over the last century since mountain climbing started as recreation on this peak. Aside from air, water is the next life-sustaining substance. And here today, the most poignant change is water, or lack thereof. Less snow and shrinking glaciers leave less water for irrigation of crops in the spring and less water to fill the aquifers and reservoirs that supply the city. This may not be on the forefront of climbers' minds because we carry the day's water in our backpacks. Nonetheless, this is an omnipresent concern for the orchardists in the valleys below and an obscure concern for the city dwellers. These lifebloods provide sustenance for our journey to the summit but are part of a more complicated, somewhat fragile ecosystem.

My three climbing partners and I are almost to the summit of Mount Hood, Oregon's iconic high point, visible from one hundred miles away on a clear day. The crisp white glacial snowfields juxtapose against the craggy dirt-gray andesite formed from the most recent volcanic major eruption in the 1790s and minor eruptions in the 1860s. We are friends and mountain rescue colleagues climbing this peak for the umpteenth time to ski it. Our backpacks are stocked with limited but highly technical climbing equipment. Our present interest is the snowpack: we have good climbing conditions with firm snow, and, more importantly, in an hour or two we expect excellent skiing conditions when the blazing sun softens the top layer of snow on the south-facing aspects. Today, we're on a half-day outing to tag the summit and ski the Zigzag Glacier, one of the twelve . . . scratch that . . . ten glaciers (after one melted, ceased flowing, and was downgraded to a snowfield and a second shrank to a tiny, stagnant ice mass) that circumscribe this peak.

We are also mindful of the hazards. The rockfall from the magnificent Steel Cliff. The steepness of the Pearly Gates. The scattered stones poking from the shallow, spring-like snowpack. The cracks in this mountain: crevasses (fissures formed as a glacier flows downhill), bergschrunds (crevasses formed where the glacier separates from a steep rock slope above), and fumaroles (volcanic vents). In fact, despite being normally sealed up this time of year, the glide cracks (fissures that open in non-glacier snowfields due to gravity pulling the snowpack) are open this January because conditions are so warm.

I do not know how many times I've been to the summit (two dozen?) or almost to the top (a couple hundred?). I do not keep track of how many times I've summited, just like I don't track my Wednesday lunch runs or my after-work bike rides up Post Canyon, the trail network two miles from my house. It's not that it wouldn't be useful. It's rather a conscious decision to eliminate this extra task, an act of cataloging that would only add complication to my outdoor activities and clog up my already-full brain.

A few years shy of sixty, I'm the most senior of our group by nearly twoscore years. And thankfully, I'm not the slowest: nothing is more nerve-racking than slowing a group of twentysomethings. Although I'm just becoming friends with this crew, I already know these mountaineers are solid, true, and authentic. Leif Bergstrom, a fit, highly skilled twenty-four-year-old, has recently begun his career as a mountain guide. Maurizio von Flotow, a fit, highly skilled thirty-year-old engineer and experienced backcountry skier, is always eager to learn and asks a lot of questions—a quality I admire and one I know will serve him well as he develops alpine rescue skills. Elliott Cramer, unsurprisingly also fit and highly skilled, is the youngest at twenty-three, and a US Forest Service wildland firefighter who is adept in emergency situations. Lifelong Hood River residents raised by parents who are "working athletes"—those who possess high-level athletic talents but also have a regular job in society—they have great work ethics and crackerjack outdoor skills: surfing, kitesurfing, Nordic skiing, backcountry skiing, climbing, sailing, and myriad others. And when I say fit, I mean able to climb a mountain on one-day notice and able to haul someone off the mountain with no notice. With this crew, we know no such concept as "getting in shape" or "training to climb Mount Hood." We are perpetually in shape and always trained to climb Mount Hood.

Today—weather, snow conditions, partners—all seems about perfect.

Until, a few hundred feet from the summit, my phone rings and interrupts the tranquility. I pull it from the left zippered pocket of my fleece hoodie, where I always carry it on alpine outings, and look at the screen. It's someone I can't ignore; quite literally, I have to take this call.

"Hey," I say. "What's up?"

"Van Tilburg, where you at?" says Deputy Scott Meyers, a good-natured veteran search and rescue coordinator with the Hood River County Sheriff's Office (HRCSO).

"You're kidding me," I say. I know exactly why he is calling.

"Yup. On the summit. Two people. Climbed up and can't get down. Not sure the problem, might be equipment failure?"

"We're on Hogsback, twenty minutes from the top," I say, describing the narrow arête of snow at 10,500 feet on the Coalman Glacier that leads up to the Pearly Gates. Fortuitously, we were just transitioning from uphill skiing with climbing skins (strips of fabric that attach to our skis to allow us to ski uphill without sliding down) to uphill climbing with boot crampons (racks of metal spikes that attach to the soles of our boots). "We're on our way up," I add.

"Okay, head up there and check it out. Let me know what you find," Meyers says. "I don't have any more info." His tone exudes confidence: he trusts me and I trust him, a relationship fostered by working together on dozens of mountain rescue missions over the years.

The crew overhears my conversation, so as I turn to them, I really don't need to explain. I relay the situation succinctly and confidently, with a hint of adrenaline. "Climbers on summit. In distress. Possibly equipment failure, not sure. Got up, can't get down." I shrug. "I guess we're on duty."

Leif, excited as always, says, "Cool, let's go." Our enthusiasm isn't meant to be at the expense of the climbers who are in trouble. Instead, it's an expression of the thrill and the honor we feel as rescue mountaineers. And we have a magnetic draw to the rescue, knowing that someone is in distress and we have the ability to help.

"I'm about ready," Elliott says. He is quiet and focused.

"What do we need to do?" Maurizio asks, ever inquisitive.

"We'll head up, find the climbers, and assess the situation. They don't sound injured. So maybe we will just need to help them down. Hard to say until we get up there," I explain. "Let's crampon up." We cast aside, for the moment, the beauty, tranquility, and excellent ski conditions, redirecting our focus to one task: saving someone's life.

The four of us quickly shuck our skis, peel off our climbing skins, lash our skis to our packs, and strap crampons on our ski boots. We slug water and take a bite or two of food: I bite into an organic peanut butter bar. Leif pulls out Swedish Fish. Elliott pulls out what looks like the remnants of yesterday's peanut butter sandwich, while Maurizio digs a burrito out of his backpack.

The climbers don't sound injured, so I'm thinking this mission will be straightforward. But then I remind myself, no rescue in the alpine is ever straightforward. Mostly, people call for help because they are injured, lost, or stuck somewhere, like on a cliff, in a canyon, or on a glacier. But every situation is unique: we have no default procedure. Communication gets muddled, and unforeseen contingencies can always arise. In this case, one climber called family, family called 911, a 911 dispatcher called Deputy Meyers, and Deputy Meyers called me. So it's a bit of the game of telephone—details can get lost or misconstrued with every transfer of information. I check my watch: we're three hours into our climb, which started at six thousand feet at the Timberline Lodge climber's parking lot—about an average pace for us.

From the Hogsback, we ascend the Coalman Glacier and cross a two-foot-wide snow bridge over the ten-foot-deep bergschrund. It's unusual for the bergschrund to be open in January; it is usually blanketed and sealed up with snow all winter. We traverse into the Pearly Gates, which is as steep as a ship's ladder, narrow as a tight hallway, and lined with thirty-foot ice walls. The tips of my skis, which are strapped diagonally on my backpack, hit the rime ice that lines the walls. Pea- to baseball-sized bits of rime slough off the ramparts, tinkle down the chute, and gently pelt Elliott and Maurizio below me. We stay close together, so if one of us knocks off a large chunk of ice, it will pass by our group before it gains enough momentum to bump one of us off the mountain.

Upward, we climb to the summit. It's New Year's Day 2022, and we have our first mountain rescue mission of the year.

OUR HOME of Hood River is a bucolic Oregon town (population 8,313) in a small county of the same name (population 23,977), bookended by this gargantuan volcano in the south and, to the north, a 26-mile section of the 1,243-mile-long Columbia River, one of the longest in America. Hood River lies at the crest of the Cascade Range, the mountains that stretch from British Columbia to Northern California and are speckled with a few dozen active and dormant, glaciated and non-glaciated volcanoes. Portland and the Pacific Ocean are to the west. Arid steppes and grasslands of the volcanic plateau are to the east. If you haven't heard of our world-class, year-round mountain climbing and skiing on Mount Hood, you might have heard of the Columbia River Gorge National Scenic Area, a eighty-mile stretch of the river known for spectacular waterfall hikes, top-notch mountain-bike trails, and legendary wind sports: windsurfing, kitesurfing, outrigger canoeing, kayaking, wing foiling, and stand-up paddle-boarding. With Mount Hood just twenty miles south of town and the river immediately to the north, it's impossible to miss these two prehistoric features.

Reportedly, Mount Hood was originally called Wy'east by the Multnomah band of the Chinookan people, who lived near present-day Portland in long-houses made of western redcedar and ate salmon, sturgeon, elk, birds, and potatoes. The moniker is wildly used in modern literature and media, but I can't find any primary source to confirm it. The mountain was given its current sobriquet on October 29, 1792, when British Royal Navy Lieutenant William Broughton navigated his ship up the Columbia River estuary to present-day Sauvie Island near Portland and spied the magnificent volcano from the northwest. "A very high, snowy mountain now appeared rising beautifully conspicuous in the midst of an extensive tract of low or moderately elevated land lying S 67 E, and seemed to announce a termination to the river," he wrote in his journal. Broughton named the peak after British Admiral Samuel Hood, despite no reports that the admiral had ever set foot on or even seen this mountain.

Legendary explorers Meriwether Lewis and William Clark would later spy the mountain on October 18, 1805, from the northeast, near present-day The Dalles at Celilo Falls. On October 29 of that year, Lewis and Clark first camped along the present-day Hood River, which flows due north from the moun-tain and empties into the Columbia River. They called the campsite Waucoma,

29

meaning "place of big trees." First, they named the stream coming from the mountain Lebeasche River, a variation of the name of expedition member François Labiche. Later it became known as Dog River, based on starving trappers who ate dog meat. The Native name for the river is not documented. Of the mountain, Clark wrote (as quoted in Jack Grauer's *Mount Hood: A Complete History*), "The pinnacle of the round topped mountain, which we saw a short distance below the banks of the river, is South 43-degrees West of us and about 37 miles. It is at this time topped with snow. We call this the Falls Mountain or Timm Mountain." Clark would later realize this was the same mountain that Broughton had dubbed Hood.

Of course, this land was not always the domain of white European settlers. The first Indigenous people lived in villages around the base of the peak. Some lived near Nch'i-Wána—the Big River, or what today we call the Columbia River. The Wasco people included the Wasco proper living in The Dalles, the Hood River Wasco, and the Watlala or Cascade Indians farther west; they fished the Columbia River for sockeye salmon and steelhead trout. Closer to the mountain, the Molalas lived on the eastern foothills near Tygh Valley and fished the Deschutes River. To the south lived the Clackamas and subtribes of the Kalapuyans. Most of these tribes spoke Chinookan or Sahaptin.

The arrival of fur traders, trappers, and explorers, including the early settlers and businessmen John Jacob Astor and John McLoughlin, brought mayhem like land grabs, disease, and the overharvesting of natural resources. European settlers began to stake claim to the Hood River Valley in 1854 when married couple Nathaniel and Mary Coe were given 319 acres by the US government. The Coes, whose name was later given to one of the mountain's glaciers, planted fruit trees in the rich, volcanic soil and irrigated them with the plentiful water that came from the mountain. A few years later, the Benson and Jenkins families followed, claiming land under the Homestead Act of 1862, which conferred land to settlers if they agreed to cultivate it for at least five years. By 1880, seventeen more families had arrived from Japan, Finland, Germany, and France. And in the following decades, the economy boomed with apple and pear orchards, salmon fishing, and timber harvest. In 1868, Mary Coe renamed the town and the stream that flowed from the mountain as Hood River, after the mountain. And, by 1895, Hood River incorporated, as it was busy with traffic on the Oregon Trail.

Meanwhile, timber was found to be a valuable natural resource. Like many glaciated stratovolcanoes in the Pacific Northwest, Mount Hood has a significant prominence (the height relative to the surrounding foothills), rising 7,706 feet above the endless greenery of forests, today mostly replanted monoculture of Douglas-fir. Back then, the forests were packed with old-growth Douglas-fir, ponderosa pine, western redcedar, white fir, and hemlock. These foothills were first earmarked as Bull Run Timberland Reserve by President Benjamin Harrison in 1892. In 1893, the reserve increased in size and was renamed Cascade Range Forest Reserve. By 1908, this land had become the Oregon National Forest, following the creation of the US Forest Service, and in 1924, it was renamed the Mount Hood National Forest. Now this forest has eight wilderness areas, including the Mount Hood Wilderness, which encompasses most of the upper mountain, above six thousand feet.

While the land was settled, fields sown, orchards planted, and forests harvested, along came recreation. The nascent sport of recreational mountain climbing had begun on Mont Blanc in 1757, when the Swiss climber Horace-Bénédict de Saussure began launching his many failed attempts on the 15,777-foot berg. He offered a reward to anyone who could successfully summit, and Jacques Balmat and Michel-Gabriel Paccard summited Mont Blanc in 1786, an ascent generally regarded as the inception of mountain climbing for sport.

I can't confirm the true first ascent of Mount Hood, but it may have been from an American Indian and wasn't recorded. It's likely wrong to say we know the "first ascent." However, the first documented ascent by a European settler was by the *Oregonian* newspaper publisher Thomas J. Dryer, Portlander Wells Lake, and an American Indian, the name of whom was not recorded, a fact that's both disheartening and typical for the era. Reportedly, the trio left Portland on August 4, 1854, and traveled via horseback to an area on the south side of the mountain. They climbed up the White River Glacier, the large south-facing drainage, to the Steel Cliff, and then over to Triangle Moraine, the top confluence of the Zigzag and White River Glaciers at ten thousand feet. They finished up a chute to the summit, arriving at noon on August 8. They used primitive crampons called "creepers" strapped to their boots, iron staffs with hooks akin to the first ice axes, and some manila farm rope. Dryer documented the summit in his own newspaper, so it was a tad bit controversial without secondary confirmation.

The second documented ascent—or first ascent, if you disbelieve Dryer—was completed by the Portlanders Henry L. Pittock, L. J. Powell, William S. Buckly, W. Lyman Chittenden, and James G. Deardorff on August 6, 1857, as reported on August 13 in the *Democratic Standard*. They reached the summit in just under six hours from tree line, on approximately the same route as Dryer.

By the end of the nineteenth century, mountaineers began climbing the peak from the north side, as it was more accessible. Hood River was now a thriving fruit-growing community and accessible from Portland via riverboat or train. A taxi service using a horse-drawn wagon took people up the valley toward the mountain. Mountaineering blossomed so much that the Hood River Post of the American Legion started climbing the mountain as a group in 1921, using local mountaineers who'd loosely organized as the Hood River Guides.

With mountain climbing came mountain accidents. Some early accidents were recorded, such as Frederic Kirn, who fell and died on the east-facing New-ton Clark Glacier on July 12, 1896. His body was recovered with the help of local mountain guide Will Langille, who, like Coe, would have a glacier named after him. Another early rescue was in August 1923. Hood River orchardist Mace Baldwin's son became lost in the mountain's foothills. Mace took his wife, Alda; his nine-year-old son, Blanchar; and his brother-in-law, Jess Puddy, on an afternoon hike near the Middle Fork of the Hood River, an idyllic stream that bisects the fertile valley spanning between Mount Hood's northern foothills and the banks of the Columbia River. During a short hike to go fishing, Blanchar became separated from his family when crossing the creek. He was instantly and suddenly lost. His father and Puddy searched all night, and then other orchard and mountain folks from Hood River Valley combed the area. (The thriving orchard community was also packed with outdoor enthusiasts who were skiing the north slope in winter and fishing, hunting, and hiking in the summer.) The orchardists set out to hike all night, tracked footprints down into a creek, and found the boy the next morning, curled against a log. He was alive and well.

In July 1924, another impromptu rescue occurred when E. C. Loveland and two companions were climbing Mount Hood from the north side. The trio ascended the treacherous Cooper Spur route, which follows the broad snowfield called Cooper Spur and then the rocky two-thousand-foot headwall of the Eliot Glacier. Once up top, the trio decided to descend via the Sunshine Route, which had been pioneered the year before by the well-known Hood River guide Mark Weygandt. On the descent, Loveland slipped on a steep section, fell, and slid several hundred feet down the mountain before stopping on the Coe Glacier, impaled in the groin by an ice axe.

The Hood River Guides, on an outing led by the local lumberyard manager Andy Anderson, saw the accident and responded instantly. The rescuers rigged a stretcher from canvas coats and alpenstocks (long wooden poles tipped with iron spikes, carried by climbers before the days of ice axes). They carried Loveland to Cloud Cap Inn, a small outpost at six thousand feet (more to come about this beloved building in subsequent chapters). From there, Loveland was loaded into a car and motored twenty miles to the hospital in Hood River.

These two rescues—Blanchar Baldwin and E. C. Loveland—piqued the interest of local mountaineers in forming a more formal search and rescue group. After all, they were active, motivated, fit men who loved to ski, climb, and hike, and many already had strong leadership skills from their time in the Hood River Guides. (The Hood River Guides also formed the Guides Ski Club in 1925. Soon after, the club morphed into the Hood River Ski Club and eventually merged in 1949 with the North Slope Ski Club, which was active through the 1960s.)

Anderson, a tall, lanky, and dominant man who was ever organized and motivated, sent out a letter on July 31, 1926, calling the men to action, loosely utilizing a couple of monikers that had been considered:

A meeting of the Mountain Goats will be held in the office of Tum-A-Lum Aug. 3, at 8. At this meeting will be discussed the need of an organization of this kind, "Crag Rats." Bring your ideas and suggestions. Kent Shoemaker will tell of the recent Jefferson trip, consented at the point of a shot gun.

On August 3, 1926, the locals sat down at Tum-A-Lum Lumber in Hood River, originally located on Fifth and Oak Street and still in operation today but at a new location, and agreed to form a club with a sole focus on mountain rescue, the first of its kind in the nation. But they adjourned without formalizing a name—that would come during the first official mission a few weeks later.

NOW, A CENTURY later, Leif, Elliott, Maurizio, and I are called to save a life on this leviathan of rock and ice, the one that dominates our county and has commandeered my life. The one where I spend two hundred days a year climbing and skiing the glaciers, trail running and mountain biking the forested flanks, and kitesurfing on the river fueled by its glaciers.

At times when I have a chance to reflect on the missions, trainings, and social outings—at least one per week—that I've shared with colleagues turned friends, I feel overwhelmed. All our activity barely leaves us time to reflect on this changing environment, the rising temperatures, the melting glaciers, the clear-cut forests, the drained reservoirs, the contaminated streams, the trampled wildflowers, the displaced wildlife, and all the many other signs of drastic change on Mount Hood, change that, ironically, also contributes to us being so busy with rescues.

Leif, Maurizio, Elliott, and I quickly redirect our focus. Notwithstanding the fact that our entire day will be shot, as we'd planned on getting back to our truck a little after noon to be home for afternoon chores, errands, and work, we now focus on a singular, immediate task: rescuing climbers from the summit. The thrill, excitement, and anxiety of a mountain rescue mission electrify my body. I have opposing feelings too: dismay that someone is in trouble, dismay that our skiing plans are ruined, and dismay that I will be putting myself at risk on this big mountain yet again. It's a complex and heady mix for someone like me, a can-do, type A adrenaline junkie.

This is mountain rescue, the way it's always been: we drop everything and head to the high peaks—crevassed glaciers; jagged arêtes; craggy andesite ridges; deep, dank canyons; and rotten, loose scree fields. In a quick twenty minutes, we reach the summit. It's utterly spectacular. Clear blue sky, with views to the north of Mounts Adams, Rainier, and St. Helens and to the south of Mount Jefferson and the Three Sisters. To the west, a cloud bank from the Pacific Ocean marine layer covers Portland, and to the east I see the arid desert.

"Have you seen a couple in trouble?" Leif asks a group on the summit.

"Yes. They started down, and the woman was helping the guy in Old Chute. The woman is okay, but the man didn't look good." They immediately point northwest, to the route adjacent the Pearly Gates, and add, "He's having trouble getting down but doesn't seem to be injured."

"Okay, thanks," Leif says.

"Good info," I say.

We walk across the summit ridge to the "catwalk," a twelve-inch-wide swath of snow that leads to the Old Chute. On one side, the cliff drops two thousand feet to the Eliot Glacier; on the other, the cliff drops one thousand feet to the Hot Rocks and Devils Kitchen fumaroles. At the top of the Old Chute, a half-dozen people are preparing to descend. We see the climbers about one hundred feet below, downclimbing the Old Chute. The man is gripped, precariously clutching the side of the mountain. The woman, exasperated, appears to be helping him.

Quickly, we downclimb the steep snow chute to the couple and take command.

"Hi, I'm Dr. Van Tilburg—are you hurt?"

"No, I'm okay," he says. "But I'm scared."

"Okay, we're here to help." I turn to the woman and ask, "Are you climbing with him?"

"Yes. He's having trouble, way out of his comfort zone."

"We'll help him from here," Leif says.

"Do you need help?" I ask the woman. She appears to be well-equipped, with two ice axes, proper boots, and crampons, but a bit unnerved from trying to get herself off the mountain and assist her partner at the same time. The man, however, has a borrowed ice axe and is wearing lightweight boots not meant for glacier travel, rendering his dangling crampons all but useless. None of this comes to a surprise to us rescuers—we've seen it all before.

"I'm okay," she says. "But we'd appreciate help down at least to Hogsback."

I nod and then turn to Leif. "Are you going to put in an anchor?"

"No, I'll just short-rope him," he says. Short-roping involves tying the climber into a ten-foot length of rope: Leif will manage the climber on the rope as they descend together. The slope is very steep, around 40 degrees, so all the climbers descend facing inward, like you would on a ladder. I think about the short-rope technique for a minute because we don't normally employ it. But Leif is a mountain guide and experienced with the procedure.

I make a quick medical assessment and determine that the man is uninjured. Meanwhile, Leif ties the man to a rope, and Elliott fixes the man's crampons and gives him another ice axe. Leif then gives his skis to Elliott, who straps them onto his own pack. I turn to Maurizio, who is just arriving.

"Can you keep the Old Chute closed for a few minutes?" I ask Maurizio. The slope is a five-hundred-foot descent until we can exit on a traverse across the Coalman Glacier to regain Hogsback. The upper part of the Old Chute is just twenty feet wide, so the climbers descending from the summit are bottle-necking above us. "I don't want people knocking stuff down on us or falling and crashing into us," I say.

"Got it," Maurizio says. He parks himself at the top and asks climbers not to descend while we are in the chute. I downclimb first and kick steps into the snow for the two climbers. The woman walks down in my boot prints and kicks the steps in deeper. The man and Leif follow. The downclimb of the Old Chute takes thirty minutes, with two stops for everyone to rest—although I'm certain Leif, Elliott, and Maurizio need no break.

At the Hogsback, we meet a group from Portland Mountain Rescue (PMR), our kindred team based in the city and deployed by the neighboring Clackamas County Sheriff's Office. They were also climbing that day and heard about the mission. We now have more rescuers, which is reassuring in case the man cannot descend the rest of the way on his own. With the technical, steepest slopes behind us, we pause to eat and drink. Leif unties the rope. Then we keep walking down the mountain with the man, sinking our boots deep into the now-soft snow, our unused skis on our packs.

Two hours later, at Timberline Lodge, we transfer the climbers to Deputy Meyers, who decides that the woman can drive the couple home. We don't take time to interview them, partly because we need to eat, hydrate, and drive home, and partly because our job is done. Thus—as so often happens—we have questions that won't be answered: *Why was the woman prepared and the man not? Who was in charge? Why was he climbing a glaciated mountain in soft hiking boots?*

We eat the little food we have left, guzzle water, toss our gear in our truck, and drive home. I'm not thinking of my to-do list or my many jobs or this book project. I am not thinking about turning sixty soon or about this fragile yet durable ecosystem of Mount Hood. In fact, I'm not really thinking about much of anything, but instead am laughing with this youngest and most talented new cohort of rescuers as we drive down the mountain, revel in the successful mission, and bask in the achievement of another fabulous day in the high alpine of Mount Hood.

CHAPTER 2

FEBRUARY: THE HOLE IN THE VOLCANO

Our volcano has a hole. A big chasm that gobbles climbers, traps them, and kills them. This sky-high, glacier-clad peak is both spectacularly magnificent and spectacularly deadly.

The favored ascent route up Mount Hood is collectively called the South Side Routes and typically follows one of several variations for the top 1,200 feet: the Pearly Gates, Old Chute, One O'Clock Couloir, Mazama Chute, and West Crater Rim. The ascent variations go right past, or over, a twin pair of fumaroles—as if one wasn't lethal enough. These deep, dark holes in the ice steam like witches' caldrons, exhausting lethal sulfur dioxide and hydrogen sulfide. The rotten-egg odor is so strong that when climbing by on a clear, windless day, your eyes water and your nose stings.

The Devils Kitchen fumarole sits just to climber's right of Hogsback, the steep snow ridge on the Coalman Glacier that leads to the Pearly Gates chute. If you fall into this fumarole, you drop thirty feet smack onto sandpapery andesite. If the impact doesn't kill you, the deadly gases can suffocate you in four minutes—as quickly as drowning. Stand up if you can, because the sulfurous gases are heavier than oxygen and congregate at the bottom of the hole.

The second cavity, the Hot Rocks fumarole, lies to climber's left of Hogsback and smack-dab at the bottom of the Old Chute, the steep snow ramp that's the second most common route to the summit. Hot Rocks vents constantly, so the heat from the steam never allows snow to accumulate on the crags of ancient black andesite lava, even in deep winter. A fall from the Old Chute or from the traverse across the top of the Coalman Glacier to and from Hogsback lands climbers in Hot Rocks.

After ascending past these cracks in the mountain, you summit, revel in the views, and then start down. Then it happens: a momentary, relatively small slip. Maybe you have a moment of inattention from the adrenaline of a successful summit. Maybe your ski edge isn't quite sharp enough to grip the firm glacial ice, or your crampons aren't on tightly enough, so they shift when you step, or they're packed with soft, sticky snow so that the spikes don't hold. Or your boots do not provide enough support climbing deep snow or bulletproof ice. Or you suddenly lose balance when the ice or snow shifts under your feet. You slip, fall, slide, and cartwheel uncontrollably. Once momentum starts, it's nearly impossible to arrest, even with a specialized ice axe, a tool invented in 1840 by the Italian mountaineering company Grivel, which was established in 1818 at the base of Mont Blanc. Down the mountain, down the snow and ice, down into the hole in the volcano, where your survival time is limited and the best chance you have for rescue is an all-volunteer group of men and women who are about to drop everything—work, family time, recreation, household chores—and race up the mountain.

One morning in winter 2022, just after the summit mission from chapter 1, at 11:38 a.m., sixty-eight cell phones from the Hood River Crag Rats mountain rescue team rattle, hum, vibrate, and ring. "Fallen climber, Hot Rocks," reads the text from HRCSO dispatch. I instantly have a concurrent cringe of consternation and frustration: the former because someone's in trouble again, and the latter because my morning, my afternoon, likely my nightly sleep, and possibly my next day will all be trashed.

In a few seconds, I quickly transition from working-at-my-computer mode to rescue mode. We have another climber in Hot Rocks, which is neither surprising nor something we're ill-prepared for. But no rescue is ever completely predictable, simple, straightforward, or risk-free. No rescue is without the potential of life-or-death consequences, both for the rescuees and the rescuers. As the first wave of rescue adrenaline hits, I uneasily consider a few background issues: my safety, the team's safety, the man deep in the hole in the volcano, the mountain weather and snow conditions. But I also know I need to concentrate on a singular duty: get my gear and drive to the county yard, where I'll meet my friends in the Crag Rats.

At this one-acre repository for Public Works, the sheriff stores search and rescue (SAR) equipment in a big metal barn. The gear housed here includes two all-terrain vehicles that can be converted from wheels to snow tracks; a couple of snowmobiles; a 1976 Logan Machine Company snowcat; a command communications truck with computers, printers, and big mast antennas; a second communications truck built from a converted four-wheel-drive box ambulance; a camper trailer converted to a command post; and two pickups we call SAR 1, a newish Ford F-250 crew cab, and SAR 2, an older Chevy 2500 crew cab, both loaded with thousands of dollars of high-tech mountain rescue equipment. The only SAR vehicle not housed here is the sheriff's Piper PA-18 Super Cub, which resides in a hangar at the Ken Jernstedt Airfield, named after a former mayor and Flying Tigers World War II pilot.

A few minutes earlier, the nineteen-year-old college kid summited, stayed for a short bit, then began his descent. He traversed the catwalk to the top of the Old Chute, where he clicked into his skis. In spring, the glacial ice can soften from both solar radiation and rising ambient temperatures, yielding a good ski descent. But in winter, like now, the slope is frozen for most of the day, and often the compacted snow doesn't soften—it can be so hard you can't get a ski edge in and need to walk down with crampons, facing into the slope, digging in the front spikes methodically with every step—a technique called "front-pointing."

The guy was likely ecstatic, having just summited. I know I always am when I crest the top. The euphoria is from the combination of athletic achievement, the stark beauty of standing atop a glaciated mountain seven thousand feet above the foothills, and the rarity of arriving at this place that few ever see.

Now, we are tasked with a mission and are driven to complete it. The fact that our mission involves saving a life magnifies both the risk and the reward when we are successful and the emotional toll when we are not. Moreover, this love of the alpine translates into a love of rescue: knowing few possess the skills to save a life in this hostile yet magnificent place compels us all the more.

The ski route down the Old Chute diverges after five hundred feet of descent. My favorite of the two paths is the less traveled: the fall line into the Zigzag Glacier is a spectacular three-thousand-foot descent when the snow is good, letting you ski all the way from the top of the Old Chute, at eleven thousand feet, to the top of the Mississippi Head Cliff, at eight thousand feet—or, if the snow is good, even another two thousand feet farther down to tree line at Split Rock, a ten-foot-tall andesite bolder that is cracked in two. But this descent is not completely straightforward. The schuss involves skiing the steep Old Chute, skirting around the Hot Rocks fumarole, avoiding a crevasse near Crater Rock, descending the Zigzag Glacier, staying right of Mississippi Head's one-thousand-foot cliff, and then cruising through gullies to Split Rock. Then you have a two-thousand-foot uphill ski out.

The majority of climbers and skiers don't take this route. More commonly, they ski down the Old Chute to 10,500 feet and then take a precarious, high traverse across the Coalman Glacier, here canted at 40 degrees, back to the Hogsback to rejoin the ascent route. The traverse can be dicey in firm snow, hardpack, or bulletproof ice, both because of its steep angle and the need to avoid bowling-ball-sized, rock-hard ice chunks peeling off the Coalman Glacier headwall (the steep rock cliff at the top of the glacier). If the snow has softened to slush, the slope can avalanche—I've witnessed a skier-triggered avalanche here more than once. If you are downclimbing without skis, it is just as hazardous, depending on how good you are with crampons. This fall today likely happened instantly—one second skiing and the next second falling. A witness said the skier "rag-dolled" and "cartwheeled" one thousand feet down the Old Chute and the Coalman Glacier, disappearing into the collection point of all who fall here: the Hot Rocks fumarole.

And then, a few minutes later, we got the call.

I call Meredith, a bubbly fiftyish entrepreneur, strong skier, and solid rescuer. When I first met her, she owned a bagel shop in downtown Hood River, which she sold to build a hydroponic basil greenhouse, which she sold to start a business making solid bars of shampoo and conditioner to eliminate single-use plastic bottles. Meredith is jovial, and we always find something to laugh about. Meredith is one of the ten Crag Rats coordinators who receive the initial call from the sheriff's office. Once a coordinator gets a report about the mission—injury, location, and other details—they send out a text to the entire team to mobilize a crew. She aptly explained once to me, "Coordinators are the brains of the mission during the early stages."

"What's happening?" I ask.

"Can you go?" Meredith asks abruptly and appropriately, because she needs to muster a squad in minutes without giving an oration to someone who might be unavailable.

"Yes," I say. "Getting gear ready now."

"Guy fell on Old Chute. That's all I know right now."

"Who else is going?"

"Just you so far."

"Okay, I'll be at the yard in ten minutes. Text me when you get a crew," I say. I won't deploy without at least one other person. But I'm confident others will rally for the call in a few minutes.

I don my ski-mountaineering kit—polyester long underwear, wool ski pants, wool-acrylic ski socks, fleece hoodie bedecked with one patch for the national Mountain Rescue Association and another for the Hood River Crag Rats—and head to my two-hundred-square-foot mudroom, which really is laced with dirt and mud because of the ski, bike, and running gear strewn across the linoleum floor, for which I specifically chose a "Caribbean" color that's both cheery and dirt-hiding. My skimo pack is mostly ready because it's in a perpetual state of either drying out from the previous day's ski outing or rescue mission or, like today, already packed and primed. I grab a giant black duffel, which is also permanently packed with extra mountain clothes, ice axes, an unusually strong thirty-meter-long by six-millimeter-diameter rope, technical rescue gear like carabiners and pulleys, a harness, spare gloves, boot crampons, ski crampons, and other rescue tools. I've started carrying extra socks in my truck because more than once lately we've had two missions in one day, and changing into dry socks can be vitally important. I grab ultralight mountaineering skis with climbing skins, jump into my 2006 Toyota Sequoia—currently clocking 220,000 miles—bolt for the county yard, and forget the one thing not preassembled in my mudroom: food.

Meredith sends a group text: "Meet at yard in ten minutes." At the top of the message, I see that Brian Hukari, Ron Martin, and Gary Szalay are all coming. Lisa and John Rust will meet us on the mountain. This is a solid, experienced A-list crew.

Lisa Rust was first a lawyer, then a Mount Rainier guide, and now a middle school teacher. She's strong, fit, and accomplished in all mountain skills and once climbed within six hundred vertical feet of Mount Everest's summit. Plus, she has a calming, matter-of-fact demeanor. Her husband, John, a lawyer turned ski race coach, is so strong and such an excellent skier that he does the work of two rescuers. Smart, good-natured, and confident Gary Szalay, a Portland firefighter and our team's rope-rescue expert, brings his firehouse humor to keep us focused in difficult situations. Quirky Ron Martin, PhD environmental engineer and Meredith's husband, brings a calm, logical approach to planning. And quiet, humble Brian Hukari, an orchardist by profession, is sixty-seven yet strong as an ox—he's summited Denali, most high volcanoes in Ecuador, and almost K2. A senior member of our team who joined at age eighteen in 1973, he has likely responded to more alpine rescue missions on Mount Hood than any other person alive.

In fifteen minutes, we convene at the county yard, and Meredith pulls up with Ron.

"I'm coming too," she says with a smile.

"Yay!" I say.

"Yeah, I was kind of expecting a rescue," Brian says. "Good weather, lots of people." He's holding a green smoothie in one hand and his bulging alpine pack in the other.

"I'm so tired from skiing all week," Ron says. He and Meredith are two of my main ski partners because we all have flexible schedules and they're always game for a tour. We tend to ski three days or more a week in winter.

"You'll survive, as long as you ate breakfast." I say this because often he doesn't eat breakfast before we ski, and then he's starving by the end of the ski tour.

"Let's go," Gary says, and we load our gear. Gary is in charge of organizing trucks and rescue gear, and he always employs careful, deliberate consideration in what we carry, from the length and diameter of ropes to spare crampons and avalanche transceivers. We jump in our three-quarter-ton Ford crew-cab long-bed pickup, which is sluggish laden down with the five of us plus our two thousand pounds of specialized mountain rescue gear. (In the coming weeks, Gary will spend an entire day of his own time getting the truck beefier springs so that it drives better.) Gary turns on the blue-and-red emergency lights as we race along the main street in Hood River and then again when we pass by the bustling Tamanawas Falls trailhead, in Mount Hood National Forest in the tight canyon carved by the Hood River.

The staging area for the South Side Routes is the historic Timberline Lodge, built on Mount Hood's southern flanks in 1937 as part of the Works Progress Administration. The fifty-mile drive takes fifty minutes from town. While Gary drives, I'm on the phone with Deputy Meyers to get GPS coordinates and information about injuries.

"Don't know much," he says. "Guy fell in a hole. Not sure the status of the guy. Portland Mountain Rescue responding, as is an AMR RAT team." The American Medical Response ambulance company's Reach and Treat is a back-country medical team that formed in 1988.

"Okay, we're on our way, twenty minutes out."

Meanwhile, Gary, Ron, and Brian are planning what gear we need. This planning-while-driving saves valuable time. They decide we need a hasty team with hypothermia gear, a litter (a stretcher with raised sides for backcountry transport), and rope. By the time Gary parks next to the ski-patrol entrance at Timberline Lodge, we have already mapped out the mission. We quickly check in with Deputy Meyers, who is sitting in his warm patrol truck.

"So, the guy's in the fumarole?" I ask Meyers when he steps out of his truck. While I'm walking to him, I'm strapping on my radio harness, turning on my avalanche transceiver, and checking that my cell phone is charged.

"Yep. Got a guy who fell skiing and landed in the hole. Don't know much. Reporting party says he's hurt bad and can't move." Meyers is affable and succinct.

"Okay, we've got a crew of seven. We're ready to head up. The Rusts are just arriving from Mt. Hood Meadows," I say, referring to the neighboring ski resort on the east side of the mountain.

"I got a ride for you," Meyers says with a grin, knowing we'll be excited to get a lift up the mountain. When the Rusts arrive, we pile into a Timberline Lodge PistenBully snowcat, which will take us to 9,300 feet above the top of the ski hill, reducing a one-and-a-half-hour climb on skins to thirty minutes. In addition to the gear in our packs, we also bring a two-piece fiberglass litter and a vacuum mattress spine board. Up at the top of the ski slopes, the air is cool but rapidly warming in the unusually warm winter sunshine, and a slight breeze blows from the west, keeping the snowpack cool and firm. This makes for fast uphill skiing. We skin at a good clip up Palmer Glacier, up Triangle Moraine, and up into the crater of Devils Kitchen, getting there about an hour and a half after leaving the lot.

"I'm hungry," I say as we ski. "And I forgot food." It's two thirty p.m., and we still have not reached the climber.

"Want some?" Lisa offers me an energy bar, switching into mom/ski guide mode as she barely slows her uphill cadence. (Lisa is the mother of two badass ski-racing, rock-climbing, Hood-summiting teenagers.)

"I forgot to eat breakfast," Ron says. "Do you have extra?"

"Ron, you never eat breakfast," I say.

"Yeah, Ron, what's up with no breakfast?" Lisa chides.

"Unless it's free," Ron fires back. "Then I'll eat it." He's known on our team for his penchant for free food. Ron and I had skied all week. I'd hydrated and eaten steel-cut oats, nuts, and berries for breakfast, but now, skiing up the mountain, I've burned through those calories. I keep a half-liter water bottle in my pack but don't want to stop climbing to dig it out because getting my pack on and off is a chore with the added rescue gear jammed inside and strapped outside.

We don't talk much, breathing heavily under the loads of our packs, which must weigh around forty pounds each. Gary and Brian have blazed ahead despite carrying the heaviest loads. Luckily this day, the sun is bright, the sky is cloudless and blue, and the temperature is a pleasant 40 degrees.

Close to four o'clock in the afternoon, we reach Hogsback, at the bottom of the one-thousand-foot slope the guy tumbled down. We see him down in the Hot Rocks fumarole, one hundred vertical feet below the ridge where we stand. Fortuitously, when the skier came to a stop, he landed on a slope ten feet deep in the fumarole but not at the bottom, another twenty-foot drop and where the deadliest air collects. He is precariously perched on a steep slope in direct sun, inches from falling deeper. Unable to move, he teeters on the brink of oblivion.

We limit the number of rescuers exposed to the deep snow around the fumarole and the falling chunks of ice coming off the cliffs above in the warming temperatures. We stash our skis, and then three of us drag the litter and vacuum mattress from Hogsback down to the fumarole. The sulfur stench is pungent and acidic: my eyes water and my nose burns. Luckily, a light breeze slightly dilutes the acridness but also brings a slight chill. I pull on a puffy coat.

The patient is in a depression that we can walk to wearing crampons. I find a paramedic from the AMR RAT team and introduce myself. "How's he doing?" I ask. Initially, I just see the AMR jacket and patches, but up closer I notice it's Robert Aberle, a highly skilled backcountry paramedic with whom I've worked several times on this mountain. "Oh, hey, Robert! Good to see you!" I say.

"Hey, Doc," he says. "Not good. Banged up: knee, back, wrist, maybe head. I gave him some morphine."

"I'm glad you're here," I say, reassuring the fallen climber—who is conscious—both that I trust Robert's medical and rescue decision-making and that I don't need to repeat a full assessment. Plus, Robert has a full advanced life support kit (a large collection of cardiac-resuscitation drugs, airway and breathing tubes, and trauma gear) in contrast to mine, which is the bare minimum (a single airway tube, minimal medication, two hemostats for bleeding, a trauma clotting bandage, one splint, and a couple rolls of tape).

"I'll take a quick look without unwrapping him," I say. The fallen climber is cocooned in a tarp and sleeping bag; unwrapping him would cause too much heat loss.

"How are you feeling?" I ask.

"Okay," the patient says weakly. "Better with the pain medicine." Robert had put in an IV to provide pain medication.

I quickly palpate the patient's chest, abdomen, and pelvis through the sleeping bag to check for catastrophic injuries that might need immediate attention. It's enough to ascertain that he has no major bones sticking out of the skin and no major external bleeding. He's alert, breathing, able to talk, and has a normal pulse.

"Good work with the assessment and pain meds," I say to Robert. "We'll get him packaged. We've got a crew of Crag Rats." Meanwhile, during my five-minute interaction with our patient, Brian, Gary, John, and Lisa have already started work on the litter. A few others from PMR show up, including Mark Morford, who walks down into the fumarole.

I look at Morford—it's technically PMR's mission because we are in Clackamas County. "You take command of the scene. Robert and I will take medical. The rest of the Crag Rats and PMR can start rigging the rope system," I suggest to Mark, whose presence I'm thankful for. Mark, a lawyer in his day job, is a highly experienced rescuer leader. He tasks someone with looking uphill for falling chunks of ice and rocks from the cliffs of the Old Chute and the Coalman Glacier headwall.

The patient moans when we slide him into the vacuum mattress and then suck out the air to create a rigid board. Then we cover him with another sleeping bag and wrap him in a blue plastic tarp. Finally, we lift him onto the litter: a fiberglass toboggan designed to slide over snow. Now that the patient is cocooned and the medication has had longer to work, the pain from his injuries subsides a tiny bit.

"How are you doing?" I ask him again.

"Okay," he says in a low, strained voice. I can barely see his face through the tarp, but it's a good sign that he's still alert and talking. The direct sun and the rising ambient temperature, which has climbed a bit above freezing after a night in the teens, helps keep him from losing too much heat. But this same heat begins to melt the cliffs above us, and ice chunks the size of baseballs and softballs are starting to zing down the slope—every few minutes, someone yells, "Rock!" or "Ice!" The ice chunks are getting larger, now the size of bowling balls. The natural tendency is to look up, but instead, we hunker down and try to be as small as possible so the chunks whiz past us and zing out of sight. The wind picks up and is now terrific, blowing from the west, causing a chill and stealthily sucking our heat. We don extra clothing—preventing heat loss is much easier than trying to warm up once you're already cold.

I hear chatter on the radio between Morford, who is coordinating the mission from his perch in the snow thirty feet above us, and Deputy Meyers, still down at the always-busy Timberline Lodge.

Then we hear the familiar *thwock-thwock-thwock* of air support. A Sikorsky HH-60 Black Hawk from the 189th Aviation Regiment of the Oregon National Guard approaches from the south. After the 2017 fatality of John Thornton Jenkins on Mount Hood resulted in a lawsuit against the Clackamas County Sheriff's Office for an alleged delay in calling a helicopter, it seems choppers are called more often these days. Good news: a quick helicopter evacuation will save us several hours over a ground evacuation and will lessen the risk to rescuers by getting us off the mountain more quickly. But helicopter missions also have their own perils. I watch the Blackhawk approach, hover five hundred feet above us, and then suddenly and violently drift sideways in forty-mile-per-hour winds. The chopper immediately backs off, takes another pass, then backs off again. *We've had a helicopter crash here in the past; it's simply not worth the risk,* I think as I recall the $7 million Air Force HH-60G Pave Hawk from the 304th Rescue Squadron that crashed in 2002 during a rescue, rolled down the Coalman Glacier, and came to rest in this exact spot, injuring all five crewmen aboard. The 2017 Jenkins lawsuit makes us want to use a helicopter, but the 2002 crash makes us dubious. These opposing motivations need to be reconciled. Sometime, but not now.

"We are getting a warning light," the pilot says over the radio. "We can't hold to do a hoist. Too much wind." I can barely make this out because of the static on the radio and the wind.

Morford and I now have to figure out a plan with the patient's condition guarded and the helicopter incapable of helping: Do we burn precious time by waiting to see if the helicopter can pluck this subject off the glacier, or do we get off the mountain posthaste with the ground team we have? The helicopter sounds like gunfire as it retreats, adding an air of urgency to our deliberations.

It's midafternoon, and with a few hours of daylight left, we need to make a decision quickly. I look at the team: Gary, Brian, Lisa, John, Ron, and Meredith compose probably one of the best alpine rescue teams anyone could assemble on Mount Hood. I'm sure we can get this guy down if we need to.

HELICOPTERS, CELL PHONES, two-way radios, ice axes, and carbon-fiber litters were not always the tools the Crag Rats used for rescue. Back in 1926, just ten days after Anderson's gathering of the Mountain Goats/Crag Rats down in summery Hood River, a gunshot pierced the air high on Mount Hood, in nearly this same location on the South Side Routes. *Pop, pop.* After a pause, a second double tap: *Pop, pop.* This was communication long before cell phones, the Global Positioning System, and handheld radios. The first mission for the newly organized Hood River mountain rescue team started on August 16, 1926. That day, the towering peak, bedecked in full glacial regalia, rose above the emerald forests of Douglas-fir, western redcedar, noble fir, western hemlock, and ponderosa pine, a varied forest so unlike today's and nearly free of trails and roads. The glaciers stretched long into the valleys, and were cream-colored and spackled with gray volcanic dust from the andesite and basalt cliffs. The streams were unfettered, their banks tangled with deciduous vine maple, bigleaf maple, and black cottonwood. The understory was a matted mess of Oregon grape, salal, rhododendrons, western swordferns, witch's hair lichen, beard lichen, salmon-berry, thimbleberry, and evergreen huckleberry. Flowers decorated the meadows and sun-kissed outcrops of andesite and basalt. Only a few cabins existed above four thousand feet: the two mountain enclaves were Government Camp on the south side and the Cooper Spur Junction on the north side.

Two days before, on August 14, 1926, Mrs. W. H. Strong (no first name or maiden name recorded, in keeping with the times) had motored to Government Camp from Gresham with her daughter (also no name in archival news reports) and three sons: Winston, age eighteen; Raymond, age twenty-one; and Jack, age ten. The community of Government Camp was unusually bustling with recreationalists that summer because the mountain road was finally paved and had been plowed for the first time ever.

To understand the origins of Government Camp, we need to go back a century to the Oregon Trail, the 2,170-mile wagon road from Independence, Missouri, to Oregon City. In the 1830s, pioneers migrating from east to west on the Oregon Trail had to take a treacherous (and expensive) ferry ride down the Columbia River to the trail's end, passing through the Long Narrows Rapids near The Dalles and the two-mile-long Cascade Rapids near Cascade Locks, which eventually were submerged by The Dalles Dam and Bonneville Dam, respectively. In 1845, Illinois entrepreneur Sam Barlow searched for an alternate path, learning of two routes from the Native Americans. One route led around the northwest side of the mountain, up and over the rugged Lolo Pass—a route passable with livestock but not wagons; it's still there today, marked with a five-mile stretch of unimproved gravel road. The other route passed around the south-east, through a notch in the hills via beautiful and expansive meadows. Barlow decided to cut a road on the southeast route, going over what became designated as Barlow Pass. By year's end, on December 25, 1845, he opened Barlow Road. Passage cost five dollars per wagon plus ten cents per head of livestock.

The Oregon Trail via Barlow Road was rough, steep, grassy, rocky, and, during rains, muddy. In 1849, US Cavalry Lieutenant William Frost led 429 wagons pulled by 1,716 mules from Fort Leavenworth, Kansas, to Fort Vancouver, Washington, via the Barlow Road. When they were hit by heavy snows on the south side of Mount Hood, they abandoned forty-five wagons at a clearing just below tree line. This small encampment became a community, which then became a town dubbed Government Camp. Along came cars and then asphalt. By 1925, the Mount Hood Loop Highway opened, fully encircling the volcano in pavement. Motorists from Portland could drive east up the Columbia River to Hood River, south up over Bennett and Barlow Passes, and back west through Government Camp to Portland, which, at the time, had a population of almost three hundred thousand. Government Camp and the Battle Axe Inn, a quaint lodge with a dining room and a few sleeping quarters opened by Everett Sickler and his wife, Belle Pierce Sickler, became popular tourist destinations.

People began flocking to the mountain for pure recreation. The first hiking trail on Mount Hood was built on the north side in 1885 near what is now known as the Tilly Jane Trail, and the Skyline Trail was built in 1909 in Government Camp. With the road finished, some trails built, and the onset of mountain climbing for sport, Mount Hood had its first surge of outdoor recreationalists.

On August 14, 1926, the Strong family motored to Government Camp on the new Mount Hood Loop Highway to spend the day picnicking and hiking around the streams, meadows, and forests of Lost Creek. Raymond and Winston took off fishing, while younger brother Jack was left to explore the Lost Creek environs alone. (The many news reports say nothing of the whereabouts of Mrs. Strong and her daughter.) The land was wild and beautiful. The understory was a hundred different shades of green. The trees were as tall as the sky. The streams were clear, pure, bubbling tranquility. For a kid, scrambling in this Pacific Northwest wonderland was divine. In mid-August, the wildflowers had likely just peaked: purple lupine, lavender foxglove, yellow monkeyflower, white or yellow yarrow, and red paintbrush lighting up the meadows. In the nooks of the crags, violet penstemon, orange-yellow columbine, tiny white spreading phlox, and pink pussypaws brightened the sandpapery charcoal-gray rocks. Up near tree line, tall, slim, top-heavy beargrass and lupine dominated. The creeks were chock-full of downed timber, so hiking likely involved bounding over rocks and logs.

Amid all this, Jack disappeared.

Some six hundred searchers descended on Government Camp over the next three days to look for Jack. The US Army Seventh Infantry sent forty soldiers from Vancouver, Washington. Members of the Mazamas mountaineering club, which had formed on July 19, 1894, on the summit of Mount Hood, and the Trails Club, formed in 1915 in Portland, showed up with volunteers. US Forest Service rangers, local law enforcement, and neighbors of the Strongs arrived. According to the *Morning Oregonian* from August 16, 1926, the searchers were "mowing through the dense underbrush like a giant rake." The first two days, no luck. No Jack Strong.

Then someone thought of contacting the group of mountaineers in Hood River, the fruit-growing and logging community fifty miles away by road on the north side of the mountain. Word had begun to spread that these expert mountain guides had been doing ad hoc search and rescue missions and were highly skilled in navigating the rough terrain of the alpine. In fact, they climbed the mountain *for fun* and guided others up the treacherous peak *for fun*.

On August 16, thirteen mountaineers motored around the mountain from Hood River, likely in a Ford Model T Runabout or Duesenberg Model A. Andy Anderson led the charge. These skilled mountain climbers had the ability to search the high mountain. They wore knee-length waxed-cotton coats and carried alpenstocks; for footwear, they'd modified orchard boots for glacier climbing by pounding hobnails into the soles for traction and cut away the backs of the boots to allow room for calf muscles when ascending steep slopes.

Although most of the search was concentrated below timberline, it was considered that Jack may have hiked uphill: up the Muddy Fork or up Lost Creek. So three of the Hood River mountaineers—Mace Baldwin, Percy Bucklin, and Jess Puddy—climbed into the alpine, bushwhacking through the undergrowth, clambering over basalt outcrops, and hiking through thick meadows. They arrived at the headwaters of Lost Creek, an area now called Paradise Park, a pristine, glacier-fed meadow replete with melodious creeks and kaleidoscopic wildflowers. After searching all day, the three mountaineers huddled in the meadow to spend a cold night out.

When Baldwin woke up the next morning, he could see the Lost Creek Canyon and the natural path an uphill hiker would likely take. Skilled in mountain travel, topography, and geography, he had a sudden realization and blurted, "I know where the boy is." The three mountaineers scrambled down into the Lost Creek drainage below timberline, where they walked right into Strong, sitting on a boulder. The boy had survived by drinking creek water, foraging for huckleberries, and trying to stomach the three raw fish he'd caught the first day. His thin shirt and trousers were torn, and his arms were scratched.

Immediately, Baldwin fired two double taps from his rifle in the early morning quiet to signal "all clear." A police officer searching much lower in the valley, a mile away and two thousand vertical feet below, acknowledged with two shots of his own. After three cold nights, the boy had been found.

A few hours later, Baldwin, Bucklin, and Puddy arrived with Strong in Government Camp. The town was bustling with searchers and media. A reporter asked Baldwin who they were. Put on the spot, he recalled Andy Anderson's wife's comment about shirking household duties and being "rats" who were out climbing the crags every weekend, so Baldwin replied spontaneously, "We are Crag Rats," forever branding what would become the first organized mountain search and rescue team in the country.

"IT'S TOO WINDY," I shout to Morford. In the fray of the rescue, the wind has picked up to twenty-five miles per hour, with gusts up to forty. So even with the blue skies and 45-degree temperature, the wind keeps us chilly.

"I don't think we should wait for a helicopter," Morford says when he walks down into conversational range with me.

"I agree. We've got a long extrication, and we're burning daylight," I say, knowing a rope extrication to drag the fallen skier up to the Hogsback and then lower him four thousand feet down to the ski resort will take three hours. "Ground evac can be done in three hours. This guy is stable now, but when the sun goes down, he'll get cold—we'll all get cold—and I have no idea, really, how bad his injuries are."

I add, directly and clearly, so that no ambiguity clouds my comments to potentially cause a snafu later, "We can always stop halfway down if the Black Hawk can do a hoist when the wind dies down."

Morford nods in agreement. "I'm so glad you're here."

"I'm glad you're here," I say with a smile. He's capable of running an efficient and safe rescue mission. But if he can defer medical decision-making to a doctor or another skilled medical professional, that's one less thing to worry about.

I look at Gary and Lisa. "We are thinking ground evac," I yell over the wind. "What think?"

"Let's get him out of here—we've got plenty of people," Gary says. "We could be waiting a while for the chopper." Lisa nods in agreement. We all seem relieved to be springing into action: standing idle is not a comfortable feeling for us task-focused rescue mountaineers. We are, as Morford will later say, a "can-do bunch." Right now, we just want to get this guy off the mountain.

Thinking ahead, John, Lisa, and Gary have already rigged up the rope with help from PMR. It's a complicated system, but we have done it before. They build an anchor using two-foot-long snow stakes called pickets. Then they connect a high-strength six-millimeter rope to the anchor and set up a 3:1 mechanical-advantage hoist using two pulleys and a few carabiners.

After we attach the litter to one end of the rope, Lisa and John haul on the other side while four of us rescuers maneuver the litter up through the snow, now softening in the sun so that our boots sink up to our knees—postholing. The rope is primarily to hold the litter in case we fall; the four of us on the litter are doing most of the labor, dragging its three-hundred-odd pounds (with the injured climber) up through three-foot-deep runnels, deep troughs in the snow formed by rain two weeks prior. Gary shouts orders to keep everyone in sync. We wear crampons strapped to our ski boots and hold ice axes in one hand to keep us from falling. Because the snow is so gloppy, it balls up on our crampons, and we must stop every few seconds to kick it off. It's even more awkward because several of us, including me, have skis strapped to our backpacks, making them top-heavy.

After a few minutes, we've raised the litter out of the hole. Then we start the traverse two hundred feet across the steep tongue of the Coalman Glacier and one hundred feet vertically up to Hogsback, where a dozen other rescuers from Crag Rats and PMR are waiting. The traverse and then climb up to them through the deep, slushy snow is accomplished only through the brute strength of us four rescuers. It takes twenty minutes to go just a few hundred feet, but finally we get the litter up to Hogsback.

Gary has already set up the anchor and rope so that right away we can transition the litter to the second rope system and begin lowering down the other side, toward Devils Kitchen and the top of Triangle Moraine.

Meanwhile, the helicopter has done something I find shocking: it lands briefly in the flat area at Devils Kitchen, three hundred feet below Hogsback. Because of the soft snow, the skids sink and the belly of the fuselage rests on the snow. It unloads a medic with extra gear: another vacuum mattress, another litter, and a medical kit. In addition to getting the patient down, Morford needs to keep track of all the rescuers from four different agencies, an added task in a complex rescue.

Now pushing four p.m., we begin a two-hour lower with a rope-rescue system called the "Hogsback kit," pioneered by PMR for exactly this situation. There have been so many missions to these two fumaroles on this most-crowded climbing route that we needed a lightweight but long rope to evacuate injured climbers in this spot. This kit consists of a high-strength, lightweight two-hundred-meter long by six-millimeter-diameter rope, made from Technora, a space-age aramid polymer (a fiber similar to the one used for Kevlar) that's stronger than other rope materials like nylon or polyester. With the Hogsback kit, an anchor is built by burying a pair of pickets two feet deep in the snow, and then the rescue rope is tethered to the anchor break bar, a metal friction device that lets you slow or stop progress at any time. Once the litter is lowered from Hogsback to Devils Kitchen, the rope is at the end. During a pause while we transition the patient from one anchor to another, Robert and I check him quickly. The morphine is wearing off, so we use longer-lasting ketamine for pain.

Meanwhile, PMR has built a second anchor with two more pickets. Here, the rope is run through another break bar, the litter is transferred to this second anchor, and then the rope is unattached from the first anchor so we can begin a second lower. Leapfrogging anchors this way lets us lower the litter in successive six-hundred-foot sections of the slope using the same rope, with a quick stop at each anchor for us to check the patient. With the soft snow in the afternoon, the rain runnels from the week before, and the occasional ridges of ice that vary from six to twelve inches tall, the litter doesn't slide. So four rescuers occasionally need to pull and push it downhill. It's exhausting, but we're making quick work of it and reach the end of the rope again after fifteen minutes, the lowering going faster than we can unbury pickets from the top and move them down the mountain to the next anchor station.

Paul Klein, a professional ski patroller and Crag Rat, shows up. He had been working at Mt. Hood Meadows, responded, and booked it up the mountain on foot after catching a ride up the Magic Mile and Palmer chairlifts to 8,540 feet.

"Damn, you're fast," I say when he shows up.

"Let's bury skis," Paul says. And then adds with a smile, "They are giant pickets—a bombproof anchor."

Gary, Paul, and I quickly bury a pair of skis and tie in the rope. Morford looks at the anchor and gives the thumbs-up, while Paul mentions that next time we might use an akja—a scalloped, lightweight toboggan with two handles at each end that's standard in ski patrol—to ski our victim off the mountain, a more efficient solution.

Gary receives the litter, attaches the rope to the ski anchor with another break bar, and keeps the rescuers moving. I peel off to ski down to the next anchor six hundred feet below, carrying another pair of skis, trying to get us down and out of the wind, down out of the rime ice and the rockfall, and away from the hostile fumaroles as quicky as possible. Slowly and methodically, we bring the patient down the mountain. It has taken two hours to get him from Hot Rocks to the top of the Palmer chairlift, where we load him into a waiting PistenBully snowcat.

By now, the helicopter has landed in the Timberline Lodge parking lot, and the rescuers are in various stages of retreat, many hauling down gear or taking turns dragging the now-empty litter. I climb into the back of the snowcat with Robert. Everyone else from the Crag Rats, Portland Mountain Rescue, American Medical Response, and the Army Reserve either clicks into their skis for a smooth, creamy ski down the groomed run or walks down. I could have made that silky ski run too—I wanted to. After all, I'd just carried my skis up and down Mount Hood for two rescues this month. But I'm also committed to getting the patient down to the pavement at Timberline Lodge, where we'll load him directly into a waiting ambulance.

Finally, with the setting sun lighting the ski run in orange and purple streaks, we're off the mountain; Robert and another paramedic will drive the patient to the trauma center in Portland. Deputy Meyers has ordered pizza, which we gobble as fast as we can, not even registering the flavor or toppings, and pausing just briefly between bites to guzzle water.

Meredith, Ron, Lisa, John, Brian, Gary, Paul, and I are elated with the success of a completed mission, one that was highly technical, involved multiple teams, and saved a life. I try to get follow-up on most missions, and in this case, I'll later pass on to the team that the man had a broken ankle and a broken pelvis and was expected to make a full recovery. Many times, however, we never hear the final outcome.

It's rare in mountain rescue that I actually get to use my doctoring skills *and* my technical rescue skills, a combination of abilities I've developed, nurtured, fostered, and attempted to master beginning roughly at the same time, way back in 1989. And I was available today: nothing bothers me more than missing a rescue. It is the worst case of FOMO possible, one that's common among the most active Crag Rats. Because in addition to missing being with friends in the beautiful alpine, we miss the chance to perform a highly specialized task that we've trained for all year. Moreover, we miss the chance to make a small difference in the world by saving a life. We are so passionate about the outdoors that to save a life in a technical mountain rescue is the apex of our lifestyle. It's like missing your kid's championship soccer game when they score the winning goal.

I later talk to Cully Wiseman, a Crag Rat who is also a general surgeon in Hood River and one of my regular ski and bike partners. He's ten years my junior, and his kids are young, the same ages my daughters were when I started rescues. He's frustrated that he missed the mission. I can empathize—like me twenty-five years ago, Cully is balancing young kids, a marriage, a household, and a job. He will, just a few weeks later, be instrumental in saving another life from deep in another fumarole.

In addition to elation, we rescuers are exhausted. After scarfing pizza, we begin the process of getting home. Gary and Brian are repacking our truck. Lisa and John pile gear in their car. We are tired, dirty, cold, wet, still hungry, and still thirsty. Our gear is in disarray. And we still have an hour drive home, where we'll have to clean, dry, and repack our gear to be ready for the next rescue. We'll also need to attend to team tasks in the next few days: clean the truck, repair gear, buy a new rope to replace the one we trashed, and restock the medical kit. Someone needs to drive the complexities of our 501(c)(3) nonprofit. We'll debrief the mission, write the report, talk to media, and, more importantly, talk to one another. We constantly train in high-angle, crevasse, and avalanche rescue. Now, we'll add a fumarole-system refresher to the training schedule, and we'll train on the akja ski toboggan to obviate the need for the rope. It's costly to be a rescue mountaineer: emotionally stressful, physically taxing, and time consuming.

As we get ready to leave Timberline Lodge, we check out with a sheriff's deputy.

"Where's Ron?" I ask.

"Still eating pizza," Gary says, pointing across the parking lot.

"Ron, let's go," Gary and I yell in unison. Ron grabs another slice, walks over, and climbs in the truck, still wearing his helmet, harness, and ski boots. Gary and I look at each other, smile, and laugh. I pat Ron on the back. No words are needed.

ONE MONTH AFTER the highly publicized Strong rescue in 1926, the Crag Rats had another mission. On September 10, 1926, Vanda York from Portland was hiking on the north side of Mount Hood at Cooper Spur Junction, the site of the Cooper Spur ski hill and the Homestead Inn, twenty miles from Hood River at the base of Mount Hood. There, she happened upon the guide Mark Weygandt, who offered her a summit trip along with a bystander, Herbert Gordon. The three set off for the summit on September 13 up the north-side Sunshine Route. As they ascended a jagged andesite ridge called Langille Crags, York slipped, fell, and slid into a crevasse. Not just down a bit into a hole, but sixty feet into the deep, dark crack in the glacier. She was wedged in the ice, unable to move or extricate herself. Weygandt shouted to a nearby party, on its way down the mountain, to summon help. He then anchored a rope in the snow, rappelled into the crevasse, and started chopping York from the ice.

The climbing party summoned four Crag Rats—Kent Shoemaker, Andy Anderson, Harold David, and C. V. Jackson—who were busy clearing brush and downed timbers to make a ski run for the winter. The four dropped their work, grabbed whatever gear they could find at the Homestead Inn—a timber axe, a stove poker, a first-aid kit, ropes, and coffee—and bolted up the mountain.

In the meantime, according to news reports, York was "embedded in the ice, the cold gradually had its effects on her, and from consciousness, she lapsed into a hazy condition and did not know what was going on above." Weygandt had chipped the ice and freed York, but she was unconscious. So, Weygandt climbed out of the crevasse by chopping steps in the ice wall, and then he and the younger Gordon hauled York out on a manila farm rope. Once back in the midday sun on the glacier, York warmed up and regained consciousness. Members of the Crag Rats arrived and carried York down to Cloud Cap Inn in a makeshift stretcher and then put her in a car for the hour-long drive down the nine-mile dirt road to the Homestead Inn.

Just like the days of yesteryear, missions can come at any time, day or night. Two days after hauling the man from the fumarole, our phones would buzz again. This time it was after dark, just as I was settling into bed with a book. The message read, "Snowshoer. Lost. Barlow Pass."

CHAPTER 3

MARCH: NIGHT STORM ON BARLOW PASS

It's midnight and we can see the stars. But the beauty of the night sky does not offset the bitter cold from temperatures in the teens and a light westerly breeze. Fortunately for the mission, it's not snowing. A few days ago, six weeks of high pressure finally broke and segued into a typical Pacific Northwest winter. While the three-day storm dropped two feet and another incoming storm is predicted to drop more snow, we still have a meager snowpack—not great for skiing.

Lisa, Meredith, and I gear up to head into the Mount Hood backcountry. We've been down this flat ski trail many times before, normally at the top of the morning to pound out ski laps in powder snow below Barlow Pass. But now it's midnight, and we are here to search for a hiker who is dangerously lost, cold, and exhausted.

Earlier that day, a woman in her forties left Barlow Pass off Highway 35 on the south side of the mountain and headed south into two-foot-deep snow, without snowshoes or skis. She was hiking solo to a steep, densely wooded feature named Barlow Butte (5,069 feet). This approach requires snow hiking south on Barlow Road, a cross-country-ski trail in winter, then turning southwest on the Barlow Ridge Trail, which is rarely used and hard to follow. This area is covered in snow and not marked well. In the wilderness, you have four ways to navigate: (1) map and compass, which are not used much nowadays; (2) a phone GPS app, which works most of the time if you have battery, you've downloaded the maps, and you're not blocked by a deep canyon, heavy clouds, or thick trees; (3) blazes (trail markers hammered onto the trees); and (4) someone else's snowshoe or ski track, which may or may not reliably follow the trail. Following Barlow Road is usually straightforward since it's tracked by prior skiers and snowshoers and marked by blazes. Once the woman left Barlow Road on what she thought was the Barlow Butte Trail, she began postholing up to her knees in the recent deep snow, with no other tracks to follow. At some point, without reaching Barlow Butte, she became exhausted, cold, and disoriented. Then she lost daylight and called 911. Fortunately, she had enough power in her phone that the sheriff's office was able to get a GPS location.

"Looks like she's right below Barlow Butte, about a half mile from Devils Half Acre," Meredith says from the warmth of SAR 1, our Ford F-250 pickup, before we click into our skis and set off into the night. "This will be fun," she adds with a smile. She knows this area well, and she's also an expert at using her phone's navigation app. Again, fun is not at the expense of the woman, but rather a key reason why we come out. Good friends, chitchat, laughs, and being in motion on skis in the beautiful forest make this experience deeply rewarding.

I grimace and say, "I'd rather be in bed," but then I grin because Meredith's smile is contagious.

"I've got a pad, a spare puffy, and hot chocolate," Lisa says, redirecting us to the mission.

"I'll grab spare snowshoes," Meredith says. She's thinking ahead and realizing that these will help the woman walk out.

We discuss our plan for a few minutes, debating whether we need more rescuers before discarding the idea, and then talk things through with HRCSO Deputy Eric Wahler, another seasoned SAR coordinator, at the trailhead. He'll stay in his warm truck while we ski into the night. We decide the information is accurate: the hiker is uninjured but cold, so we'll need to hurry before she gets hypothermic. The sky has cleared between storms, and temps are in the mid-teens, headed for single digits. I worry that, without a rescue, she may not survive the night.

"Ready," announces Meredith, who is way too much awake and bubbly given the ungodly hour. She's a night person and always grumbles when I force our ski-day departures at six a.m.

"Me too." Lisa hoists her pack.

Meredith, Lisa, and I ski into the night through the hauntingly dark forest, lit by the white glow of our LED headlamps. We mostly have a sense of urgency, but we're also lighthearted. If we didn't laugh and chitchat, we'd not be able to do this avocation. Most rescues end up with a positive outcome: we find the lost, rescue the stranded, carry out the injured. But we still have the physical toll of the mission, and when the outcome is a bad one, an emotional toll—a covert cause of stress. Once we searched for a week for a missing skier only to find him deceased in a creek. We become all business in these moments, our energies poured into bringing the body out for the benefit of the family. In those grim and sorrowful situations, humor, laughter, and finding the positive aspects of the mission—skiing with friends—are what let us persevere.

Now, amid the trees and the stars, there's little evidence of human impact: the tall trees here are mostly preserved, and the evidence of melting glaciers is out of sight. Being lower on the mountain with fewer hazards, on relatively flat ground, and on a known trail also means we can be more relaxed. And we only have to ski a little over two miles and about an hour to a subject who is uninjured and alive.

Yet, at any moment, Mount Hood could change, going from a cuddly puppy to a tempestuous wolf. And at any time, the woman's condition could change. She could become hypothermic. She could start walking, thus changing her location. I have this nagging feeling that this may take all night.

"I really hope we find this woman uninjured and only two miles away," I say. "I have to work tomorrow."

"We will," Lisa says, ever the optimist. "I have to work too."

These missions occur regularly: searching for the lost or stranded. Hunter at Frog Lake, hiker on Mount Defiance, snowshoer at Tamanawas Falls. Not injured but cold, tired, hungry, and thirsty. Maybe slightly disoriented because they lost their way or they have no headlamp. In days past, folks in trouble on Mount Hood often had to figure out how to be more self-reliant because there was no instant communication. Now we've got comms: good ones. Cell phones and satellite locators and radios. In the Jack Strong rescue from 1926, a gunshot was used to communicate while on the mountain. Back in those early days, the Crag Rats had to use landlines for mission callouts. For those without phones, someone had to drive over and pound on the door.

After the Crag Rats formed, found the Strong boy, and rescued the York woman, they would have their first official mission on the foreboding, dominant Mount Hood, at night, in the middle of winter, in the middle of a storm, on an evening not unlike the one we're out in, looking for a stranded hiker. As I mentioned, the year 1926 marked the first explosion of outdoor recreation on Mount Hood, fueled by the completion of the Mount Hood Loop Highway and the establishment of Government Camp. Better and more available mountain equipment that was often war-surplus gear, like waxed-cotton parkas, crampons, waterproof "bunny" boots, and wool clothing, brought more people to the mountain as well.

On New Year's Day 1927, a group of Portland teenage boys drove to Government Camp, from where they skied and snowshoed up Little Zigzag Canyon into the alpine in a snowstorm. Calvin White, seventeen, was reported to have better ski skills, better fitness, or better wax—no one is exactly sure. But he forged ahead. When the group retreated in the storm, White kept going. And then he got lost.

A search was launched from the Battle Axe Inn in Government Camp. A small forest service cabin at six thousand feet, at the present-day site of Timberline Lodge, was used as an advanced incident command post. To facilitate communication, a phone line was run six miles from the Battle Axe Inn to the Timberline Cabin, where a large electric light was set up on a pole. The group now known as the Hood River Crag Rats was called out during a blinding, bitter-cold snowstorm.

For two days and nights, searchers battled the storm, then rested in the Timberline Cabin. Clothes hung from the rafters. Rescuers scarfed food that had been delivered by the Portland Advertising Club and then curled up in the bunks to rest. Three Crag Rats—Bill Cochran, John Annala, and Paul Hoerlein—deployed on Sunday, January 3, 1927, at four a.m. after driving over from Hood River. They followed what they thought was White's trail over the Little Zigzag River: down into the canyon, through deep snow, and up the other side. In a newspaper story, Cochran later wrote, "I followed a trail and soon after found out where he made a bed of fir boughs. It was in a protected spot." White had been going up and down and crisscrossing the giant canyon haphazardly. After following White's zigzagging tracks, Cochran made contact: "Here I hollered and got his reply, which was clear." By midmorning, the Crag Rats had found White in the deep snow of the Little Zigzag Canyon, alive. "He was underneath a tree with a big boulder beside it. The boulder was five or six feet high. It would have protected him from rain or snow coming straight down," Cochran wrote.

As was customary, Cochran signaled with a rifle shot. Crag Rats descended upon White with dry clothing and hot soup. "I've been without sleep for three days and nights! If I go to sleep now, I will sleep for a long time," White was later quoted as saying in the *Oregonian*. Cochran stripped White's wet clothing, helped him change into dry clothes, and gave him water and food. They started carrying him out using skis as a sled. To cross the ice-cold creek, two additional Crag Rats, Aatto Annala and Everett Philpoe, stood in the water and bent over so the rescue sled could be passed across their backs. A dog team sent from Government Camp pulled a toboggan to haul White the final mile to the Battle Axe Inn.

White was driven to the hospital, where he would have a few frostbitten toes amputated. White's father, Dr. Calvin White Sr., would later state in the news, "I fully realize I owe my son's life to Bill Cochran of Hood River. And it would be futile for me to even try to sound the depth of my gratitude to him. Had he not speeded ahead of the rest, had he not pushed on without slackening, even when he himself was all but exhausted, and had he not acted quickly and wisely when he found Calvin, doubtless my boy would not be alive." This rings familiar to me, as we get similar thanks from the rescued and their families to this day: a thank-you note, a donation check, a plate of cookies, a formal letter of commendation, and sometimes just an anonymous contribution. Often, thankful families unknowingly focus on just one rescue member, like Cochran, not understanding the overall teamwork involved in a successful mission.

The Calvin White mission was both exhausting and a success. But the Crag Rats didn't leave the mountain, because another mission had unfolded simultaneously. Also on New Year's Day 1927, Leslie Brownlee and Al Feyerabend, both twenty years old, wanted to be the first to summit Mount Hood in the new year. (This is the forerunner to today's craze of setting FKTs, or fastest known times.) They departed Government Camp early in the morning of December 31, clad in heavy "submarines"—waxed, wind- and water-repellent US Navy parkas—and wood-framed, rawhide-laced bear-claw snowshoes. They had hot food in insulated bottles, flashlights, and a compass. The two climbed two thousand feet to the Timberline Cabin, and then they continued at one thirty a.m. on New Year's Day up the mountain. The storm rolled in and started dumping snow. Newspaper reports stated that visibility was only ten feet, with snow falling at an inch per hour: twenty-six inches piled up in one day.

The two fell asleep on the snow, somewhere around seven thousand feet on the south side above the Timberline Cabin, without a tent or sleeping bags. They awoke a few hours later and were cold. Despite the storm, they continued up White River Glacier's west moraine, the large slope above the Timberline Cabin, and expected to find Crater Rock, the volcanic monolith at the summit crater at ten thousand feet. But with the wind, snowfall, and poor visibility, they couldn't see and became exhausted. Brownlee turned back. Feyerabend continued for a bit, then also turned back. But the two had become separated in the whiteout conditions.

On January 2, Feyerabend blindly walked down the fall line from Crater Rock, which led him to Mississippi Head, far west of the Timberline Cabin. When the storm cleared for a brief moment, he saw his mistake, traversed east back to the Timberline Cabin, and made it down to Government Camp without Brownlee, right about the time the Calvin White mission had concluded. Brownlee was still missing.

January 3, 1927, was a long day for the tired, hungry, and thirsty Crag Rats just off the White mission. Nonetheless, Crag Rats Bill Hukari, Aatto Annala, Joshua Pierson, and Eino Annala climbed back up the mountain to Crater Rock high on the south side and then over to Illumination Rock—another volcanic monolith at nine thousand feet—and the upper Zigzag Glacier. The thought was that Brownlee may have descended to the right into Little Zigzag Canyon near where White was found. They searched deep snow with snowshoes. They spent the cold night of January 3 camped in Paradise Park, right near where Jack Strong had been found the autumn before. They built a fire on the glacial ice, but the embers kept sinking into the snowpack, so it created a giant hole. They had no sleeping bags and one army-surplus wool blanket. Bill Hukari tried to fall asleep on the soggy blanket, but the others prodded him awake for fear he'd freeze to death. However, when the Crag Rats later recounted the mission in the meeting minutes, they simply explained the night as "interesting."

Another Crag Rats team led by Bill Lenz, who was also just off the White search, spent the day of January 3 and well into the night following snowshoe tracks that went into the Salmon River, thinking Brownlee may have descended to the left into the Salmon River Canyon and down into White River Canyon. They, too, spent the night searching down to the Mount Hood Loop Highway. By the time Lenz was ready to quit, he had spent twenty-seven hours searching for Brownlee without rest.

Brownlee was never found.

NOW, NEARLY ONE HUNDRED years later, Lisa, Meredith, and I chitchat and laugh. As Lisa watches the phone GPS, we reach Devils Half Acre in a half hour, then bushwhack straight uphill toward Barlow Butte. As we converse easily, I remark—twice—that I hope the hiker can still walk, giving voice to a thought that's been rattling around in my brain.

"What if she can't?" Meredith asks.

"Two go back for the litter, and one hunkers in to keep her alive," I say.

"That will take a couple hours," Lisa says.

"Yes. That will be awful," I scowl.

Our mood turns more serious and focused when we get within a few hundred feet of the subject's GPS coordinates, in forested terrain with deep, untracked snow. I imagine it's like when Lisa runs her middle school classroom: it's fun to joke and laugh and be merry, but at some point, she has to say, "All right, class, it's time to learn algebra." As we break trail slightly downhill in the newly fallen snow, it's as if our skis are giant, awkward snowshoes. Lisa and Meredith have their phones out, following the GPS signal. The blazes are no longer present. As we get closer, we start yelling.

"We should be right on her," Lisa says, referring to the GPS. Meredith yells again. We hear a rustle from a tree just above us, off-trail. All three of us light up the tree with our headlamps.

"Hello?" I shout.

Meredith and Lisa ski to the tree, a fifteen-foot-high Douglas-fir whose snow-covered boughs shake violently. The woman, who'd been fully hidden under the branches, pokes her head out.

"Hi," she says meekly. "I'm here." She clambers out of the tree, afraid to miss us passing by.

"Hi, we're mountain rescue," Lisa says.

"Oh, thank you."

"Are you injured?" I ask, being direct to find out *Can she walk?*

"No, but I'm cold." She scoots on her knees out of the tree well, the limbs showering her with snow. Lisa, Meredith, and I encase her in a huddle.

"Let's get some food and water in her and then get moving," I say, knowing she needs calories to warm up but also needs to start walking. I do a quick scan to make sure she's uninjured.

I also check her clothes, which seem to be mostly dry. She's alert and able to stand. Meredith straps the spare snowshoes on the woman's boots while Lisa digs in her pack and pulls out a thermos.

"Here, drink this," Lisa says. She holds the thermos up to the woman's mouth, helping her chug its contents in one gulp.

"What is that?" I ask.

"Lukewarm hot chocolate made with milk and extra sugar. Just like you taught me," Lisa says, citing my guidance that hypothermic people benefit more from calories than hot liquids.

"Perfect," I say. I'm glad Lisa remembered to bring the cocoa, because I certainly did not. Lisa's elixir is like magic, rejuvenating the woman in minutes.

"We should get moving, but slowly," I say. I'm worried her core temperature might drop now that she's out from the tree and moving around, which pushes blood that was likely being conserved out to cool extremities, an effect like a radiator. "You ready to start walking once we get the snowshoes on?" I ask the woman. She nods. "We'll go slowly, and we'll help you," I say, trying to be reassuring but also prompt.

After a few minutes—we don't waste time—we start the long walk back to the lot where SAR 1 is parked. Meredith's spare snowshoes are key, because instead of sinking up to her knees, the woman floats on the surface of the deep snow downhill to Devils Half Acre. After fifteen minutes of awkward walking and stumbling, we reach Barlow Road; it's a relief to be back on a well-trodden trail with compacted snow.

"I'm warming up," the woman says. She is fit and strong, so once we rejuvenate her with calories and comfort, we make good time. I'm relieved—as long as we keep moving, speed isn't too important. Lisa and Meredith walk in front, further packing down the snow for the woman. Meredith chats with the woman. She had set off without snowshoes, thinking it would be a quick, hour-long hike, and was actually quite prepared, carrying extra food, water, gloves, and a puffy jacket in a backpack. She just got into a bit of bad luck by somehow losing the trail, which is easy to do with all the snow. She had no map or cell phone trail app.

This search has been successful, but not all of them are. Once near here, at Mt. Hood Meadows ski resort, we searched for three days for a missing snowboarder who was found deceased, having suffocated in deep snow. Another time on a nearby trail, we searched for four days for a missing cross-country skier; their remains were found two years later. Now at night with the woman on snowshoes, it takes an hour to hike a mile back to the parking lot, stopping just twice for brief rests. In addition to Deputy Wahler, the woman's family is waiting in the parking lot. We get greetings and thanks and oh-my-Gods and more thank-yous. Despite the goodwill, Meredith, Lisa, and I don't want to talk anymore. We just want to go home. It's three o'clock in the morning, and Lisa and I need to be at work in a few hours.

The next evening, I chat with Skylar and Avrie via FaceTime. I recount the mission, playing it down because we had no good ski turns because it was basically an out-and-back along a flat trail. I recount Lisa's preparedness. "Good thing Lisa came along," they say. They both took middle school classes from her and recall their time as her students fondly. We quickly move on to other topics, including our next trip—a rendezvous in Tenerife.

Later in the week, at a Crag Rats meeting, Lisa, Meredith, and I recount the mission in a brief two minutes—this routine mission has few lessons to impart. I praise Meredith for bringing snowshoes and for her fine phone GPS skills, and Lisa for bringing the magical hot chocolate elixir. Then we move on. No one asks why the woman was out solo, without snowshoes. We all probably think about it fleetingly but know that there's no good answer. Sometimes people just do things without being fully informed or paying attention to the skills required.

One hundred years ago, after the White and Feyerabend/Brownlee missions, the *Morning Oregonian* on January 6, 1927, made a statement that could easily be reproduced today verbatim, as it's the same advice we have been giving people for a century:

> *Mount Hood is growing more popular every year, and we can not afford to neglect this matter any longer. It is impossible to keep people off the mountain and while it is one of the safest and easiest to climb,*

it is not a parlor game, particularly for novices without guidance or proper equipment.

But Crag Rats are not judgy. Because we are in the mountains nearly every day, I suspect we all know that we, too, might someday need to be rescued. Although I don't voice this to the group, I'm happy people are out enjoying the world, even if occasionally underprepared, to give them an appreciation of this beautiful land we love so dearly.

CHAPTER 4

APRIL: FELLOWSHIP OF THE HIGH ALPINE

Finally, after a couple more long stretches of mild weather, a late winter storm unleashes two feet of snow on the mountain. At the top of the morning, Meredith, Ron, Cully, and I gather our gear, which is nearly perpetually packed. When I ski with Eric Peterson, a Crag Rat, seasoned flight nurse, and former ski patroller and park ranger—and one of the most graceful skiers I know—we are wheels-up at six a.m. But without Eric, Meredith and Cully push for a later departure. Ron is always instantly agreeable to leave early, as long as I drive. Not so much because he doesn't want to drive, but because he's frugal. Cully needs to drop his kids off at preschool first, and when he begins to apologize for the later departure, I brush him off. "I've been there before; I remember the days," I say.

When Meredith, on the other hand, wrangles for a later departure, I get good-naturedly argumentative. She and Ron don't have kids.

"I want to sleep," she says.

"I'm rolling my eyes," I say unapologetically over the phone. "Go to bed earlier and you'll get the same amount of sleep." I apply logic every time. It's jovial banter, a tone we've adopted partly to help keep mountain rescue missions less stressful. Although now we're not scouring for a lost person but hunting for deep powder.

We drive up to Mt. Hood Meadows, where, on a busy weekend, several thousand people a day enjoy the slopes. The sky is clear in town, but as we drive thirty-five miles up Highway 35, we enter the clouds and find snow flurries and slight wind. Rather than take chairlifts, we ski into the backcountry just a quarter mile out of bounds and find smooth, untracked, late-season powder. At the top of a ridge, we spend five minutes to transition from uphill-ski to downhill-ski mode, peeling off our climbing skins and locking down the heels of our bindings. The eight-hundred-foot run took thirty minutes up and will take ten minutes down.

"How are you so fast at transitions?" Meredith asks as I peel the sticky skins from the bottom of my skis and stuff them inside my parka without taking off my backpack.

I shrug. "Before I met you two, I skied a lot solo. You get fast when you don't have to wait for people."

"Wait for me," Meredith jokes.

"We're always waiting for you," Ron counters. I'm lucky to have Meredith, Ron, and Cully as ski friends. On any given ski day, our group is likely to include Eric and Heiko Stopsack, who are currently at work. Because in addition to having flexible schedules, this group is almost always willing to ski, provided no work or family duties are pressing. The physical euphoria of gliding over snow is powerful and addicting, but doing so with friends is even better.

We are all smiles. Today our hedonistic search for deep powder has been fruitful. But it is a bit of an obsession or, at the very least, a deeply ingrained habit. The last thing I do at night and each morning is check various weather apps to track storms, precipitation, wind speed, temperature, and incoming moisture from the Pacific Ocean as it blows, drifts, or rages over the Portland metro area and up the Cascade foothills. Resort ski report: check. Radar: check. Telemetry: check. Webcams: check. All this in search of smooth, lofty, silky turns in deep powder and the peacefulness and euphoria that accompany being in motion in the natural world.

Ron, Cully, and Eric do the same because, often, if I text our group at nine thirty p.m. with a weather synopsis, Ron will text back, "Yeah, I just saw that." And Cully will text, "I'm checking a few other sites." Whereas many people plan their days and weeks around work or family duties, we plan our lives around skiing and the mountains.

The four of us spend the morning skiing, making lap after lap. When I get home midafternoon, I hang my jacket and pants to dry in the mudroom, put my ski boots on an electric air dryer, and then fire up my computer to work. Just before I drift off to sleep, I hear the wind pick up as it wrestles with the giant ponderosa pines outside my bedroom window. A few minutes later, the rain arrives and pelts the side of my house loudly like hail. Rain in the valley means snow in the mountains.

I've been asleep a half hour when my phone rattles on the nightstand. Yes, it's another mountain rescue callout. This time a skier is injured on the Tilly Jane Trail, the main access point to the Cloud Cap–Tilly Jane Historic District and the north side of Mount Hood. The Tilly Jane Trail is a 2.5-mile-long, two-thousand-foot-elevation-gain climb. In winter, you need skis or snowshoes; in summer, a pair of light hiking boots or trail-running shoes. At the top, you'll find a collection of buildings from yesteryear: an A-frame cabin; a collapsing, uninhabitable cookhouse built by the American Legion in the 1920s; a US Forest Service guard station; the private Snowshoe Club Cabin; and the historic Cloud Cap Inn.

I look at my phone again. In addition to me, Ron, and Meredith, the crew will be Lisa, Brian, Cully, and Heiko. Good crew. No, *great* crew. Nearly the same crew as always. Our entire club has a roster of one hundred, including inactive members, rescuers, and those who help with the many tasks of running our nonprofit: dealing with our finances, insurance, two trucks, two snowcats, and two buildings. Of the sixty-eight in the field-deployable callout group, around forty of us do most of the missions. This is not an easy task, considering we get around forty mission days per year, and this year is shaping up to be a record.

Now, another night mission. I pull myself out of bed. This is getting a tad more difficult. Not so much being in the mountains all night, but recovering the following day. For a decade, I worked one night shift a week in the emergency department. One day, I finally stopped abruptly, because I was spending the entire next day tired, unfocused, and discombobulated. These Crag Rats night rescues are beginning to have the same effect. But the thing getting me out of bed now is the thrill of the mission, the love of this mountain, the camaraderie among friends, and the fear of missing out. If I don't get up, I'm likely to lie awake wondering about the good times my friends are having, wondering who is in trouble and needing help while I'm cozy under the comforter, and wondering who will come get me if I need help someday. But, as the years wear on, night missions are becoming more difficult.

Because I'm in mountaineering clothing 150 times a year, getting dressed to ski is robotic, and I jump into my kit as easily as someone else might put on Saturday sweatpants and a T-shirt. Like Steve Jobs wearing the same clothing every day so as not to use brain power on trivial decisions, I pull on the same outfit—or a variation of the same outfit—every time. On top: base layer, full-zip fleece hoodie with a cell phone chest pocket, and wind jacket. On the bottom: polyester long underwear and one of two ski pants, either a wool midweight pair for being in motion in good weather or burly wind- and waterproof storm pants, the ones I pull on today.

Into the mudroom, it's the same procedure as always: get my ski pack, pull my ski boots off the dryer, grab gloves and climbing skins off the drying rack, and get the SAR radio from its charging dock. I load my backcountry skis and poles. Sitting in my truck, I take a tactical pause to run through a list in my mind: skis, boots, skins, backpack, radio, phone. *Same as always.*

I meet Brian, Ron, Meredith, Cully, and Heiko at the county yard, hauntingly lit by the dingy yellow of mercury-vapor lights. We are picking up Lisa on the way. SAR Deputy Chris Guertin has just arrived.

"What's the story?" I ask.

"Skier in a group of three injured on the Tilly Jane Trail. About halfway up. Leg injury. Can't walk, and the two other people can't bring him down."

"At least we know where they are," Meredith says.

"Sounds like a ski out," Brian says.

"Okay, let's roll," I say. "Who's driving?"

"I can," Heiko says. He fires up SAR 1, and we jam our packs and skis in the back. They barely fit because the Ford F-250's bed has a slide-out tray that is loaded with three litters, a dozen ropes, avalanche rescue gear, crevasse rescue gear, and medical equipment, including a high-tech vacuum mattress and a military-spec hypothermia bag wedged next to old-school basics like inexpensive sleeping bags, foam camping pads, and blue plastic tarps. We pack ourselves shoulder to shoulder in the cab. I wedge my ski boots on the floor in front of the heater so they stay warm during the drive.

As we head into the night, I call the skier's friend via cell phone. I find out that after a day of skiing in the trees, this group of three skiers was headed down the Tilly Jane Trail in the dark when one skier twisted his ankle and was rendered immobile.

"Let's get moving," I say. "I have to work in the morning."

"Me too," says Heiko, who commutes to King County, Washington, where he works as a paramedic and helicopter rescue specialist.

"I always have work," says Brian, who runs his family's orchard of pears and blueberries.

At ten p.m., I send out a quick text to the entire team of Crag Rats: "Hasty team departing the yard." A hasty team is the quick-response crew that goes up to do an initial assessment and rescue. If more resources are required for a complex rescue, we have a secondary team soon follow.

AFTER THE WHITE and Feyerabend/Brownlee missions of January 1927, more mountain rescue missions immediately commenced for the Crag Rats, and they organized robustly. To learn more about this time, I dissect our archives, which are housed in the basement of the Crag Rat Hut. The hut was built by Crag Rats in 1966 on a small, unfarmable knoll surrounded by an orchard called Winchell Butte, just five miles from Hood River on land donated by the orchardist Riddle Lage. The hut has an in-your-face view of Mount Hood and the expansive orchards of Hood River Valley. It's not really a hut but a two-story building with a commercial kitchen, two giant great rooms, and a back patio. We rent it out for weddings in the summer to help defray our SAR operating costs. In a dark, panic-room-sized walk-in closet under the stairs in the basement, there is an antique six-foot-tall steel fireproof safe jam-packed with materials.

I start here, sorting through reams of archives: correspondence, meeting minutes, logbooks, financial statements, loose newsclips, and scrapbooks from founders like Andy Anderson. I read meeting minutes, which were typewritten or handwritten in cursive and organized in three-ring binders, neatly categorized by decade from the group's inception in 1926 through 1973. Outside the safe, records from 2000 to 2013 are stored in a metal file cabinet and are in various states of completeness, likely depending on the personality of the Pip Squeak (Pip Squeak is the secretary, Little Squeak is the vice president, and Big Squeak is the president). Some years, comprehensive records are stored in their respective manila folders: meeting minutes, financial records, and correspondence. Other years, the paperwork is minimal, with everything stuffed into one folder. In 2013, our recordkeeping went electronic, with everything stored on Google Drive thanks to the diligence of Tom Rousseau. To give you an idea of what sort of badass joins the Crag Rats, the retired oscilloscope engineer used to bicycle to work from Hood River to Beaverton on Monday, eighty three miles, stay the week, and then bicycle home every Friday. Tom's calm, quiet, unassuming demeanor is exactly why he excels in organizing both our radio program and our electronic records.

Outside the safe in a walk-in closet, cabinets store cleaning materials, a fridge stores beer, and the corners house miscellaneous outdated and retired rescue items like several hundred feet of rope wrapped around a wood spool as tall as my knees. And there's a back closet within the closet with more stuff from the past century. I'll have to come back to search that—on my first orientation to the basement archives, I could not find 1974 to 1999, which are possibly cached in the extra closet.

According to the records, in 1927, the Crag Rats were busy running their first-of-its-kind startup in the United States. Meetings were held the second and fourth Thursdays of the month, something we still adhere to. Crag Rats bought "khaki fur trimmed parkas" for $4 each, and in June 1928, they adopted a black-and-white buffalo-checked wool shirt as the official garb, bought at the famous Portland department store Montgomery Ward for $3.95. We still wear these wool shirts today for social outings more than missions. By May 1927, the Crag Rats reached an agreement with the US Forest Service to help fight forest fires in the summer (although, after a few years, this function of Crag Rats ceased). And they assumed guide responsibilities for the annual American Legion climb on the north side of Mount Hood, which they continued to guide through 1948, although the legion climbs continued until 1953.

The early meetings, much like today, had an air of jovial camaraderie, which comes through in the meeting minutes. Although little information exists on early rescues, one mission on July 18, 1927, garnered national attention when a 103-person group of the Mazamas climbing club was ascending the peak via the north slope, via the icy Sunshine Route, which menders through crevasses and seracs on the Eliot and Coe Glaciers and then gains Cathedral Ridge to the summit. About two thousand feet below the summit and five hundred feet below Cathedral Ridge, they were cutting steps with ice axes to cross the top of the Coe Glacier when one member slipped—no account exists of exactly who. But that was all it took, just one person. The climber rocketed down the 75-degree slope, pulling off other climbers, as they were all tied together by a hemp rope wrapped around their waists. The *Oregon Daily Journal* recounted climber Harry Krebs's story: he was on the rope line, felt a tug when someone fell, heard a shout, felt a jerk, and tried to self-arrest. But his alpenstock jerked out of his hand, he slid, and his speed increased. Eight climbers fell in a jumble over a precipice and into a crevasse. They landed in a pile, stacked on top of each other. One had a broken leg, another took an alpenstock to the face, and Portland dentist W. H. Stryker had been impaled in the gut with his ice axe.

Crag Rats responded immediately. The *Morning Oregonian* reported on July 19 that "in less time almost than the telling requires, Crag Rats were off to the Legion Camp for stretchers." The Legion Camp was established by the Hood River Post of the American Legion on the site of the present-day Tilly Jane A-Frame. Crag Rats ran up the mountain, extricated the group from the crevasse with a rope, and found Stryker critically injured. Eventually, all the fallen went on to Hood River and Portland hospitals. Mary Malloy had a compound right ankle fracture. Gerald Moore had a head injury, causing him to be "irrational" all night. William Harris had his nose pierced by an alpenstock. E. M. Bergen had fractures of both collarbones. Hilda Roes fractured both ankles and injured her spine. Harry Krebs ended up with chest and abdomen injuries. One other had been injured but not seriously. Stryker died.

Not unlike today, the Crag Rats had little time to process the tragedy. Work, family, and recreation of their own beckoned. And then more rescues. Reports in news articles say they had scores of rescue missions per year, although I found little information except for sporadic yellowed clips from local newspapers, which were probably hastily written judging by the typos and brevity. Meeting minutes from the 1920s and 1930s were detailed with social outings and club business but left out nearly any mention of rescues.

In the following years, the Crag Rats flourished. Using member dues, they bought property in Hood River—not at the present site of the hut, but on the west side of town close to the Columbia River. Although the building has long since been razed, the chimney of the original Crag Rats Hut still stands at Interstate 84 Eastbound Exit 62. This first hut was constructed between 1931 and 1932, and the first meeting in the new digs was held on October 27, 1932. During this time, membership expanded, but the Crag Rats, like today, were selective. They voted in a handful of members per year and rejected many. To become a member, the vote needed to be nearly unanimous: just two unfavorable votes prohibited any person from becoming a member, a policy that holds true to this day.

Mountain safety—much like today—was a timely topic. From this early era of burgeoning outdoor recreation, I found references expressing concern that people were heading to the mountain unprepared. During the meeting on January 14, 1927, Andy Anderson had an idea of "posting signs that would tell where the trails lead and the dangers of the glaciers." A monograph typed on onion-skin paper, wedged into the meeting minutes around the same time but without a date, is titled "Safety Suggestions for Climbing Mount Hood (North

Side), When Not Accompanied by a Competent Guide." It lists some timeless dos and don'ts that readers might see today nearly verbatim in a guidebook or on a climbing website. The dos include "Have an Ice Axe or Metal Pointed Alpenstock" and "Wear Proper Clothing," while the don'ts include "Don't climb with less than two companions, unless properly equipped, unless physically fit, and without knowledge of the mountain and its surroundings."

I find another article glued to a paper scrapbook with no date, source, or author but in a folder marked "1930s." It's titled "Mountain Safety to Be Considered" and regarded a plan to "Prevent Lives Lost on Outings." It was a plan sponsored by two Portland-based clubs that were instrumental in the Strong, White, and Feyerabend/Brownlee searches—the Portland Advertising Club and the Portland Chamber of Commerce. The article suggests that in cooperation with the Mount Hood National Forest, the chamber of commerce, the state highway commission, and the state traffic department, changes should be considered in recreational facilities. For example, instead of government-only buildings and trails for forest protection, the US Forest Service should also maintain sanitary conditions in forest campgrounds, build shelter huts, mark trails, provide first-aid supplies, and develop better parking. In the post-Depression era, utilizing the Civilian Conservation Corps and Franklin Roosevelt's New Deal, shelters were constructed, some of which still stand today on landmarks like McNeil Point, Cairn Basin, and Cooper Spur.

And not unlike today, I also find some blame and shame. This same articles states that the Portland Chamber of Commerce advised the US Forest Service to consider ways to prevent tragedies on Mount Hood. "It is felt, a member of the committee said yesterday, that Calvin White and Feyerabend/Brownlee would not have been lost on the mountain if proper efforts had been made to prevent attempts to climb the peak alone or to go any distance from camp alone during the winter." This statement has a familiar ring, a theme echoed throughout the upcoming decades and one we still hear today.

Meanwhile, rescue missions kept coming in the 1930s and 1940s, many below timberline, according to brief news reports stuck to scrapbook pages and even briefer meeting minutes. At the US Forest Service Ditch Cabin on the north side of the mountain, Crag Rats found two lost men. On the Coe Glacier, they rescued a climber who stepped on a snow bridge and fell twelve feet into a crevasse. In the Salmon River Canyon on the south side, they searched for a man who got lost. In the Hood River, they helped a logger who was trapped by the "boiling torrent" of rising water on an island. Logs were "racing down in the milky flood and making a continual boom from boulders clanking." Using a sling, pulley, and lifeline, Crag Rats pulled him to safety. Similarly, on the Lake Branch, a man was fishing, slipped from a rock, fell into a deep pool, and drowned; Crag Rats recovered his body. Near Wapinitia, they found a man who got lost after walking out of a "sanitarium." They found him at a sheep camp by following his distinctive tracks, as he was wearing a pair of his wife's sandals.

Occasionally, Crag Rats would have a mission in the alpine. The first in several years came in 1940. Velma Hathaway, age twenty-six, was climbing with a large group when she felt ill and left the party to descend alone on Cooper Spur around eight thousand feet. The party turned around a little farther up and returned to Cloud Cap Inn, but found no Hathaway. At least twenty-five Crag Rats turned out to search all night. Hathaway was found seven hours later at two a.m. suffering from "shock and exhaustion." A theatrical newspaper clip without a date or byline reports:

> More than seven hours alone in the dark and silence, more than seven hours of bewilderment among the crevasses and perils of the gashed mountain, powerless through every movement to know where to turn or what to do to deliver herself—her forlorn predicament through the night makes you wonder why unfamiliar girls and men permit themselves to wander away from guides or the beaten path in a mountainside that has been the sepulcher of so many lost amateurs and the doom of so many whom fate finally snatched from the snow and merciless glaciers. Doom holds revelry on the heights of Hood. Death dances and feasts in every crevasse. Ghosts flit from hummock to hummock and laugh at the amateurs who stray and novices unskilled in mountain

lore. Happily there are Crag Rats nearby and mountain guides who now own Hood.

As the Crag Rats' reputation grew, they were called out of county, no easy task considering the automobile of the day was a Ford Model T. To get to the busy south side in Clackamas County, they had to drive fifty miles over Bennet and Barlow Passes to Government Camp, which took a couple of hours in bad weather.

In 1929, the Crag Rats were called to Mount Rainier to search for missing apprentice guide Forrest Greathouse. Led by Andy Anderson, eleven members responded to Paradise Inn and joined the search on day three. Crag Rats found Greathouse's frozen corpse deep in an Ingraham Glacier crevasse, lowered a rescuer down, and pulled the body out. They had left Hood River at three p.m., arrived in Paradise at one thirty a.m., finished the rescue before dark, and were back home thirty-five hours and 480 miles later.

In 1933, they were called to Mount Jefferson to bring three deceased climbers off the central Oregon peak. According to the *Oregon Journal*, "Their bodies found Friday afternoon frozen into the crevasse into which, borne by avalanche, they plunged while attempting to ascend the peak last Monday Morning, were chopped from the ice, carried to Jefferson Park, then borne out to the road at Olallie Lake Saturday."

The Crag Rats made a name for themselves during this time, but likely unintentionally. Under Anderson's leadership, they responded to missions for the love of rescue and love of community, a side effect that was attracting national notice, as no other team in the country then specialized in mountain rescue.

First, on August 23, 1931, the *New York Times* published a short column on the elite team, titled "Crag Rats Rescue the Lost: Like the Monks of St. Bernard Pass, They Are Always Ready to Endure Hardships in the Mountains." The article reports that the Crag Rats are like no other group: "Leaving their occupations at a moment's notice, without pay or expenses of any kind, they have fought blizzards, traversed glaciers, and have been lowered by ropes into the great crevasses of the Cascades." In the short five years of their existence, the Crag Rats had logged around a hundred rescue missions—and were logging about a dozen notable rescues a year. In the article, they self-described their twenty-seven-person group as "cosmopolitan," with "fruit growers, two bankers, one photographer, one electrician, one doctor, one druggist, one service-station man, and Anderson, the lumberman." The article pointed out, "Many applied, few were accepted."

Then, in March 1932, the magazine *American Forests* ran a feature story by Stewart H. Holbrook titled "The St. Bernards of North America," which further catapulted the Crag Rats from the rural orchards of Hood River to national fame. Holbrook described the Crag Rats as the only group dedicated to the rescue of persons in the mountains, responding to Mounts St. Helens, Jefferson, and Rainier. He wrote, "To be a Crag Rat one must have climbed to the tops of Mounts Hood and Adams to one's credit; must be fit physically; must be at home on snow-shoes and skis; must know how to use an ice ax; and, most important of all, to be on call at all times for the névé, glaciers, and the deep crevasses of the peaks."

A 1935 *Popular Science Monthly* article by Sterling Gleason explores the team esprit de corps, describing a camaraderie we still share today:

> *Like hounds on a hot trail, they took it up, plunging down through timbers and snowdrifts into a deep canyon. Throughout the night they tramped, covering every possible foot of the mountain side, the beams of their flight lights hardly penetrating the swirling snow, their voices but faintly audible over the roaring wind. . . .*

> *Their code is as strict as that of the sea. No SOS goes unheeded. Neither may any pay or reward be accepted, for mountaineering is a hobby with them. They spend their own money on rescue trips, finding reward in the satisfaction of saving lives. . . .*

> *Membership is by invitation only. Of the hundreds who have made application, only a few have been accepted, and these only after a long*

trial period. To qualify, a man must have a good character and rep-
utation in the community, and must keep in training by climbing at
least one major peak each year. He must own an ice ax, a pair of skis,
snowshoes, compass and a fur-lined parka.

NOW, ON THE TILLY JANE TRAIL, well past midnight, my one-thousand-lumen mountain-biking headlamp brilliantly lights up the snow-covered track. Brian does the work of two people without speaking much: he skis up the trail, dragging the entire two-piece toboggan. The specialized toboggan has handles for skiers—the pilot steers and the stoker brakes. It's made from fiberglass with aluminum skegs in the bottom to grip the slope. One hour up the Tilly Jane Trail, we find the group of three skiers, including the one with the injured leg. He's bundled up and insulated from the snow, sitting on a backpack.

"You okay?" I ask. "What happened?"

"I crashed coming down the trail. Twisted my ankle. I can't ski or walk."

"Okay, let me take a quick look," I say as I examine his leg briefly through his pants. I do a quick palpation to make sure it's not dislocated and that no broken bone protrudes. In thirty seconds, I'm finished with an exam that would normally take much more time in the ER. I explain our plan: "We're going to load you into this toboggan and ski you down." Then I look to the two companions and say, "You two are skiing down. You okay with that?" They nod. "We have extra headlamps for you," I add. And then, knowing from past missions how far even just a quick bit of reassurance goes, I say, "We do this all the time. We'll take care of you."

We're working by headlamp on the trail, which is about twenty feet wide and lined with giant Douglas-fir snags, burned from the Gnarl Ridge Fire. We quickly lift the man, who clocks in at six-foot-two and 250 pounds, into the toboggan, bundling him with clothes and the sleeping bag we brought up. Then, once our patient is loaded, Brian grabs the handles and I take the tail rope. Brian first skied this trail over fifty years ago; he can navigate it in the dark as quickly as most can by day.

"We'll head down," I say to Lisa. "You got these two?" I ask, pointing at the companions.

"Got it, Doc," she says. As skilled as Lisa is at technical rescue, she's also willing to pitch in and do the unglamorous but no-less-crucial jobs.

"Ready," Brian says.

"I'm good," I say. Then Brian and I scoot off down the trail, which is marred by ski tracks, snowshoe prints, and holes from hikers' boots. This makes it bumpy. Still, with Brian at the helm, we're able to descend in fifteen minutes what took an hour to climb up. The trail narrows as the forest thickens, and Brian zips through effortlessly, if not a tad fast for my comfort. But I keep up, holding the tail rope. A few times, I get spooked because we are going so fast and I can't see ahead of Brian. I relax and trust him. This implicit trust isn't necessarily fostered intentionally; it just happens. We have a relatively strict vetting process to join Crag Rats: not only do you need to be an alpinist, but you also need to have a calm temperament and be willing to work in a team. And instead of a long list of formal skills checks, we self-select into jobs. If someone takes the handles of the litter, we trust they can operate it safely. In my early days as a Crag Rat, I went on hundreds of missions with Brian and learned much from him, accruing knowledge I still use to this day.

Down at the trailhead, we accept profound thanks, say goodbye, and prepare to head home to bed.

"That was pretty easy," Lisa says once we're back at SAR 1 and the man has been transferred to his friend's car.

"Yep," Brian says, then chuckles. "Although I thought I was going to sling CVT right off the back of the litter," he says, referring to me by my Crag Rat nickname, taken from my abbreviated email signature.

"Not sure why you needed me or anyone else," I say with a smile. "You could have just done that whole mission solo."

"With your eyes closed," Lisa says.

"That was fun," Heiko says. He means no disrespect to the injured man, but is simply acknowledging our love of this mountain and skiing, as well as our deep friendships. Seriously, we are so obsessed with skiing that our lives would have a big hole without the thrill of gliding down snow.

"I'm glad I didn't miss another rescue," Cully says.

At home, I'm tired, but before collapsing into bed, I still obsessively and hurriedly unpack my gear: boots on the dryer, gloves and skins on the rack, SAR radio on the charger, getting everything prepped for the next rescue.

WHEN HEIKO AND I ski up the Tilly Jane Trail a few weeks later on a recreational outing, we have a quiet conversation and regard the landscape. The Bluegrass Fire of 2006, the Gnarl Ridge Fire from 2008, and the Dollar Lake Fire from 2011 have burned much of this region, leaving wide swaths of tall snags. Wildfires opened the glades and created excellent skiing, but the cons of our weather's and the climate's wide and erratic extremes surely outweigh this singular benefit. The glaciers are falling back, including the ginormous Eliot Glacier on the north side, which has receded from a terminus at five thousand feet elevation to seven thousand feet. At least two Mount Hood glaciers are no longer glaciers, and two more are soon to follow. The trails are widening from more people, with shortcuts around switchbacks causing erosion. And animals are displaced by the construction of buildings, cell towers, and roads in the foothills where there once were none. These changes are more visible on a quiet ski day.

"We're lucky to have this place so close to home," I comment.

"We are. And I'm lucky to have such a good friend," Heiko replies.

In less than two hours, we reach the Tilly Jane A-Frame and then continue up through thick forest. Once we pop out at timberline at seven thousand feet, we encounter blustery, cold wind and hard snow. The skiing is bad above timberline because the wind has either blown all the powder from the ridges or compacted it. We find a gully that has filled in with soft snow and make one run down. It's a bust for making epic ski turns, but any day on skis in the alpine with a friend is a good day nonetheless.

In my two previous memoirs, I tried to explain why we love this mountain and this avocation of mountain rescue. I realize now, two decades after *Mountain Rescue Doctor* was published, that our love for mountain rescue is more complex than I originally thought. My ideas are bolstered now by twenty-five years of rescues, research into decades of Crag Rats archives, and talks with my best friends and fellow rescuers—who are the same people.

Introspectively, we seek the thrill of the rescue, the immediate reward of helping someone. We love and, to some extent, are addicted to the euphoria of being in motion, being fit, and being outside in nature—especially on skis, but also on a bike, surfboard, or kiteboard. We gain satisfaction in exploring novel and beautiful landscapes. We are immensely rewarded by utilizing highly specific technical expertise—avalanche mitigation, rope rescue, and ski mountaineering. We are also drawn to this avocation with some sense of empathy, and the singular purpose of helping others. And, undoubtedly, we do it to some degree for the recognition—I would be remiss not to mention this piece.

But probably the most important to me is the unparalleled friendship and camaraderie—to be in an intense situation in a beautiful location, focused on an all-consuming, life-affirming task alongside kindred souls like Lisa, John, Brian, Cully, Heiko, Ron, Gary, and Meredith, completing high-stakes, life-and-death, foul-weather, middle-of-the-night, high-mountain rescues that few people on Earth would be able to.

And then we have this place. The high alpine. We have deep respect, love, and devotion for Mount Hood. The thick evergreen forests. The deep canyons sheltered from sunlight and bedecked in moss, ferns, and Oregon grape. The high cliffs of andesite. The creeks trickling from the springs and lined in wildflowers. The expansive glaciers. The top of this peak—to me, not some obscure point in the distance but a familiar place I've visited dozens of times.

Our time on Earth goes by, and the window in our lives during which we can participate in mountain rescue is only one piece of it. I realize on this day out with Heiko that Mount Hood and its environs have changed, altered perhaps irreversibly by human impact. We are drawn to this mountain to be with our friends, to be in the outdoors, to help others. Other people can get this same satisfaction in other settings, like volunteering in the inner city, building homes for the disadvantaged, or working in a lab to eradicate malaria—I have friends who do all of these with great reward and while forming deep relationships. But for us Crag Rats, the one thing we can't take away, inseparable from everything that embodies who we are, is this place: Mount Hood.

Which makes me wonder: What if the mountain as we know it is not here anymore?

PART II
SPRING

MOUNTAIN CLIMBING EXPLODES, 1940 TO 1965

CHAPTER 5

MAY: PLANE CRASH ON ELIOT GLACIER

The high-alpine glaciers are vast, ambiguous, and formidable to those who have not skied, climbed, or otherwise explored them. Those of us who spend time on these daunting, disquieting features regard them with an uneasy mix of titillation and circumspection. Snow falls on the mountain, consolidates, and compacts into ice, the sheet of which flows, the sine qua non of a glacier, down the gullies and ravines and canyons. Sometimes, the ice is hard and slippery under our climbing skins. When the glaciers are too steep or firm for skinning uphill, we'll use ski crampons—spiked plates that clamp onto our bindings and add grip. For even steeper and harder slopes, we switch to a burlier traction tool: boot crampons, multi-spiked racks of steel or aluminum that attach to boots, stick to the ice, and crackle when the spikes pierce a few millimeters of ice.

This place, a broad, open mass of snow and ice, is not totally barren. Occasionally spiders or beetles will linger on the surface. Pink snow periodically shows up in the spring, caused by an alga that forms on the surface of the ice: no one knows where it comes from or how it lives here. Sometimes a crow might alight on the ice, looking for insects or scraps from climbers.

The peak's rugged, difficult-to-climb northern facade is elusive and less visited for several reasons. For one, the approach is more time consuming. From late October through late June, the road is open only to Tilly Jane Sno-Park, at four thousand feet at Cooper Spur Mountain Resort. From there, you need to ski or snowshoe two hours up the Tilly Jane Trail or take a snowmobile or snowcat up the nine-mile Cloud Cap Road. This road opens for car travel only once the snow is melted and the dirt dries out, sometime in late June or early July, and then closes again in early November with the first snowfall. Once up to the Cloud Cap–Tilly Jane Historic District, you can find glades and gullies to ski, but the terrain is low angle, which can be great with light, fast snow, but not so great with heavy, dense, deep snow. On a typical day out, if we have enough time and are moving quickly, we like to head above timberline, where we find expansive glaciers, two large snowfields, and challenging summit routes.

The Eliot Glacier, the mountain's largest by volume—73,000 acre feet, almost double the next largest—dominates the north side and flows almost directly northward. Its moniker comes from Dr. Thomas Eliot, a late 1800s Oregon mountaineer. The Eliot is flanked by massive moraines of boulders, their facets tumbled for centuries by the retreating and thinning glacier. To get to the Eliot, you need to ski past tree line to the east moraine above six thousand feet elevation and then climb five hundred vertical feet down onto the ice. At one time the tongue, or lowest point, of the glacier flowed to five thousand feet but has now receded to around seven thousand feet.

The Eliot Glacier was first photographed in 1901, and measurements in melting rates, ice thickness, and surface velocities started in the 1940s. So we know the Eliot is retreating and thinning like all the glaciers on Mount Hood. This has all been confirmed by Portland State University faculty Keith Jackson and Andrew Fountain in 2007, and again in 2023 by Portland State University glaciologist Kiya Riverman. Riverman spoke at a Crag Rats banquet in Hood River on January 6, 2024 and explained her research in a fascinating, dynamic lecture. She and a squad of grad students measured the Eliot Glacier using radar and found that it is receding in surface area but not as much as we'd think. The real melting comes from depleting thickness: during summer 2023, she measured the ice at 30 meters thick, which, compared with past measurements, showed a melting rate of 1 meter per year. This means that at the current rate, the Eliot Glacier may be gone in three decades.

To the east of the Eliot lies a wide, crevasse-free snowfield called Cooper Spur, which offers good skiing in winter and good hiking in summer because you can climb up to 8,500 feet without technical gear and ogle at expansive views to the north of Mount Adams, Mount Rainier, Mount St. Helens, Goat Rocks, and the Simcoe Mountains. Farther east lies the Newton Clark Glacier, named after a local surveyor and farmer. The largest by surface area at 491 acres, the Newton Clark is shrinking too: it lost 32 percent of its surface area from 1907 to 2004.

To the west of Eliot, across the north side, lie several glaciers and the remnants of glaciers, slowly melting in the direct sun and warming climate. The small Langille Glacier, named after the mountain-guiding Langille brothers, offers good skiing midwinter through spring. Crag Rats call the bowls and glades near the Langille "Private Reserve" because few others ski this area in winter due to its remoteness.

Next comes the Coe Glacier, named after initial Hood River European settlers Nathaniel and Mary Coe and their son Henry. It's riddled with giant serac fields and terminates in beautiful Elk Cove, a summer hiking and backpacking destination replete with wildflowers, huckleberries, marmots, bears, and elk. Continuing farther west, Ladd Glacier, named after William Ladd, early climber and builder of Cloud Cap Inn, has mostly melted, losing 37 percent of its volume from 1907 to 2004. The lower half has disappeared, while the upper section is barely one square kilometer. It's almost no longer a glacier. Similarly, the former Glisan Glacier, dubbed after the climber and Mazamas member Rodney Glisan, existed in 2003 but as of 2020 had melted so much that it's now just a stagnant bit of ice.

The remaining glaciers encapsulate the southern hemisphere of the mountain. From east to west, these are White River, Coalman (named for the climber Elijah Coalman, with a reported 586 summits of Mount Hood), Palmer snowfield (the climber Joe Palmer's namesake glacier stopped flowing in 1980 and has been downgraded to a permanent snowfield), Zigzag, Reid, and Sandy. All of these on the south side drain either south into the White River or west into the Sandy River.

While these glaciers remain ever enchanting to climb and ski, we feel the impact of climate change under our skis and in our town. The melting snow and ice mean we have longer approaches on rocks, dirt, and boulders to reach the snow. More importantly, these glaciers supply Hood River with its drinking and irrigation water, not currently of concern at this moment, but an issue that's clearly coming.

This is not a book about glaciology or climate change, but I cannot ignore the fact that human-caused factors are impacting our well-being, both that of the Crag Rats and of Mount Hood. The wild climate swings produce erratic weather patterns. The clear-cut forests are replaced with monoculture and reduce biodiversity. The roads, buildings, dams, and bridges disrupt the natural flow of streams and cause erosion. Even lately, record hot temperatures have caused rescuer fatigue and heat cramps, problems never recorded in past missions. The Pacific Northwest's once-in-a-millennium summer 2021 heat dome is just one example, with Oregon reaching all-time-high triple digits and Washington's Mount Rainier losing four feet of snow, or 30 percent of its snowpack, in a week. Today, however, is a cold, clear spring day—no stifling summer heat yet—as we are deployed to the Eliot Glacier on a mission for a downed airplane.

"How often do you get to respond to a plane crash on the side of a mountain?" Wes Baumann says, quickly making me change my mind after I told him I would need to miss the mission to work. More than a decade younger than me, Wes is a professional ski patroller at Mt. Hood Meadows, and he spent five years as a climbing ranger on Mount Rainier and another couple as a climbing ranger on Mount Hood. He's highly skilled and an excellent teacher, and he has the calmest leadership and broadest situational awareness I've seen on missions.

"Oh, you're right. Let me see if I can figure it out," I say.

The call for help comes late in the afternoon. After a small plane was reported overdue, HRCSO Deputy Sheriff Joe Wampler—who served as sheriff for two decades and now works part-time flying the HRCSO Piper Super Cub airplane—spotted the crash debris high on the Eliot Glacier, right where the glacier meets the cliff, at the bergschrund. Then a helicopter from the 189th Aviation Regiment of the Oregon National Guard in Salem flew over the crash site. From the air, the crew chief determined the pilot was deceased, and we are called in to recover the body.

I drive up the mountain with Wes, Eric, and Asa Mueller, a part-time ski patroller at Mt. Hood Meadows and a full-time EMT firefighter for Tualatin Valley Fire and Rescue. We need to get up to Cloud Cap Inn at night to be ready for an early morning departure the next day to the upper reaches of the Eliot Glacier, so we meet at the lodge at Cooper Spur Mountain Resort. I arrive expecting to have to ski two hours up the Tilly Jane Trail. But when I spy Dennis "Deno" Klein unloading the Crag Rats' 1976 Logan Machine Company snowcat, I am elated. Deno, the father of Paul, a fellow Crag Rat who helped with getting the fallen climber from chapter 2 down the mountain, is a wiry, fit, and experienced retired ski patroller and firefighter, as well as the caretaker for our snowcat. We are getting a lift.

After jostling around in the back of the deafening snowcat, we reach Cloud Cap Inn. This beloved cabin is a two-thousand-square-foot lodge hand-built from big timbers and perched at Cloud Cap saddle. The giant Douglas-fir logs are capped by a cedar-shake roof, wrapped by a rough-hewn deck, and bedecked with a twenty-foot lava-rock chimney. The inn has a storied 135-year history that starts near the end of the nineteenth century, when a network of roads connected Hood River Valley and proceeded as far south as Cooper Spur Junction and the Homestead Inn. In 1884, the developers David Cooper, Oscar Stranahan, and Henry Coe built a cabin near Tilly Jane Creek and constructed a primitive road up to six thousand feet, where the trees terminated and the glaciers commenced. The Mount Hood Trail and Wagon Road Company dubbed the road "Wagon Road"; it climbed 2,500 feet over four miles and had a 22 percent grade at a spot called China Fill, so named because it was built by Chinese laborers. Soon after road construction was completed, a summer tent camp was established at a saddle at six thousand feet. The developers had grandiose plans of putting in a hotel and gondola—neither of which materialized. Nonetheless, the developer William Ladd built a lodge in 1889, constructed from giant Douglas-fir hewn by giant handsaws and hauled to the saddle by horses. Drinking water came from nearby Tilly Jane Creek. The place was dubbed Cloud Cap Inn, after the lenticular cloud that forms frequently on the summit of Mount Hood in the spring and summer.

Cloud Cap Inn opened to the public on August 6, 1889. The lodge was initially run as a deluxe hotel by Lewis Adams, and guests were brought up by horse-drawn wagon. That first winter, it was unclear if the building could survive storms, so in February 1890, the mountain guides (and brothers) William and Doug Langille ascended on home-built skis to find the cabin intact. This marked the first documented ski-tour in the Pacific Northwest. However, with the mounting costs of running the hotel and the stage ride up, Adams struggled to find financial success. In 1891, the inn was taken over by Sarah Langille, mother of William and Doug, who ran it more like a spartan bed-and-breakfast. Following that, in 1893, the Langille brothers used Cloud Cap Inn as a base for the first attempt on the Cooper Spur route to the mountaintop but failed to summit.

At the turn of the century, the north side became the region's mountaineering hub. This was in part because of Cloud Cap Inn and the Wagon Road, and also because the railroad ran from Portland to Hood River. The Mazamas ran ski expeditions for members as early as February 1903 from Hood River. Spring and summer trips started with a train from Portland to Hood River, and continued with a horse-pulled wagon up to Cloud Cap Inn. The trip from Hood River to the inn required eight hours and at least one change of horses, despite the distance being only thirty miles. By 1910, the Mount Hood Railroad spur brought passengers south from Hood River, which shaved fifteen miles from the trip. (The scenic rail line still functions for tourists.) The inn was used as a base for local guides leading clients up the north side, including the Langille brothers and the famed guide Mark Weygandt.

Over the years, Cloud Cap Inn was hard to manage, as the idea of a mountain inn wasn't exactly supported by the transportation infrastructure, weather, or general population. It was simply too remote and costly. Ladd turned operations over to Horace and Olive Mecklem in 1907. They used a Pierce-Arrow automobile, which cut transit from Hood River from eight to two hours. But the Mecklems couldn't make the inn profitable either and sold it to the local Hood River resident Homer Rogers for $5,000 in early 1919. Rogers was banking on the Mount Hood Loop Highway, which was still under construction. Around that time, the remarkably steep Wagon Road needed to be reconstructed. So, in 1926, a new road was routed to be more gradual, meandering nine miles and utilizing ten switchbacks. But still, Rogers had no luck in running a successful inn. The inn changed hands again in 1927 to Noyes Tyrell, and then again in 1934 to Boyd French Sr., who closed it during the war. No one could make Cloud Cap Inn function as a business. Finally, French sold it to the US Forest Service for $2,000 in 1942. The US Forest Service left it dormant.

The Crag Rats, meanwhile, had essentially no alpine missions during the war years—likely because few people were out recreating, with the nation's focus on the war—and only a smattering of callouts in the lowlands. Nonetheless, the group kept busy guiding the American Legion up the mountain.

Then, on April 12, 1948, this sleepy period came to an end when a single-engine airplane crashed on Cooper Spur. The sheriff asked for six Crag Rats and got fourteen in less than two hours. They must have been eager to participate on an alpine mission—I know I would have been. Up in the alpine, the Crag Rats found cold, wind, and fog. Most turned back, but three—Bob Sheppard, Rob Hukari, and Bob Moller—continued into the night to the upper Eliot Glacier. According to meeting minutes, the trio was "fumbling around on the glacier dodging crevasse and ice seracs always climbing upward." Weather inhibited the night search, and the trio bivouacked on the glacier. In the morning, a search airplane spotted the wreckage on Newton Clark Glacier. The three Crag Rats climbed out of the Eliot Glacier to the east moraine, crossed the Cooper Spur snowfield, and descended onto the Newton Clark. They found the plane without a pilot, quickly picked up a trail of footprints and blood, and tracked the pilot into the trees, where he was found alive.

Following the 1948 mission, another dearth of alpine rescues ensued. But the Crag Rats responded more frequently to the newish forest playground between Portland and Hood River—the Columbia River Gorge, a draw for hikers, climbers, hunters, anglers, and foragers. In the 1950s, for example, they scoured the Wahtum Lake area for a missing sixty-year-old man, searched Benson Plateau for two missing teenage boys, and rescued a fisherman on the West Fork of the Hood River. The minutes after one rescue recounted colorfully that "the brush in that locale [was] so thick that a homesick rabbit would have a difficult time getting through."

After the war, recreation rebounded, and the Crag Rats were sporadically supplicated to assist out of county. In September 1954, they responded to Mount Jefferson to search for the climber Bill Morley, whom they found deceased at 6,800 feet; they brought the body down the Milk Creek Glacier and then five miles down the trail to Pamelia Lake. In April 1955, they assisted in the search for a pilot who'd crashed in the Simcoe Mountains near Goldendale, Washington. In September 1955, they searched North Sister for Frank Gilbert, who had fallen down a chute and was eventually evacuated by helicopter. Later that month, they were called to Spirit Lake on Mount St. Helens to search for two elderly prospectors who were camping, got lost, and were found alive after a week. In 1957, they rescued a man stuck on Beacon Rock, an 848-foot-high basalt monolith in the Columbia River Gorge. In the 1950s, they responded a half-dozen times to Mount Adams in Washington for missing huckleberry pickers, missing cone pickers, and for three men who were stranded at ten thousand feet on the Adams Glacier in a storm in 1958.

But missions, especially those in the alpine, remained few. In addition, following the war, other rescue groups started forming. The Alpinees of Hood River established on February 23, 1947, as a mountain rescue group akin to the Crag Rats. After coming back from World War II, some folks led by the Seabee Jack Baldwin wanted to do technical rescues and, according to Jack Grauer's seminal *Mount Hood: A Complete History*, "advance general and scientific info and knowledge about mountain rescue." These Alpinees were less keen on social outings and community service outside of rescues. They immediately aligned with the Hood River detachment of the Civil Air Patrol, developed a technical cable-extrication system for a litter, and joined the National Ski Patrol, which was formed in 1938 to provide "service and safety" to the burgeoning ski-resort industry. Baldwin and fellow Alpinee member and Hood River resident George Howell were instrumental in putting a tow motor and warming hut at an area known as Jump Hill at the Cooper Spur Junction (more about this in chapter 6).

Wy'east Climbers, a highly skilled mountaineering club, also helped. This group of badass alpinists formed in the 1930s and put up many of the most challenging climbing routes of the time, many of which are still climbed today. Similarly, the Mazamas and the US Forest Service helped with SAR missions.

Despite few rescues in the 1940s and 1950s, the Crag Rats were not idle, and embraced other forms of community service. In 1950, they agreed to help Hood River County Sheriff Rupert Gillmouthe in a postwar Civil Defense program. The sheriff wanted to protect against an aerial attack from a foreign military and, according to Crag Rats meeting minutes, he wanted to deal with "facing the problem of caring for, feeding and housing those evacuated from the metropolitan areas." In other words, if a foreign adversary struck Portland, city folk might flee to and seek refuge in Hood River. On February 22, 1951, some twenty-two Crag Rats attended "Police School." And on July 2, 1954, according to the *Hood River News*, Crag Rats staffed a roadblock to help capture three people who'd robbed Hood River's Pastime Tavern. During a summer heat wave, according to an article in *Hood River News* on June 10, 1955, several swimmers needed to be rescued at Koberg Beach on the Columbia River in 90-degree temperatures, so the sheriff asked Crag Rats to lifeguard there for a week.

In addition to fire, police, and lifeguard duties, the Crag Rats was a thriving social club driven by a profound passion for mountain climbing. The minutes from the 1950s are jam-packed with reports from year-round ascents of Cascade volcanoes: South Sister, Middle Sister, North Sister, Mount Adams, Mount St. Helens, Mount Jefferson, Mount Washington, Three Fingered Jack, and Mount Rainier. Often, the *Hood River News* would run a few column inches about the Crag Rats' climbs. The Crag Rats even created a "life membership" category for those who climbed eight snowcapped stratovolcanoes: Mount Rainier, Mount St. Helens, Mount Adams, Mount Hood, Mount Jefferson, North Sister, Middle Sister, and South Sister. After Mount St. Helens erupted in 1980 and was closed for climbing, Glacier Peak was deemed the alternative.

Although that tradition is still active, it's an infrequent goal. Crag Rats members John Rust, Hugh Brown, and Paul Crowley, as of this writing, were the most recent to achieve the milestone, a decade ago.

The Crag Rats also skied scores of days every year and planned annual winter ski outings. Annual summer outings were often held at Wallowa Lake in eastern Oregon or at Camp Westwind on the Oregon Coast. The trip reports are filled with fun, adventure, and humor. For example, after a climb of the Sunshine Route on Mount Hood on May 24, 1951, they reported that the Crag Rats tried to mitigate the effects of an overnight bivy on the rocks at Langille Crags: "Doc stated he administered sleeping pills and aspirin to those who slept on the ridge, proving his theory that they were lighter to pack than an air mattress and gaining the same effect."

Business meetings were filled with discussions about hut maintenance, insurance, first-aid courses for rescuers, trip reports and trip planning, plaques for deceased members, summer outings, rescue maps, and radios, which, in the 1950s, were just becoming available for civilian use and were about the size of a shoebox. From what I can tell reading the meeting minutes, other than an annual first-aid refresher, they did no organized training.

One of the most significant, longest-lasting contributions to the community, which started in the 1950s and continued into the late 1980s, was snow surveys. The meeting minutes are crammed with reports of these ski trips for the Hood River Soil and Water Conservation District to measure snowpack depth and water content, gauging spring and summer water availability for the booming orchard industry in the fertile Hood River Valley. From December to April, almost weekly, the Crag Rats skied to three locations—Green Point Reservoir (3,200 feet), Red Hill (5,000 feet), and Tilly Jane (6,000 feet)—while hauling up four-foot-long, four-inch-diameter aluminum tubes. They would pound the hollow pipes into the snowpack and then weigh the snow-filled pipe. In this way, they could both measure snowpack depth and calculate water content using the weight. The hundreds of trip reports are ripe with sarcasm, humor, and sendups of members who crashed while skiing or burned dinner. One report reads, "After what seemed like an eternity, a roaring fire was going in the fireplace and stakes were sizzling on the stove." For breakfast: "Side pork, sausage, bacon, eggs and hot cakes provides a fair breakfast, but for some reason or other there was less fervor over Les Hukari's coffee."

For the snow surveys, Crag Rats utilized cabins at the three locations. The Green Point and Red Hill cabins have long since been demolished, but up in the Cloud Cap–Tilly Jane Historic District, they used a variety of cabins, including a US Forest Service guard station and the Tilly Jane A-Frame, both available today for the public to rent for outings. (There's also the Snowshoe Club Cabin, built in 1910 and still owned by the eponymous club that formed in 1904.) In the late 1940s, Crag Rats started using the then-derelict Cloud Cap Inn. Near as I can tell from reading meeting minutes, the Crag Rats just sort of moved in with verbal permission from the US Forest Service or no permission whatsoever. The US Forest Service discussed razing the inn, as first reported in the Crag Rats meeting minutes from September 28, 1950. The roof had collapsed, and the cabin had succumbed to the weather and fallen into disrepair: the shingles had blown off in storms, the windows were broken from gales, and mice had eaten through the textiles. The Crag Rats started negotiating permanent use of the cabin with support from the Hood River County Historical Society. This permit process took the better part of five years, until it was signed in 1955.

The Crag Rats took good care of Cloud Cap Inn. They kept it stocked with wood, repaired the doors and windows, kept the water line patent, fixed the gas stove, installed a rescue radio, shored up the walls, reshingled the roof, rehinged the doors, and tried to keep the rats from pilfering the cabin food by using metal lockers and war-surplus ammo boxes. They were using the cabin so much that on January 8, 1953, they purchased a used Weasel for $200, using the World War II tracked snow vehicle with room for four people (plus gear) to get to and from Cloud Cap Inn.

Thus it is that for seventy years, Cloud Cap Inn has been our beloved base for missions and training. We've made upgrades over the years, including dual woodstoves, a wood-fired hot-water tank, a flush toilet, and a shower. We have a solar panel to run lights, a cell phone charger, and a rescue radio. The full kitchen is equipped for serving large groups. And we have a cache of rescue gear. One of our $5,000 carbon rescue sleds, an akja, is housed here, along with its aluminum precursor, purchased in 1950 for $113 and that now hangs on display from the inn's rafters.

AFTER OUR SNOWCAT ride up that evening, Eric, Wes, Asa, and I reached the inn after dark. I love doing rescues with these three—they are calm in a crisis and, thanks to hundreds of hours of patient care on ski slopes in the resort and on the helicopter calls, are skilled at managing patients and scenes, as well as looking at a mission's big picture. And all three are graceful skiers, appearing to descend the steepest terrain almost effortlessly.

We open up the cabin, no simple chore because the propane and water are turned off and large, heavy, aluminum-encased plywood shutters cover the two dozen windows. Inside, the inn looks like a cross between a worn and weathered trapper's cabin and an expansive ski lodge. The great room has woodstoves, rocking chairs, a double-length picnic table, and a hand-crank dumbwaiter that is lowered to the basement, where it can be filled with firewood. The south-facing abutment comprises wall-to-wall single-pane, multi-panel windows that give an in-your-face view of Mount Hood's entire north slope. The kitchen has a propane stove, oven, and griddle. Running water comes piped in from a spring a quarter mile up the mountain. A dozen rooms have bunks and mattresses. Every Crag Rats member keeps a mouse-proof bin to store a sleeping bag, hut shoes, a toothbrush, extra clothes, and nonperishable food.

After unloading packs and skis from the snowcat, we sit around the table and plan the recovery mission. It should be straightforward: climb up to the body with the akja, and then ski the body down. Then we make our way to the back of the cabin to each find a bunk. As I wander toward the east wing, I pause to look at the cabin's walls, adorned with a century of climbing ropes, photos, old Forest Service trail signs, ski-resort plaques, letters from other mountain clubs, old splints, outdated litters, antique ice axes, and various other forms of memorabilia haphazardly tacked on. One back bunk room still has graffiti—hand-scrawled signatures—dating back one hundred years.

For the midcentury Crag Rats, alpine rescues were infrequent, with just one mission from 1940 to 1956. The dry spell ended on the morning of July 10, 1956. That day, Alice Nielson, a twenty-five-year-old Salem stenographer, was climbing with a group of Mazamas on the Cooper Spur route. Near Tie-In Rock, where the ridge meets the Eliot Glacier headwall and climbers need a rope because the slope steepens, she became ill. According to an *Oregonian* article published on July 10, 1956, Nielson said, "I didn't feel right when we set out in the assault on the summit at midnight on Saturday. I thought I could hike it off. But when we reached the 8,500-foot level and they tied me to the rest of the party for safety I couldn't stand it any longer. The rope around my waist made me feel ill." She started walking down solo but then missed the slight westward traverse from the Tilly Jane Creek drainage to Cloud Cap Inn. This happens on a conical volcano: if you are off by a few degrees, the farther you descend, the more you deviate from your route. So Nielson accidentally descended Cold Spring Creek, where she got lost.

"I was afraid of dying of thirst," Nielson reported. Adding that she never wanted to die that way and that it had always frightened her, she stayed close to Cold Creek Falls after stumbling upon it and began to pray. As she followed the creek's waters downhill, she reached some tall timber and realized that she could no longer see the summit—and that she was totally lost. Nielson continued, "Then I became afraid and climbed back across the snow field to a place I thought was near where I had set out. It didn't look the same and I didn't know what to do. First I knew I had to get off the snow. It was knee deep and moving all the time. When I got back to the timber, I tried to light a fire, but I had fallen in the snow so much my matches were wet."

Nielson was missing for thirty-six hours before being spotted by an airplane and then rescued by Crag Rats near Lamberson Butte, a rocky outcrop at 6,600 feet.

Despite the dearth of alpine rescues, the highly skilled alpinists of the Crag Rats still carried out ongoing missions in the surrounding lowlands. In meeting minutes, Crag Rats discussed their commitment to the lowlands, even if rescues there were perhaps beneath the group. They agreed to respond to all Hood River

County missions—alpine or not—but opted to forgo calls for out-of-county assistance that didn't involve alpine travel. This was a discussion quite like the ones we have today: Should we send folks out-of-state to join a ground search for a lost mushroom picker, on what the old meeting minutes labeled a "brush beating" and we now call "ground pounding"? Regardless, according to later meeting minutes, Crag Rats kept responding to *anyone* who called for help, out of county or not, alpine or not, brush beating or not. The thrill of adventure and the desire to help were too strong.

With many other groups now participating in rescues, the Crag Rats leader Dick Pooley recognized the need for greater organization. Pooley was a small, wiry guy with impressive strength and a more impressive list of peaks bagged. A natural leader, he had helped form the National Ski Patrol as well as local ham radio clubs. (Pooley took on the Crag Rats leadership role after Anderson moved to California in the 1950s.) I met him twice before he died, in 2015 at age ninety-five, at which time he was still attending Crag Rats banquets.

On Mount Hood, rescue missions were completed by an assortment of clubs and organizations: the Crag Rats, Alpinees, Wy'east Climbers, Mazamas, and US Forest Service, among others. Similarly, up in Washington State, many groups responded to alpine missions. The Mountaineers, Washington Alpine Club, and National Ski Patrol Northwest Region were busy during the early 1950s with avalanches, lightning strikes, crevasse falls, glissading injuries, cliff falls, rappelling accidents, rockfall and icefall, and four aircraft crashes. Mountain rescue teams formed in Tacoma, Everett, the Olympics, and Yakima, eventually banding together to form the Washington Mountain Rescue Council in 1952. The council was instigated by the famed Washington rescue mountaineers Ome Daiber, Wolf Bauer, Kurt Beam, and Dr. Otto Trott, an early mountain rescue physician who was one of the first to bring advanced medical care to the mountains. The men had immigrated to the Pacific Northwest from the Alps and got the idea for a council from a short documentary movie called *Die Bergwacht*, which highlights the first German mountain rescue team, founded in Saxony in 1912 as a section of the Sächsischer Bergsteigerbund (Saxon Climbers' Federation). A few Crag Rats attended the 1953 conference at Snoqualmie

Pass to learn about snow evacuation techniques, how to make a makeshift litter out of skis, helicopter use, and a "mechanical mule" motor-driven stretcher.

At a Crag Rats meeting on February 10, 1955, the group discussed creating a similar Oregon council. Discussions coalesced into the formation of the Mountain Rescue and Safety Council of Oregon, or MORESCO, spearheaded by Pooley. The various teams officially inked the deal at Cloud Cap Inn on October 13, 1955, with sixty-nine people from the Crag Rats, Alpinees, Wy'east Climbers, and Multnomah County (MORESCO Multnomah County would become MORESCO Portland Unit, and eventually Portland Mountain Rescue). But the next day's scheduled training was canceled, as the Multnomah County sheriff asked for help searching for missing boys near Multnomah Falls, in the Columbia River Gorge. Cloud Cap Inn emptied for the rescue.

After its formation, MORESCO held regular meetings. Then, in Crag Rats meeting minutes from April 17, 1959, I found the first reference about forming a national group, a task also organized in part by Pooley. Washington and Oregon had their statewide councils, and similar coalitions were forming in Colorado and California. At the May 14, 1959, meeting, Crag Rats initially opposed the idea but cited no reason why. I can speculate. It may be that Crag Rats valued their tightknit group culture, independence, and camaraderie too much to try to share with or bond to outside groups, and forming a statewide coalition was enough. They may not have seen any benefit to a national group. Also, when working in a high-stakes alpine rescue, one needs to know their rescue colleagues confidentially and intimately, and any sort of state or national oversight potentially encroaches on this. As Asa once artfully articulated, "We need to know who's on our rope." But other things took up more ink in the meeting minutes, such as someone's successful procurement of hard-to-find wool in a one-inch black-and-white buffalo-plaid pattern at Meier and Frank Co. in Portland, with 22 yards available at $3.95 per yard, to sew up for shirts, plus a lengthy discussion about what should be done with the propeller that was retrieved from the wrecked aircraft from 1948. This was important stuff.

Nonetheless, teams in the western United States eventually felt the need to band together beyond their state organization. Pooley provided leadership to gather eleven teams to form the Mountain Rescue Association (MRA) on June 6 and 7, 1959, at Timberline Lodge. He became the MRA's first president. This camaraderie would turn out to be a lifelong connection for me, somewhat following in Anderson's and Pooley's steps. I did a stint as a Crag Rats officer and have long been medical director. For a decade, I served as chair of the MRA's medical committee. Now I am the MRA's alternate delegate to the International Commission for Alpine Rescue (ICAR) Medical Commission, which is one reason why I ended up in the Dolomites doing CPR on that Sellaronda cyclist.

NOW, IT'S BEFORE sunrise in the alpine, and I'm not thinking about Crag Rats minutes or MRA or ICAR meetings. I'm thinking about the unadulterated loveliness and peacefulness of the alpine and the gratitude I feel to be here with trusted colleagues who have become great friends. The sky glows with the faint light of predawn. After strong coffee brewed from an old-school percolator, we pull on cold ski boots and strap on packs. From the windows, we see a cloudless, sunless, starless cerulean-turning-azure sky.

Hard, cold snow crunches under out boots as we exit the warm cabin into the frigid morning. *More people should experience this peacefulness, exhilaration, and clarity,* I muse. *Like politicians, world leaders, government officials.* But I understand that it's not possible for many, not of interest to some, and wildly foreign and frightening to most. The familiar sounds of preparing to ski uphill disrupt the quiet—the peeling apart of our climbing skins sounds a bit like peeling Velcro, before we silently affix them to our skis. Someone lets out a moan as we tighten ski-boot buckles with a snap. The small click of stepping into our ski bindings. The sandpapery noise of skins sliding on firm snow. Our flexing boots squeaking subtly with every glide.

Our mission is much less rushed, given that the pilot we are retrieving is dead, no other people were reported in the airplane, and the location is known. So we can take our time and enjoy the high alpine.

We ski up the east moraine of the Eliot Glacier as Eric sets a solid pace, one that means we are here to do a job. We drop down into the glacier at seven thousand feet at the Pooley Trail, a unofficial, rough-hewn path through the andesite boulders on the east moraine, which is marked by a giant cairn and named after the great contributor to mountain rescue. The rocks are exposed, so we step out of our skis, strap them on our packs, and walk down. Then, back in our skis, we skin up the glacier. Eric leads, and I follow second. We avoid the center of the glacier, which is littered with water ice, seracs, and crevasses. Eric and I are the only two with ski crampons; with better traction, we get to the pilot first, in about two hours, as the sun warms the snow and ice. At the crash site—not my first—I notice the indentation on the snow where the plane impacted and left an impression: a round hole for the fuselage with the imprint of two wings. Then, getting closer, we see the mangled remnants of the fuselage and motor, with the wings and tail strewn in thousands of pieces across the ice, some as small as paperback books.

"I'm happy you're here with me," I tell Eric, breaking the morning silence. "Let's get this wrapped up." Although we are both emergency medicine professionals, we are still humans who must process death in our own way. For now, in the high alpine, we package the body quickly and efficiently. It's simply a task that needs to be done, and we complete it businesslike, robotically. Later, we will likely move on and not think too much about the accident, but that's not to say we don't think about it at all. Earlier in my career, I was more easily affected. The 2003 plane crash on Vista Ridge, which I wrote about in *Mountain Rescue Doctor*, stayed with me for a year, recurring in my dreams in its grisly particulars.

We quickly bundle the deceased in a tarp and wait a few minutes for the rest of the crew, who are carrying other parts of the akja. Once Wes and Asa arrive, we assemble the sled, strap in the pilot's body, and ski down. It's still not that easy, because the glacier ice is hard on this shaded north side of Mount Hood. But Wes and Asa have many years of experience as ski patrollers. They are the best suited to ski the pilot down. We may have hundreds of ski patrollers in the United States who know how to use an akja, but I imagine that few of them have skied an akja across a crevassed glacier like Wes and Asa have.

After ten minutes of descending the steepest section of the upper Eliot Glacier—a pitch that would take a climber thirty minutes to walk down—we come to a low-angle spot at the seven-thousand-foot bench. Wes looks at me and says, "This would be a good time to practice with the akja."

"Okay, I'll take a turn," I say, grateful for the chance to pilot the toboggan. I take the handles of the heavy sled and ski five hundred feet down, with good purchase because my ski edges are sharp. When we come to a steeper section, I stop and look to Wes, silently indicating I need to turn the package back over to him and Asa. He nods. In just a few minutes, Asa and Wes have skied the sled down the Eliot—a two-hour uphill skin becomes a twenty-minute ski down. At the tongue of the glacier, a second team of Crag Rats has dropped a sixty-meter rope. They haul the sled up the rocky moraine, from where it will be skied down to Cloud Cap Inn, put in a snowcat, and shuttled to the Tilly Jane Sno-Park.

Up on the moraine, I see Walter Burkhardt hauling the rope hand over hand, quickly and with great strength. This gives me great reassurance. Walter is a strong and highly skilled Crag Rat. He grew up skiing and climbing, and works as a rope rigger for Hollywood movies. Walter knows the mountain better than almost anyone (except perhaps Brian Hukari)—on his days off, Walter scours the mountain for adventure, cross-country skiing, ice climbing, rock climbing, and exploring glacial caves.

Aside from running the akja and supervising the packaging of the dead body, I take the time to observe Wes's and Asa's leadership styles. They are calm, direct, and think ahead, sometimes many steps ahead, especially in calling for resources and asking for solutions early. I make a mental note to emulate them.

A few weeks later, at the next business meeting, I learn Walter has been doing something that surprises me. He has started making trips up to the plane crash site on his personal time to bring down the wreckage. Otherwise, it would have remained on the mountain, first being devoured by the Eliot Glacier, and later—perhaps decades later—turning up lower down Mount Hood. (In 2017, Crag Rats were sent to the Eliot Glacier to recover a backpack that had been discovered by a climbing party; it turned out to be from a man who was rescued by Crag Rats in 1997. Brian Hukari was on both missions.)

"Why are you doing that?" I ask.

Walter, a big smile blossoming across his weather-worn face, beneath his frizzy, uncombed hair, looks at me and says simply, "I want that fucking plane off my mountain."

I stare at him nonplussed, first because I'm in awe of Walter's physical capabilities, but second, and more importantly, because I'm awed that anyone could care so devoutly about this mountain.

Back in the 1950s, the thriving Crag Rats had little time for environmental causes. Environmental or ecological impact was a rudimentary notion in our nation, and Crag Rats were busy with work, family, rescues, first-aid classes, police school, lifeguard duties, snow surveys, running the hut, and climbing for recreation. Requests for environmental support were infrequent and intermittent and seem to have been glossed over. For example, according to minutes from April 13, 1950, Crag Rats received a letter from the Federation of Western Outdoor Clubs "concerning the breaking up of certain primitive areas by commercial enterprises." Crag Rats sent back a letter of support and then proceeded to devote more ink to spending a four-dollar REI dividend on a 120-foot 5/16-inch nylon climbing rope. Similarly, in 1954, Crag Rats were asked to help protest the proposed Echo Park Dam in Colorado, in Dinosaur National Monument. They sent a letter and moved on to other topics, like deciding where to hold the annual summer outing.

However, retrieving plane crash debris would become something Crag Rats did more than once. In the search for the plane crash in 1948, described above, once the pilot was rescued from the Newton Clark Glacier, Crag Rats went back up to the crash site a few days later and retrieved the motor and propeller. In 1959 on Mount Adams, climbers found airplane wreckage from a crash in 1948. Crag Rats thus went up on August 26, 1959, to retrieve the remains of the pilot and push the wreckage into a crevasse; it would reappear from the crevasse in 1972, and Crag Rats would go back up again to retrieve the airplane.

I truly admire Walter for hauling junk off the mountain. Although Mount Hood is in crisis from climate change, we often depreciate the mountain, directly and indirectly, by overlooking the small, tangible things, like removing debris and garbage, to focus instead on less tangible tasks like preventing the melting of glaciers through climate action. But we need to form good habits in the first place, contributing to the health of the macrocosm by caring for the microcosm.

For example, the US Forest Service built a fire lookout on the summit of Mount Hood in 1915, first a tent and then a cabin, which was initially staffed by Elijah Coalman and then decommissioned and dismantled in 1933. In 1940, the US Forest Service sent wood up to Crater Rock on the South Side Routes to rebuild the cabin. The cabin was never reconstructed, but both the steam engine winch used to haul up the lumber and the lumber itself were left piled at ten thousand feet in the Mount Hood Wilderness. Just left there. Similarly, an abandoned and partially collapsed summit cabin on Mount Adams is still on the peak—the tip used to be visible in the late summer, but in recent years with a melting snowpack due to climate change, the whole cabin is usually visible by August. Again, just left there. During the pandemic, the US Forest Service had a garbage problem in the Columbia River Gorge National Scenic Area. With folks flocking to the trails, the trailhead garbage cans quickly over-filled, with people just leaving garbage on the ground nearby, as if it's okay to do so when the can is full. Empty oxygen bottles are abandoned at the South Col of Mount Everest: climbers use them to ascend but then have no energy or motivation to bring them back down. We no longer have just one Great Pacific Garbage Patch, but five ocean collections of plastic garbage. We're so arrogant and presumptuous as a species that we leave garbage in space: we have some 3,000 nonoperational spacecraft, thousands of satellites, and an estimated 36,500 objects of human origin in space greater than 4 inches, 1 million between 0.4 and 4 inches, and 330 million smaller than 0.4 inch. Quick math: that's a lot of garbage in a place we don't fully understand, probably the same way Lewis and Clark didn't fully understand the Pacific Northwest landscape they were "discovering."

So while we can and should focus on lessening human-caused climate change by doing things like converting to more efficient and cleaner energy, we also need to curtail our consumption and not leave garbage from that consumption on Mount Hood or in space. I find it disheartening that we tend to think otherwise. At the same time, I admire what Walter is doing.

Slowly and stealthily over the years, the environmental impacts on Mount Hood have grown, some of which are yet unknown to us. Fortunately, the north side is still relatively pristine, untraveled, intact aside from the melting glaciers, clear-cut forests in the lowlands, and the few roads that have not been expanded onto the upper mountain. The north side remains Hood's less-visited hemisphere.

LATER IN THE YEAR, we ski up to Cloud Cap Inn for a ski-tour and overnight: me, Eric, Cully, Heiko. We open the cabin's heavy shutters, turn on the water, fix a leaky pipe, thaw the toilet fittings, turn on the solar lights, open the gas valve to make tea, and build fires in each of the woodstoves. Then, we make several short, five-hundred-vertical-foot laps in light, dry powder below the cabin on a run called Ghost Ridge. We track up the slopes, and then at dusk, we retreat to the cabin to make dinner. While the rescues are always intense, purpose-driven times, I cherish these mellower moments skiing with friends in the alpine just as much.

Inside the cabin that evening, we pull books from the shelf. The eighth edition of Jack Grauer's self-published *Mount Hood: A Complete History* and Eino Annala's self-published 1973 book *The Crag Rats* are two that Heiko and I leaf through. When I pull down Bill Mullee's 2014 *Mount Hood: A Climber's Guide*, Cully says, "I can sit and read that book for hours." These books capture the routes and the history and the peak's majesty but do little to capture the camaraderie and the thrill of skiing, climbing, and rescuing together. The solace of the high alpine.

After a ski day, an overnight, and another ski day, we close up the cabin and ski back to the car. Cully volunteers to take out our one bag of garbage. After all, it's the small things that count.

CHAPTER 6

JUNE: MASS CASUALTY ON THE SOUTH SIDE ROUTES

Many of us have two temperaments. Sometimes we need a quiet evening at home on the couch watching a movie or reading a book. Other times we revel in a social outing, such as seeing our friends at a dinner party. Mount Hood is like that too: it has one quiet, less-visited side and another where most of the people go.

While the north side was the hub of mountain climbing and skiing in the 1920s, the completion of the Mount Hood Loop Highway in 1925 and the construction of Timberline Lodge in 1938 soon brought most of the recreational interest to the peak's south side. With the new, easier access, this majestic mountain quickly became the most climbed glaciated peak in the world, the result of one route that collects nearly all the climbers: the South Side Routes—the scene of Mount Hood's first large-scale mass casualty, in 1956.

"Girl Loses Life. 16 Climbers Injured by Plunge into Mt. Hood Crevasse," read the *Oregonian* headline on July 30, 1956. This mass casualty still stands as the largest number of climbers involved in a single accident on Mount Hood that I could find. And resulted from a technique that has caused loss of life both in the past and in the modern day.

In the 1950s, the war was over, and the economy was booming. Most people had modern conveniences like cars, electric household appliances, and telephones. Air travel was flourishing, and ski resorts were popping up around the world. The second boom of mountain climbing was surging, with Timberline Lodge taking over as the hub on Mount Hood.

In July 1956, a group of eighteen teenagers on summer break from the East Coast hired the young guide Carl Schnoor, a Mazamas member, to lead them to the top. The *Oregonian* described the teenagers as "hardy physical specimens used to outdoor life."

They left Timberline Lodge at six thirty in the morning, riding a snowcat to the upper mountain. When Schnoor and the students reached the steep section at Devils Kitchen, all of them tied onto a single 120-foot rope. It took them until early afternoon to reach the summit; this is very late in the day for a climb in July if temperatures are warm and the sun is out, because the snow softens to slush and the thawing ice and loosening rock start falling. Still roped together, they began climbing down, which is generally regarded as usually more dangerous than ascending. Another climber that day, George McCreary, who passed the group, said later, "The snow was getting soft and fouling the group's crampons."

The *Oregon Journal* reported that at 3:05 p.m. one person fell, but no one remembered who. The whole group—all nineteen affixed to a single rope—careered down the mountain, each person yanked off the snow in rapid succession like dominoes falling. One sixteen-year-old boy reported trying to dig in with his ice axe when the slide began, but the snow was too soft—he flipped over and landed on his face. Judy Hart, also sixteen, said, "One minute we were walking along and the next minute we were sliding. I was just pulled along into the crevasse." The jumble of kids slid four hundred feet and dropped deep into a fissure at ten thousand feet—the Hot Rocks fumarole, the hole in the volcano from chapter 2. One unnamed climber said, "The sulfur fumes were terrible,

terrible. Some could not breathe. And we couldn't move. It was awful cold." Louise Kuflik, thirteen, said, "All I remember is tumbling and tumbling head over heels. Then we shot into the air and fell past two big open spaces on the side of the mountain. We landed all on top of each other. Some of the kids you couldn't even see after we landed." One had a fractured shoulder; another had a broken wrist and a back injury. In all, sixteen were injured. And one would die.

Rescuers from the Crag Rats, the Alpinees, and MORESCO's newly formed Portland unit were called at five thirty p.m. It took an hour to drive to Timberline Lodge and another two hours to get up the mountain. Ralph Wiese, Mount Hood district ranger, was the first on the scene and supervised the rescue. (He would later become a common figure on Mount Hood south-side rescues. But in 1960, after ambiguity over who was in charge, US Forest Service Region 6 officially bequeathed SAR responsibilities to county sheriffs, a responsibility that would later be codified into Oregon law.)

As rescuers arrived, they based out of Silcox Hut, a cabin a few hundred feet above Timberline Lodge. Workers brought blankets, milk, and cans of coffee. Another climber, Tom Pfau, was in the vicinity of the accident and scurried to the site: "I had a jackknife and I tried to cut them apart," Pfau said. "They were all tied close together and screaming. It was just a bloody mess. There were arms and legs sticking up everywhere. They were gouging each other with their crampons. The men were moaning, and the girls were screaming. I tried to unbury one girl whose feet were sticking out of the snow. She died while I tried to pull her out. I tried to move another man and he screamed at me not to touch him. He said his back was broken."

Rescue crews spent all night and most of the next day extricating the teens from the crevasse and hauling them down the mountain. The *Oregonian* reported, "Hundreds of rescue workers toiled through the night to unscramble the mass of broken bodies they found lying at the bottom of a 35-foot hole reeking of sulfur fumes."

The cause of the mass casualty: too many climbers tied to a rope that wasn't anchored to the snow. It's a pattern that I first described in chapter 4, dating back to the accident in 1927, when 8 members of a 103-person group of

Mazamas were tied into one rope, fell, and landed in a crevasse. This same mistake has continued to repeat itself, including in 2002 when nine people were roped together in three groups, an accident I wrote about in my first book, *Mountain Rescue Doctor*. In that accident, one group fell and, because they were tied together on a rope, slid and took out the other two groups, also tied to their partners unanchored. Nine climbers ended up in the Coalman Glacier bergschrund, and three died. During the mission, a heavy US Air Force Pave Hawk was trying to hoist a patient, lost lift, crashed, and rolled, causing more casualties but no more fatalities.

Now, one spring day in 2022, Crag Rats are called to yet another accident because of climbers utilizing the same misbegotten technique. Just home from a long bike ride, I scarf a bean-and-cheese burrito and doze off in the noonday sun. I have a bazillion things to do today, after spending two days the week before on the mountain for a mission, but right now I need a nap.

The phone buzzes loudly and nearly rattles off the table. Still bedecked in bike spandex, I reach for it. *Oh no, not now,* I think. *I'm so damned tired.* That lament leaves my brain instantly when I look at the text: "Two climbers injured. Below Summit. Devils Kitchen."

I wait for a few seconds—a tactical pause to let the adrenaline run through my body—and take a deep breath. I need to be clear-thinking when I pack so that I don't forget anything. I walk deliberately and slowly inside to my closet, shuck my cycling spandex, pull on my alpine kit, walk to the mudroom, and assemble my gear. While I'm getting ready, I text Meredith, who has picked up the coordinator duty.

"I'm available. Getting gear together now."

"Okay, you and Brian so far," she replies. Like me, Brian Hukari is dropping work—for him, at the orchard he runs with his brother, Bruce, a Crag Rat, and that he inherited from his dad, who was also a Crag Rat until he died. Meanwhile, Meredith gathers information about the rescue and rallies a crew. We plan to meet at the county yard in fifteen minutes. I grab my ski pack, skis, boots, and poles, plus my alpine glacier gear: harness, crampons, ice axe, and a small rope-rescue kit. I add climbing skins and gloves: the two items still on the drying rack from two days prior. And then I pull my SAR radio off the charger, fire up my Toyota, and drive to the county yard.

There, Brian has just pulled up, a green smoothie clutched in his hand.

"I'm coming too," Meredith says, smiling as she pulls up with Ron.

"Two climbers," Ron muses. "We may have to split up." I like this about Ron: he's already thinking about the mission logistics.

Cully texts me: "I can't go, on call." He, like me, hates missing rescues. "It's the one thing that makes me depressed," he once confided in me. Recently, Cully and I cut a ski day short because he had to be home for another family's roller-skating birthday party. That day, as he started to apologize, I waved him off, saying, "You should Strava the roller-skating party." Later, he sent me his track: 4.16 miles going round and round in a high school gym.

"FKT?" I texted back.

"Unofficially, yes," he replied.

Now at the county yard, I meet the crew. "Let's get up there and figure it out," Brian says, speaking from experience. Gary has arrived, but Heiko is taking a bit more time. I text Heiko, "We'll pick you up at the park and ride." We're anxious to roll.

We jump in SAR 1 and are pulling out of the yard when, at the last minute, unannounced and without texting, Walter shows up.

"Hey, guys, just give me a minute," he says. From his tiny Nissan Leaf, he pulls out a big duffel of gear and a giant backpack. His hair is frizzier than usual, like he just got out of bed. I'm glad he is here. Like Brian, Walter knows the arêtes, ridges, glaciers, and headwalls on Mount Hood, because, as you'll recall, on his days off he is constantly exploring this mountain.

"Lisa and John are up on the mountain, climbing with their kids," Meredith says. "They are responding."

"Great!" I say, knowing that we once again have an excellent crew, with the added advantage of having John and Lisa—two of the best alpinists in the area—responding immediately. "Are their kids coming on the mission too?" I ask of their teenagers. Meredith says the kids will descend the mountain with some other parents. Meanwhile, and fortuitously, Steve Rollins from Portland

Mountain Rescue (PMR) has been climbing with a friend and is nearby. "And AMR is there too," Meredith says, referring to the American Medical Response team.

This is a good crew and a fast response: lucky for the climbers.

We wedge ourselves into the double cab after jamming skis and packs into an already-full truck. Gary expertly negotiates the curvy Highway 35; fifty minutes later, we arrive at a busy Timberline Lodge, where we're waved past the roadblock keeping cars out of the VIP parking lot. We park haphazardly next to a sheriff command truck and the AMR ambulance.

"Same day, same location, different people." The ever-affable and good-spirited Deputy Scott Meyers smiles. "We have two this time."

"Okay, give us a few minutes and we'll be ready," I say.

"Snowcat isn't available at the moment—we need a driver," Meyers says.

We're burning daylight—darkness compounds almost every aspect of a mission—and we're itching to get going.

"Take the chairlift," Meyers says, once again smiling confidently. He's never stressed—he seems to know that either our mission will turn out fine or we'll do our very best. He has total trust in us.

"Copy," Gary says. We load up our heavy packs and rescue gear, catch the Magic Mile chairlift, and then switch to Palmer chairlift, which delivers us to 8,470 feet. From there, we skin toward Hogsback, some 1,500 feet higher and a little over an hour's ski. Same mountain, same place, nearly the same situation as the mission from chapter 2—only with two subjects instead of one.

Like opposite siblings, the two sides of one mountain offer different experiences. The north side is guarded by a thirty-minute, rough, nine-mile dirt road in the summer to reach Cloud Cap Inn that becomes a two-hour ski approach in the winter. And this just gets you to the beginning of the climbing routes, which are highly technical, with steep, exposed slopes like those found on Cooper Spur and the Sunshine Route. It's rugged wilderness.

The south side's vibe is much different. First, it's accessible via the paved Timberline Road. At Timberline Lodge you can get a burger, brunch, or a room for $300 a night. Downhill skiers are here nearly year-round, as Timberline

Lodge Ski Area is one of the few resorts in the world open nearly all year. And it's not unusual to see tourists in street clothes just up for a visit to the lodge, even in midwinter.

Second, when the weather is clear, the climbing route is almost completely visible from the parking lot, and it's straightforward. The first 1,500 vertical feet ascend adjacent to the ski resort, which gives people a sense of security and makes navigation easy in clear weather. In winter and spring, the route is busy with skiers heading to Illumination Saddle and Devils Kitchen without even considering the summit. And the South Side Routes only have relatively short, steep technical sections, just the top 1,200 vertical feet up the Coalman or Zigzag Glaciers. All these factors combine to make the south side way more crowded.

A couple of hours earlier, two climbers had summited and were descending, tied together but not anchored. We are not surprised to hear this, because this is exactly how many people fall and die on this mountain, again and again.

Generally, climbers use different rope techniques for different situations. On less steep glaciers, where one might fall *down* into a crevasse from an uphill climbing or skiing position, climbers often tie into a rope together but have no anchors. The hope is if one person falls in, usually the one in front, the weight of the other climbers will be enough to stop the fall. But once climbers (whether climbing up or down) switch to high-angle slopes, like the 40-degree Pearly Gates chute, the worry becomes a fall leading to an uncontrollable slide. In this situation, the rope must be anchored if it's to stop falling climbers. Again: *The rope must be anchored.* The anchors are usually two-foot-long snow stakes called pickets or six- to eight-inch-long ice screws. For some reason on Mount Hood, people erroneously use the glacier-travel technique, roped *without* anchors, on the Pearly Gates, which requires a rope *with* anchors or no rope at all if one's skills and equipment are commensurate to the terrain.

So these two climbers, a man and woman, were downclimbing after reaching the summit, roped together without anchors. One tripped, fell, started sliding, and gained momentum so quickly that he or she yanked the other climber off the mountain. The two lost their footing instantly and tumbled down the Pearly

Gates chute. They plopped right into the Coalman Glacier bergschrund, which, at this time of year, was three feet wide and thirty feet deep, sitting at eleven thousand feet on top of Hogsback.

Fortunately, because of the hordes on the mountain this sunny Sunday, someone saw the accident and called 911. The Rusts and Steve Rollins, who were high on the mountain, received the text, abandoned their climbs, and responded immediately. At the bergschrund, they find that a group of bystanders has pulled the climbers out relatively quickly and that they slid only ten feet inside the fissure. The man has a back injury and can't walk. Rollins, John, and Lisa dig out a platform in the snow, bundle him in extra clothes and a tarp, bury two ice axes to the hilts in the ice, and tie him to this anchor. The woman has an ankle injury, face abrasions, and is "sore all over." But she can walk. Both are wearing ill-fitting crampons on boots made for hiking—not mountain climbing—and tiny backpacks, and carry no extra clothes, food, or water. This is not the first time I've written about inadequate equipment: it's a regular occurrence on this route. Once, when climbing the Mazama Chute, Maurizio and I looked to the adjacent One O'Clock Couloir and saw a crampon sliding down the chute: it had popped off someone's boot.

Luckily, the sky is clear, the sun is bright, and the air temperature is climbing to 45 degrees in the south-facing amphitheater of Devils Kitchen. The crater receives direct sun most of the day. But this welcoming sun can also be a hazard, melting the ice and sending projectiles of rock and ice zinging down the mountain. This is in addition to steep slopes, the risk of avalanches, and sudden changes in weather.

Rollins stays with the man on the flat platform in the snow, while the Rusts decide to help the woman walk down off the Hogsback into safer terrain—the flat spot near the Devils Kitchen fumarole. From here, the downclimb back to Timberline Lodge, while long and difficult, is neither technical nor crevassed like the upper mountain. At Devils Kitchen, Lisa and John make an excellent decision: Lisa will keep slowly walking downhill with the woman, while John will climb back up with an extra rope to help Rollins with the immobile man.

Meanwhile, Gary, Ron, Walter, Brian, Meredith, and I skin up to meet Lisa at 9,500 feet. She's with the injured woman, who looks exhausted.

"She can't walk anymore," Lisa says. "She'll need a litter. But we've made it this far."

"Good work!" I say. "PMR is coming up with a litter right behind us." I call the team on my radio to let them know the situation, then Lisa briefs us on John's plan.

"The guy up top needs a litter. He can't walk," Lisa says. She points way uphill, where we see the tiny specks of Rollins, John, and the man in the snow just a few hundred feet below the summit.

"If you can stay with this woman to wait for Team 3, they have a litter. We'll keep heading up," I say.

"Sure," Lisa says. "These guys are unprepared and not doing too well." As a guide, she's skilled at assessing people.

I see that Ron, Brian, Walter, and Gary have kept ascending right past us, quickly and wordlessly: their task is to get equipment and personnel high up the mountain, where it's needed most urgently.

I introduce myself to the woman: "Hi, I'm Dr. Van Tilburg. Okay if I check you quickly?" I have my hospital ID and Crag Rats patch affixed to the radio harness on my chest to identify myself.

I complete the primary survey in about ten seconds: airway, breathing, circulation, disability, environment. In mountain rescue, it's too difficult to complete a full exam with dangerous and difficult terrain, the inability to unclothe a patient, and such. I decide that the woman is stable and then turn to a more immediate task: allocating resources. I do a quick count in my head of how many rescuers we have with the man at eleven thousand feet: Rollins, two medics, and five Crag Rats. I think I may be more useful up higher.

"Can you stay with Lisa until a second litter comes up?" I ask Meredith.

"Sure," she replies. Meredith is an expert skier and highly skilled rescuer who knows basic medical care, not just because she attends my medical trainings but meaningfully and quizzically engages to learn the skill of mountain medicine.

The injured woman will be in fine hands with Lisa and Meredith. I call command to let them know the status. Then I keep climbing, following Gary, Ron, Walter, and Brian, who are a few hundred feet and ten minutes above me. In twenty minutes, we reach Hogsback, where we join John and the small group of bystanders.

"What do you think?" I ask John, who, because of his mountain guide experience, has already figured out a solid plan.

"We take the litter up, package him, lower him down with a rope. Pretty straightforward. But anchors will be tricky because the snow is so soft," he says.

"We've done this before," I say. I'm about to start up Hogsback with John when we hear the familiar rotor blades of an inbound helicopter, in this case a Sikorsky HH-60 Black Hawk from the 189th Aviation Regiment of the Oregon National Guard. Like déjà vu, I see it far off to the south, rapidly approaching. And also like déjà vu, the Jenkins lawsuit from 2017 and the Pave Hawk crash from 2002 come to mind. With everyone staged at 10,500 feet on Hogsback, I climb up five minutes to the top of Hogsback to conference with Rollins.

"Helicopter inbound." I point.

"Yeah, good thing—he's not doing too well. In a lot of pain."

"With the helicopter inbound, I'd like to get everyone down lower on Hogsback, and just keep me and one medic," Rollins says.

"Good idea," I say. I defer to him, a skilled rescuer and, by default, in command of the situation. The helicopter swoops in, makes a pass, and flies away, undoubtedly trying to assess if a safe hoist can be accomplished. As the chopper comes in for another look, it creates a nerve-racking downdraft, blowing snow and ice everywhere. Even though the climber is anchored to the two ice axes, the snow is softening in the pressure cooker of the Devils Kitchen. At least we have the litter at Hogsback, carried up by Gary and Brian. I retreat lower, to a safe zone out of the rotor wash, and wait with Gary, Brian, Walter, and Ron. I'm worried about the helicopter but also excited because it's thrilling to watch, and I know this means we might make it down the mountain before dark and be home by bedtime.

Just as the helicopter flies back to do a dangerous hoist, the radio crackles: "All teams, we have another mission on the mountain. A reporting party said they saw a skier enter White River Glacier from the headwall"—the top of the glacier, a five-minute ski away—"and not come out."

"Fuck," I say, looking at Rollins up high and then at Gary. Now we've got another problem. We have a total of three injured or missing climbers on the mountain, including one immobile at eleven thousand feet.

MUCH CONTROVERSY FOLLOWED the 1956 mass-casualty accident, not unlike today. In fact, it's nearly exactly like today. An *Oregonian* editorial on July 31, 1956, said, "This accident raised anew the old question of why safety regulations for climbing Mt. Hood are not formalized or enforced." And the paper noted that "approved practice calls for groups of no more than five or six to be roped with ten-foot intervals, each climber holding a couple loops of slack in one hand to be wrapped quickly around the handle of his implanted axe should a fellow climber lose his footing."

Another letter by the mountain guide John Scott cited his thirty-five years of experience and membership on the Mazamas climbing committee. Scott wrote, "I will state unequivocally that the irreducible minimum distance between climbers in a roped squad is not less than 20 feet. On 120 feet of 7/16 inch line, the present accepted standard, the Mazamas will allow only five climbers." Scott goes on to say that tying nineteen into one rope is "preposterous" because "if one slips on a dangerous, steep slope, the rest go down like a line of dominos before anyone has time to get set and dig in." This is exactly what happened to the students and their guide.

In another letter, Kent Simon of Lake Oswego wrote, "Use proper equipment, never climb alone." Simon cited a climb earlier in the week when he wrote the letter, describing a boy who summited Mount Hood in galoshes without crampons and then had the audacity to "falsely advertise to future climbers by entering in the forest service climbing register 'this goes to show that you can make it without crampons.'" Per Simon, however, the boy had omitted the fact that he was accompanied by an experienced climber who wore crampons, he was roped to the experienced climber, and he carried ice axes. "But anyone who reads that account will think that those who want to can climb without crampons," Simon concluded.

These back-and-forths are much like what you find on today's social media: blame, questionable advice, misleading information, blatantly wrong information, fiery emotions, arguments, and so on. But there's one big difference: the speed with which information propagated back then was slower, and much less information was available, as communication was via a print newspaper.

When MORESCO debriefed the accident on August 9, 1956 (according to Crag Rats meeting minutes), they made clear recommendations: one guide for eighteen clients is not adequate. (In 2023, most guides follow a 3:1 client-to-guide ratio for climbing and 6:1 for skiing.). One rope is not sufficient for nineteen people. And the climbers started up far too late in the day.

At a meeting on October 25, 1956, MORESCO leaders critiqued the rescue operation. Communications were not great—a problem we continue to have today even with modern radios, GPS, and cell phones. Too many unauthorized people were on the mountain getting in the way. Coordination of crews at Timberline Lodge was poor. And so, regulation was discussed. Per the minutes, "The advisability of MORESCO going on record as recommending Forest Service regulation of mountain climbing in Oregon was discussed and finally tabled without any action." We have similar discussions today: challenges with communication, with multiple agencies working together, and rescuers scattered along the rescue-operation area.

At a later meeting, on January 24, 1957, MORESCO met with the US Forest Service to discuss legislation to regulate mountaineering. They decided again to defer a formal recommendation because the groups felt that legislation was not the answer. Instead, it was decided to stress education programs and the posting of signs requesting and encouraging climber registration. Sound familiar? The same issues would go on to be discussed for many decades; in both 1999 and 2006, after accidents, the US Forest Service considered climbing regulation. But it wasn't until January 1, 2024, that the US Forest Service would commence a climbing permit system on Mount Hood—a decision that was met with much controversy, despite permits being required to climb Mount Rainier, Mount St. Helens, Mount Adams, Denali, Mount Shasta, and other western mountains. Given how new this system is on Mount Hood, it will take time to see if there's a meaningful impact on climbing, crowds, and mountain rescues.

After the 1956 mission and well into the early 1960s, Crag Rats had few rescues, sometimes less than a handful per year, and less than one per year in the alpine. This is possibly because other teams were available for missions, or because we simply had a lull in accidents. Little is documented on these rescues in the Crag Rats meeting minutes. I found just four alpine missions during these years, namely on the Chisholm Trail on the north side. Don't go trying to find this trail, because it's neither a trail nor a climbing route. Rather, it signifies a route people fall *down*.

On the north side on June 25, 1961, twenty-five Mazamas were climbing the Sunshine Route up and the Cooper Spur Route down. Colin Chisholm and his twenty-two-year-old son, Douglas, lost their footing near a rock formation called the Chimney. They slid and tumbled two thousand feet onto the Eliot Glacier. Luckily, they survived by landing in snow that had avalanched a few days before and had softened from the sun. Crag Rats were already at Cloud Cap Inn, and so they immediately deployed when word of the accident reached them. The rescue was completed in six hours with support from a helicopter. "This was probably one of the best coordinated rescue operations we have participated in in some time," noted a write-up in the archives. This most popular route to fall down on the north side would thereafter be dubbed the "Chisholm Trail" by the Crag Rats.

Similarly, on September 15, 1962, five students from Reed College descended the Chimney, slipped, and fell down the Chisholm Trail. Crag Rats again were already on the mountain, so they were able to respond quickly and extricate the group from a crevasse on the Eliot Glacier. Then, a Kaman HH-43 Huskie from Portland's 304th Air Rescue Squadron landed on the Eliot, loaded the five climbers, and whisked them to safety.

On July 22, 1963, another accident occurred in the same spot. The *Oregon Journal* reported that Dr. Eberhard Gloekler, Mark Hanschka, and Robert

Shoemaker had summited and were caught in a predicted storm. Gloekler later said the "wind was hard and ugly. I didn't realize the other two were very tired, and couldn't react normally in case of a fall, and I had perhaps taken in too much rope—it was rather tight." All three were downclimbing eight hundred feet below summit when one person slipped at the Chimney, taking all three down the express descent of the Chisholm Trail. Gloekler was "jerked free" of the snow, failing to self-arrest because the snow was too soft. Shoemaker dislocated his shoulder and broke several ribs. Hanschka injured his back and broke his right arm. Since Rob Hukari and other Crag Rats were at Cloud Cap Inn for a quiet weekend after the cherry harvest, a team deployed immediately. Eventually, nineteen Crag Rats and eleven Alpinees used litters to bring the three off the mountain while being whipped by rain, sleet, and gusts that hit fifty miles per hour. According to Crag Rats meeting minutes, it was a "long, bumpy and dangerous trip back to safety. Several times members of the party slipped on the wicked slopes letting the akja down with a bump, but Hanschka never uttered a sound. Bounding rocks, many of them propelled by the fierce gusts of wind, made the exhausting trip even more dangerous."

And again near the Chisholm Trail, on October 13, 1966, Charles B. Gibson Jr. and Louis Siegel were "glacier hopping" when Gibson slipped, fell, and pulled Siegel down with him. They tumbled five hundred feet; when they stopped, Gibson had a broken leg. It took Siegel nine hours to reach Cloud Cap Inn, where, as usual, some Crag Rats—Bill Bryan, Elwood Samuels, and Al Combes—were bunking. Crag Rats rescued Gibson, and Sheriff Rupert Gillmouthe was quoted in the *Hood River News* as congratulating the Crag Rats on a "perfect operation."

I found three consistencies across these sparse missions. First, the Chisholm Trail was the main venue of mayhem. Second, Crag Rats hung out at Cloud Cap Inn a lot! They loved the alpine and spending time at the cabin. Third, this era marked the onset of using helicopters for missions. In the 1960s, the technology boom was exploding. By the end of the 1960s, radios had shrunk from the size of shoeboxes to bricks, airplanes were used for scouting, helicopters were used for rescues, and snowcats aided ground transportation. Someone brought the first plastic drinking bottle to a Crag Rats meeting and asked for orders. Crag Rats upgraded their rope to nylon from farm hemp: 1/2-inch diameter for $0.02 per foot and 3/16-inch diameter for $0.03 per foot.

During this era, another problem was brought up. At a meeting on December 12, 1962, Bill Pattison, a young, up-and-coming community leader who eventually became Hood River fire chief, town mayor, insurance salesman, and Pooley's successor as a Crag Rats titan, questioned if the organization needed "new younger life blood" and if "something should be done about the number of empty seats at the meetings." At subsequent meetings, Crag Rats acknowledged the lack of missions also. According to the minutes from March 11, 1965, the decrease in the number of missions was thought to be from "increased efficiency of MRA [Mountain Rescue Association] units in Northwest" and a "higher level of climber accomplishment, better coordination between units, and more rescue units equipped to handle problems in their own areas." More rescue teams had been formed across the West. At an MRA meeting in Seattle in 1962, attendance jumped to a whopping seventy-five attendees, up from twenty-five in prior years.

During this time, Crag Rats were busy with snow surveys, ski trips, climbing trips, and repairs to Cloud Cap Inn. The meeting minutes are filled with the jovial camaraderie of social outings. At one meeting, a primary discussion resolved a chief issue: "Remove empty beer kegs and bottles from the hut after each party." In a trip report about skiing Mount Bachelor, Lefty Leavens was quoted as saying, "The operators of the Bachelor Butte area were not very happy to see the checkered shirt boys return because of what they had done to the Poma lift last year." No further explanation was given, but I infer some tomfoolery.

Also in the early 1960s, Crag Rats had a building project. As Interstate 84 was quickly becoming busy, with a new interchange planned in Hood River, Crag Rats sold their original hut near the freeway for $60,000 to Texaco to build a gas station in 1965. Immediately thereafter, they constructed the new hut on Winchell Butte in 1966, for $44,700; it is still used today as our meeting hall and training center, albeit remodeled in 2018.

Again, in the 1960s, the Crag Rats had a few more brief discussions about the mountain environment. In meeting minutes from April 27, 1961, they reviewed the Federation of Western Outdoor Clubs' request to help block Forest Service roads from being built in wilderness areas near Waldo Lake and the Minam River in Central Oregon. The Crag Rats decided that "members should investigate to see whether it is worthy." But the matter was not mentioned again.

In early 1961, word spread about the new ski resort proposed for the east side of Mount Hood. This piqued the Crag Rats' interest, as they had a long history of skiing. In fact, skiing in the Pacific Northwest had started after the turn of the century right here, on Mount Hood. In Lowell Skoog's book, *Written in the Snows: Across Time on Skis in the Pacific Northwest*, he traced the first mention of skiing in the Pacific Northwest to the Langille brothers, who skied to Cloud Cap Inn in 1890.

Skiing is not only a requisite component of being a Crag Rat but also a passion indelibly woven into the fabric of my own life. The first ski areas in the country started out as jump hills. Howelsen Hill in Steamboat Springs, Colorado, which opened in 1915, is thought to be the first and is still operating. On Mount Hood, Summit Ski Area opened on December 11, 1927—not long after the Feyerabend/Brownlee and White searches—as there was so much interest in mountain recreation. The initiative was spearheaded by the Portland Advertising Club, which formed the Winter Sports Committee, and received permission from the US Forest Service to build a ski jump, toboggan slide, ski slope, and rental shop. Soon thereafter, they built a rope tow, then a T-bar, and then a chairlift. (The first rope tow is generally thought to be the one that opened in Woodstock, New York, in January 1934.) Now Summit is owned by Timberline Lodge, which boasts the ski run with the most vertical drop of any ski area in the country: a 4,540-foot descent from top to bottom.

Back in the 1920s, the site of the present-day Timberline Lodge had a Forest Service cabin and two private ski-club cabins at tree line. The Works Progress Administration helped fund Timberline Lodge's construction in 1937, and the Magic Mile chairlift was installed a year later as the second chairlift in the United States. (Sun Valley, Idaho, is generally thought to have the first chairlift, built in 1936.) The war years took a toll on the lodge business, and after shuttering the lodge in 1955, the US Forest Service gave the operations permit to Richard L. Kohnstamm, whose family still operates the lodge and ski resort today. By 1969, Timberline Lodge was receiving 750,000 visitors annually.

Two additional resorts started on the south side, right in Government Camp on twin hills. In 1928, Everett Sickler of Portland developed a jump hill on Multorpor Mountain (a portmanteau of *Multnomah County* and *Portland*). In 1938, he built a rope tow powered by a Dodge truck engine—cost: $0.05 per ride or $1 per day. A chairlift followed in 1961. In 1937, literally next door at Tom, Dick, and Harry Mountain, French Boyd installed a 2,100-foot rope tow powered by a car engine. He called the new area Skibowl and put in a chairlift in 1946. By 1964, Everett Darr and Carl Reynolds bought both ski areas and joined the two; they installed night lights in 1966, making one of the largest night-skiing areas in the country.

Meanwhile, on the north side, Jump Hill at the Cooper Spur Junction had been maintained by the Hood River Ski Club since around 1927. A primitive rope tow was installed in 1938 by putting a motor in the center of the hill, with the rope running above and below. The ski hill was eventually purchased in 1956 by Jack Baldwin and George Howell, who also acted as ski patrollers and ski instructors, were early members of the Crag Rats, and later—after World War II—formed the Alpinees. Cooper Spur would get a T-bar in 1971 and eventually a chairlift. Dan and Sharon Dillard bought the resort in 1974 and ran it until they sold it to Mt. Hood Meadows in 2001. According to the archives, in the 1950s the Crag Rats, Alpinees, and Hood River Ski Club volunteered many hours constructing the ski trails and improving the roads. I asked Crag Rat Roger Nelson about this time, as he is one of the few members of both the Crag Rats and Alpinees. He said the Cooper Spur Ski Area helped the two groups, who were otherwise gentle rivals, form a common bond. (The Alpinees disbanded in the 1990s after becoming what Roger called "mostly an outing club.")

While the ski areas around Government Camp and Cooper Spur had been ongoing hubs of recreation since the 1920s, in the early 1960s a new area was being considered for development on the lee side of Mount Hood, protected from the wind by a pair of massive moraines from the Newton Clark and White River Glaciers. These rocky ramparts shield the gentle glades and open meadows. Development of the resort began with a US Forest Service feasibility study in 1964, with a group including Hood River locals Jack Baldwin, L. R. Steeves, Dr. J. Allan Henderson, and two Crag Rats: Roland "Rusty" Leavens and Tony Krivak. Several spots were investigated, including Lamberson Butte, Cloud Cap, and Wy'east Basin. But today's present site of Mt. Hood Meadows was settled on. After two years, in April 1966, the US Forest Service awarded Portland's Franklin G. Drake a permit for two chairlifts, a T-bar, a rope tow, and a lodge. But this was not without controversy, according to Jack Grauer's book *Mount Hood: A Complete History*. First, not everyone wanted another ski resort—including some private citizens, the Sierra Club, the Mazamas, and the Seattle-based Mountaineers. The concern was the impact of roads, buildings, and a parking lot on the scenic Umbrella and Sahale Falls, a popular destination for hikers. Second, a group of Hood River residents called Hood River Improvement Corporation, composed of local skiers, business owners, Alpinees, and Crag Rats, had put in a bid of their own, though they lost out to Drake.

Mt. Hood Meadows opened in 1968. The Drake family still owns the resort today, and like Timberline, it remains a standout independent resort among the majority of conglomerate-owned US ski resorts. Long ago, my brother gave me a book called *Northwest Ski Trails* by Ted Mueller, published in 1968. In the introduction, Mueller discusses concern for the environment, the impact of ski resorts, and the mining industry's resistance to the creation of Washington's spectacular North Cascades National Park. Back then, like today, people were concerned that resorts would bring crowds and environmental degradation. At the same time, we love skiing, socializing, friendships, and the security that ski resorts bring to the mountains. But still, these resorts—the chairlifts, logged runs, buildings, cars of visitors, parking lots—are not impact-free.

I grew up skiing on Mount Hood. When I was seven, my parents took me, my sister, and my brother up to Summit Ski Area on Mount Hood. The first day, we had to sidestep up the hill and attempt to ski down. Although I only vaguely remember the skiing, I can distinctly recall my robin's-egg-blue Sportscaster coat, which I would eventually bedeck with patches from regional ski areas including the Mount Hood resorts and Mount Bachelor. Later, we rode the T-bar. As I rode up with my dad, the T-bar hit me across the shoulders and him in the legs—I struggled to stay on.

I skied frequently but not obsessively in college, and I learned to snowboard at a tiny, four-hundred-foot-vertical, now-defunct resort called North–South Ski Bowl in Idaho during my first year of medical school, in 1989. Built by the Civilian Conservation Corps through the Works Progress Administration in the late 1930s, the place consisted of one tiny lift and one tiny bowl lit up with lights. Boots were floppy, and the snowboards were one step above plywood.

I learned the basics of backcountry snowboarding during my medical internship in Salt Lake City. In 1995, I cut my first snowboard lengthwise and installed a split kit, which allowed me to skin up the backcountry using the two halves like skis, reassemble the snowboard at the top of the slope, and glide back down. In fact, I made my first climb of Mount Hood, in 1994, with that snowboard. In 1998, I wrote my first book, *Backcountry Snowboarding*. With kids, I later migrated back to skiing and eventually to backcountry skiing. I started picking off volcanoes and kept a list of my descents, which I'd later develop into the book *Backcountry Ski and Snowboard Routes: Oregon*.

I taught both my daughters to ski, in part to give them the skill and in part to pass on my love of skiing, ski culture, and the high alpine. I fondly recall those days of loading up the truck, driving to the mountain, and shushing in the sun—even though some were marked by the frustration of storms or lousy snow or hunger or missing nap time. As my kids got older and became good skiers, and my career matured, I started combining skiing and travel. This started when my family skied Portillo, Chile, twice. I funded these family trips by keeping my overhead low, driving an old truck, building a simple house, working extra shifts in the ER, and consulting in wilderness medicine. And then, when my kids got older, I became obsessed. I saved money, hoarded vacation time, and kept the old truck. I skied the trifecta of Alps grand tours: the Haute Route, the Bernese Oberland, and the Ortler Circuit. I jumped on a sailboat-based ski trip to Svalbard, Norway. I skied Hokkaido, Japan—twice.

How many days do I ski every year? I don't even know. Maybe one hundred? Do I count the one run off the tip-top of Mount Hood, or the one run at night on the flat Barlow Pass with Lisa and Meredith? Or the one run where Brian basically dragged me down the Tilly Jane Trail at night? Skiing is more than an obsession; it's a deep connection between me, the Crag Rats, and our mountain.

NOW, PRESENT DAY, we are on the mountain with a complicated situation. While waiting for the helicopter to reset, I climb up Hogsback to talk with Rollins, perched on the snow ledge and anchored by the two ice axes. He's with an AMR medic, while everyone else has evacuated to lower, safer terrain.

"You got this? The patient stable?" I ask. "We have another mission."

"Yeah, I heard. This guy is stable but could go bad at any time. Looks favorable to hoist with the helicopter."

The AMR medic gives me a briefing. The main thing I hear is, "He's stable." I lean over, pull a tarp away from the patient's face, and take a quick look, not wanting to unbundle him or repeat an assessment completed by the medic, whom I trust as a highly skilled wilderness medicine expert. The patient is alert, and his eyes are open—that's good enough to confirm he's stable. For now.

"Okay, if you two can handle this patient, I'll take the second call," I say to Rollins. "Someone apparently skied into a crevasse below the White River headwall."

"Okay, I'll radio command," Rollins says.

I climb back down to the lower Hogsback and inform Ron, Brian, and Gary of the plan. We decide we need just three of us to search White River and leave everyone else to stage at Hogsback in case the helicopter hoist is aborted. Plus, the gear we brought up needs to be hauled back down anyway. Still cognizant of the 2002 disaster, I pause for a few minutes to make sure the helicopter hoist works as planned. I watch as the helicopter makes four dangerous passes in a matter of ten minutes. First, it flies in, lowers the medic, and flies away. Then it flies back three times, in succession, to lower the empty litter, to pick up the litter with the patient, and then to pick up the medic. With no wind and clear skies, it's successful. Rollins can now organize the crew to get gear and rescuers off the mountain safely.

"Let's go," I say to Ron and Walter, adding, "You lead," to Walter because he knows the terrain better than me and just skied White River Glacier the week before.

The snow is smooth from the sun and warm temperatures; it's just softening to corn—an apt moniker for snow consisting of tiny balls of melted ice that hasn't yet turned to slush. It's fabulous: creamy, smooth, and delightful. After a few minutes, we ski to the crevasse, a horizontal crack spanning nearly the entire three-hundred-foot-wide glacier at 9,300 feet. On the ski down, we see two sets of ski tracks that traverse across the top of the crevasse and exit the glacier on the west moraine. We peer into the bottomless fissure and yell. No response. We decide no one fell in.

I call command on the radio. "We are at the White River crevasse. Tracks come down to the crevasse and clearly exit to the west. No tracks lead into the crevasse. All clear."

Walter sums up the situation, saying, "So someone saw a skier drop onto the glacier but didn't see an accident. They probably just saw all the search activity for the two climbers and thought they should call it in."

"Clearly there's no tracks and no missing skier," I say to Walter.

"Agree," he says.

"Let's go home," Ron says. "I'm tired and hungry."

"Agree," Walter says again.

We ski back to Timberline Lodge just as the mission for the two climbers completes: the one climber was successfully airlifted, and the other was brought down in the litter and transported to the hospital in an ambulance. All teams are down by five p.m.

At the next business meeting, during the debrief, we bring up communication again. At the time, I think that it's something we should address. Later, after researching this book, I realize this is a long-standing problem in search and rescue, dating back at least to the 1950s. High-stakes, time-critical missions are completed with many different groups, from several jurisdictions—a mix of paid and volunteer people. It's no wonder communication challenges persist.

Later, Gary bird-dogs a Portland Fire and Rescue specialist to lead a training in the National Incident Management System (NIMS). I'm enthralled and soak up the information. I'll later ask Gary many questions and read several briefs about NIMS. Gary takes this on because we noticed a safety problem and because Gary, like me, sees a simple way to foster better, safer, and more efficient missions. Later, I recount the mission to Cully, who's genuinely interested in the procedure and the outcome. We wonder why people still climb roped without anchors. In medicine, when we have an unsafe, outdated, or incorrect procedure, we change it and hold people accountable to it. But it doesn't seem to be the same up in the mountains for recreationalists.

"I wonder how this erroneous message gets propagated?" I ask while we discuss the mission.

"Not sure—social media? Guidebooks?"

"People gain comfort in tying a rope around themselves, even if it's not going to help and potentially makes things worse."

But this just makes me recall my own fallibility outside of mountain rescues. Alas, we are humans, and humans are not perfect. We all make mistakes, myself included. The key is to not make lethal ones.

PART III
SUMMER

GROWING UP GEN X,
1966 TO 1999

CHAPTER 7

JULY: NIGHT MISSION ON MCGEE CREEK

It's a midsummer day in peak tourist season. Hood River is bustling with mountain bikers, hikers, trail runners, and folks who ride the wind and waves of the Columbia River by way of windsurfing, kitesurfing, stand-up paddling, outrigger canoeing, kayaking, and wing foiling.

Back in the 1980s, windsurfers discovered that the Columbia River Gorge was windy all summer. The cool marine air drifts in from the Pacific Ocean and stalls when it hits the Cascade Range, while out east the arid grasslands heat up. Cool air gets sucked up the gorge, a natural wind tunnel that accelerates via the Venturi effect. Since the current flows opposite the wind, giant swells form on the river. As a result, Hood River became a global hub of wind- and watersports.

As the sun drifts low in the sky and the westerly breeze blows, evening finds the town filled with folks coming off the trails or the water; strolling through the downtown boutiques; sipping beverages at the wineries, vineyards, and brewpubs; or wrapping up the Hood River Fruit Loop, the moniker given to the loop of Highways 35 and 281 that allows visitors to stop at the many roadside stands selling locally grown fruits and vegetables. The orchards thrive as one of the world's leading producers of Anjou pears, along with other varieties of pears, apples, blueberries, peaches, cherries, and more recently, wine grapes and beer hops.

Amid yet another busy summer in Hood River, my phone buzzes with an incoming text message. The moment this happens, I suspect I'll be hiking up the mountain, into a forest, or through a thick-brushed, steep, rocky canyon. If you are getting tired of every chapter starting with the annoying buzz of my phone, welcome to the lives of Crag Rats.

"Injured hiker, McGee Creek."

Where the fuck is McGee Creek? Even after a quarter century of rescues and five decades of adventuring on this mountain, some places remain mysterious to me. My personal terra incognita is much larger than I can even imagine: drainages, forests, cliffs, and ridges. The glacier sections I've never traveled on, the waterfalls I've never seen, the bucolic meadows chock-full of wildflowers that I have never crossed. I search my brain. I pop open the GPS map app on my phone, scroll to the Mount Hood map, and plug in the name. *That's way the fuck up the mountain.* Then I look at my watch, it's six p.m. *This will be all fucking night.* I don't always have such profanity coursing through my brain, but the year is wearing on me: so many missions. It's only July, and we're already at thirty calls, usually our total for the year.

Of late, Timberline Trail #600, the forty-mile track that circumnavigates the mountain, has become increasingly popular among adventure athletes. For decades, backpackers would hike the trail in a span of three to ten days, usually starting at Timberline Lodge. Hikers can start at a few other trailheads: the Cloud Cap trailhead on the north side, or the Ramona Falls and Top Spur trailheads on the west side near the Sandy River. A loop taking two or three days would be considered fastpacking, a mode of backpacking that involves fast hiking, long days, and minimal gear. But lately, the trend is for trail runners to complete, or attempt to complete, the trail in a *single day*. This is no easy task, even for an ultrarunner, as Timberline Trail #600 climbs (and descends) ten thousand feet in its forty miles. In fact, I've jumped on this trend, running the trail twice in a day, once with a friend in fourteen hours and a second time solo in ten hours twenty minutes. This was something not even on my radar back in 1989, when I first moved here. But times have changed.

"Hiker on McGee Creek, shoulder injury," Deputy Scott Meyers says when I call him, being his usual direct but cheery self—not rushed, not judgmental, not frustrated. It's more of a here-we-go-again, matter-of-fact, let's-get-'er-done tone, one honed over years as a SAR deputy. "Five people, one injured, on the Timberline Trail. They have minimal gear," he adds.

"Where on McGee Creek?" I ask. The creek, I can see in my GPS app, begins in the high country near McNeil Point and trickles down the mountain into roadless, trailless areas. And then I ask, "If they've got backpacking gear, can they camp tonight and we can fetch them in the morning?" Just as I say this, I know without Meyers answering that we will go tonight—we almost always do. I put Meyers on speaker and spread a frayed paper map of the Mount Hood Wilderness on my scarred kitchen counter, preferring this to the app. I locate McGee Creek.

"Okay, I found it."

"Well, not sure the situation, and she sounded pretty worried," Meyers says. A woman in the party had called in for the rescue from her cell phone.

"I'll get a crew," I say, then, while still on the phone, I pull up the text-messaging app and start an all-team callout. "Send me the coordinates." I plan to plug those into the CalTopo mapping app after sending the callout.

"Can you go?" I ask when Ron calls in.

"Yes, I'm available. Meredith can come too. Where are we going?"

"On Timberline Trail at McGee Creek. Might take a while. Not sure which trail to access from. Maybe Vista or Top Spur? We'll figure that out on the way."

After I hang up, my phone pops with text messages. In ten minutes, we've assembled a great crew. Elliott Cramer, the strong, young climber I summited Mount Hood with in chapter 1, and Jon Gehrig, another young, skilled lifelong Hood River resident, are coming. Plus, part of the over fifty-year-old club: me, Ron, and Meredith.

I want Lisa to join, to add humor and help organize logistics, but she can't. I want John Rust or Walter or Brian to come, because they each bring the strength of two people, but they are unavailable. Heiko is also unavailable, since he's working at his paramedic job, so we'll have to do without his calm and deliberate contributions to safety. Cully is also unavailable but says he can take over coordination. Like me, he hates missing rescues, but work and family duties are a priority. Right now, I'm glad for Cully's help because trying to answer texts and phone calls from Crag Rats is too difficult while simultaneously trying to pack my gear. He will follow our progress on the mapping app most of the night.

I grab my summer rescue pack. It's quite different from my winter ski pack because it has minimal gear: a climbing harness, a helmet, basic rope-rescue hardware, a headlamp, and a two bottles of water. I grab my advance life support kit, which, over the years, has been whittled down to a six-liter, zippered pouch—small enough to fit in my pack with just the essentials to save a life. I head to the yard. We chitchat while we load our gear into SAR 1 and drive through the evening crowds. We head up Dee Highway toward Lost Lake and then continue farther up Forest Service roads to the Vista Ridge trailhead: an hour drive despite being only twenty miles from town. I can't remember who is driving because we've had so many missions this year—they all blur together. But on this mission, I will remember the biting bugs. We all will.

On the drive up, Ron and I scour the map. The group of hikers is at the top of the Mazama Trail, at its confluence with the Timberline Trial. The Top Spur Trail comes in about a mile to the west, and the Vista Ridge Trail comes in a mile to the east of this junction.

Then, as if he can overhear us needing help, Wes calls. I put the phone on speaker.

"Hey, Wes, can you come?"

"No, I'm busy. But I thought I'd give you info on the trails. I've been up there recently, and I talked to the Forest Service. They've only just started to clear trails. Where is the group?" He speaks in a slow drawl, one that's indicative of his calm and deliberate manner.

"On the Timberline Trail at the Mazama Trail."

"Many of the trails haven't been cleared yet. Downed logs everywhere. There are a few ways to get to the backpackers," Wes says. "Mazama Trail is the closest, but it hasn't been bucked out. It's full of blowdown. That will be hard with a litter. Top Spur is really steep and a little longer, but it's clear for sure. Not sure about Vista Ridge. Might take Vista up as it will be quickest, and then take Top Spur down since it's cleared."

Ron and I look back and forth between the map and the subjects' GPS waypoint.

"That's good info. We're just looking at the map. So no go on Mazama?" I ask to confirm.

"I wouldn't recommend it," Wes says.

"What about Vista? That's the fastest?" Ron asks.

"Not sure. Forest Service said some trees but mostly passible," Wes replies. "But at least consider taking them down Top Spur, because that's clear for sure."

"Okay. Great info. I wish you were coming," I say.

"I don't. It's going to take all night, and I have work in the morning."

"Me too," Elliott says.

"Me too," I say.

"Not me; I can sleep in." Meredith smiles triumphantly. I give her my best stink eye, and her eyes go wide and her eyebrows shoot up like the surprise emoji. Then we both laugh.

We decide the quickest way is to hike up the Vista Ridge Trail to the Timberline Trail and then figure out the rest later. We try to reach Meyers by cell phone, but we are out of reception. After several tries, we rouse him by radio and agree to meet at the Vista Ridge trailhead, at six thousand feet elevation and down a dead-end dirt road deep in the subalpine woodland.

"The injured guy thinks his shoulder is dislocated and back is thrown out," Meyers says. With cell phone technology, things are so much easier nowadays. Yes, people call for a rescue when they don't need to, but those types of calls are the minority. Cell phones give us great information: we can find out injury, the gear on hand, the situation, and a precise location before we even leave the trailhead.

Meredith, Ron, and I set off on a brisk walk up the Vista Ridge Trail at dusk. Elliott and Jon take a few minutes to assemble the litter and start up behind us twenty minutes later.

Scarlet Indian paintbrush, blue chicory, white oxeye daisy, and purple lupine line the trail. The air is fragrant with the Christmas-tree aroma of alpine fir. The glow in the cloudless sky is soothing, and I see Venus sparkling to the southwest. I take a picture of us hiking without pausing my gait, and then abruptly trip on a root and catch myself from face-planting. The photo comes out blurry. Thereafter, I keep my eyes on the trail, as every few minutes we scramble over a downed log. Ron and I start counting the logs blocking the trail to use in decision-making later: I lose track after a dozen. We leave our headlamps off when dusk turns to twilight. Then, when the sky turns black speckled with stars, I turn on the small red light on my headlamp to preserve my night vision.

"I don't think we can come down this way," I say when we reach the top of the Vista Ridge Trail, at the confluence of the Timberline Trail, an hour into our slog.

"I agree," Ron says in his quiet, contemplative voice. "I counted thirty logs."

"What if Top Spur and Mazama are just as full of logs?" Meredith asks.

"Wes said Top Spur is clear. It's much longer but all downhill, and we have plenty of people to help," Ron replies.

"Ron and I have it figured out," I say, teasing Meredith. "Not sure what you were doing on the drive up: Facebooking?" I joke, and she flashes a big smile that's contagious.

It's dark now as we traverse westward on one of the remoter sections of the Timberline Trail. Fortunately, the trail is wide and mostly clear of blowdown. It undulates over various glacial streams, many just a trickle this time of year. When we reach Ladd Creek, which is two feet deep, we find a way to keep our feet dry by hiking upstream ten feet, scrambling down an embankment, hopping across dry boulders, and climbing up the other side. I imagine that, in years past, the creek was raging when the glaciers were bigger. I can see the ancient high-water mark twenty feet above me, at a line where the vegetation starts.

"That won't be easy with a litter," Ron says.

"Nope. We need another way out of here," I say.

"Yeah," Ron says. I know he's evaluating the terrain to figure out the best course of action.

We cross a small, unnamed creek that's trickling through a meadow and then pass Glisan Creek. A few minutes later, we see the five people huddling across the stream below a twenty-foot-tall embankment. Again, we scramble down a small embankment and cross the creek by hopping rocks, finding the injured man and his four hiking partners all in good spirits. It's ten thirty p.m.

"Hi, I'm Christopher; we're mountain rescue," I say. "This is Meredith, and we're going to help." Ron is getting information from one of the other hikers. Apparently, they were looking for a place to camp when the man stumbled, fell into a creek, and popped his shoulder on a rock. Just three minutes into our assessment, we see lights across McGee Creek. Although the litter crew started twenty minutes behind us, they've arrived quickly. "Damn, they are fast," I say.

"They are young. And full of energy," Meredith says.

Meredith and I quickly look at the injured man's shoulder. It's probably dislocated. I ask Meredith to hold him from the uninjured side, and I gently pull down on the shoulder. We both feel and hear a *klunk* as it jumps back into the socket.

"Oh my God, that's better," he says. "But my back is killing me."

Not wanting to waste time, Meredith and I put a sling and swath around the shoulder. We discuss the exit plan amid the warm midsummer darkness. I know, frustratingly, that this evacuation will take all night. One option is to go back the way we came—but we would need to cross both Glisan and Ladd Creeks, hike uphill to the Vista–Timberline confluence, and then portage over the thirty downed logs on the Vista Ridge Trail. Ron shakes his head. Option two is to continue west on the Timberline Trail, which we know is clear, and hike down the Top Spur Trail. This is a five-mile pack out dropping nearly two thousand feet, and exiting on the one-mile-long, steep, and rooted Top Spur Trail—imagine a dilapidated staircase with uneven and listing risers loaded with obstacles like kids' toys. This will also require that someone down at the Vista Ridge trailhead move SAR 1 to the Top Spur trailhead. In the end, we decide to take this second option, following Wes's advice.

"Can you guys all walk?" Ron asks the uninjured hikers. They all nod.

I'm having trouble radioing Meyers, so Elliott calls in using his more pow-erful Forest Service unit. We load the patient into the litter, and then four of us hold the litter three feet off the ground while Elliott attaches the wheel. After a few minutes we realize our old wheel doesn't fit our Cascade 200 litter pre-cisely. We grabbed the 1982-designed Russ Anderson wheel because our more state-of-the-art Cascade Rescue wheel broke an axle while we were hauling a patient out of Eagle Creek a few weeks earlier.

"Just a sec," Elliott says as he and Jon rattle and fuss with the loose, ill-fitting wheel. Elliott pulls out polyurethane ski straps, and they lash the wheel frame to the litter.

"Will it hold?" I ask.

"Sure," Elliott says, smiling. "We got it."

I trust that Elliott and Jon have rigged the litter safely. A keen-eyed Ron looks it over to double-check. We'll need to use the brute strength of these strong, young rescuers to compensate for whatever sloppiness we encounter with the wheel.

"Looks good," Ron says.

As this all unfolds, with nightfall and the proximity to water, the bugs come out. And they are awful. Thousands of tiny gnats swirl around our heads and bite our exposed skin. We all switch our headlamps from white to red beams, because the latter don't attract as many bugs. Except Meredith, because her headlamp doesn't have a red light. So she holds her headlamp awkwardly in one hand, down by her hips, to keep the bugs away from her face, while carrying the litter in the other hand. Later, we will have many laughs about Meredith's lack of a red light—it's fodder for several jokes, as in "Maybe you should be better prepared?"

The pack out is slow, with the wobbly, ill-fitting wheel, the murkiness of the dank subalpine forest, the tortuous trail that has the occasional downed log or root staircase, and the annoying bugs. We are mindful of the back-jarring descents, the ankle-twisting roots, the jagged rocks. And did I mention the bugs? We all keep one hand on the litter and use the other to constantly swat the critters away from our faces. At some point, a foursome from Clackamas

County SAR catches up and rotates in with litter-carry duties. Past midnight, amid the toil and rickety wheel that shifts every few minutes, all banter has ceased. Then Jon wisecracks, "Glad we have the old wheel. I wanted to get a better workout," uplifting our spirits and breaking up the monotony.

Meredith asks to trade me headlamps, since I have a red light. I smile and shake my head.

Finally, at three thirty a.m., we make it down to the Top Spur trailhead. Meyers arranged to have a few trucks moved, including SAR 1. An ambulance is waiting in the parking lot to take the injured man to the hospital. Meyers will give the other four hikers a ride to their car back at Timberline Lodge. We jump in SAR 1, piling our packs in haphazardly. No one wants to drive, so Elliott climbs behind the wheel. I want to sleep, but we end up talking all the way home to keep Elliott awake. Except Ron, who sleeps.

I walk into my mudroom at five o'clock a.m., with work starting in three hours. Methodically and without pause, I put my radio on the charger and leave my pack on the floor to remind me to repack it later, for the next mission. These night missions are fun . . . at the beginning. We had a spectacular sunset and hike . . . at the beginning. Meredith and I had many laughs . . . at the beginning, especially at the bugs encircling her head with her white light. But the mission stopped being fun after midnight.

At work, I'm foggy and have difficulty concentrating when talking to patients, reading emails, and writing medical chart notes. However, this is nothing new. As I document these stories, especially the Timberline Trail mission, I recall how awful I typically feel at the end of a night mission: like I'm suffering from a bad hangover. When I was young, night missions rarely bothered me. But now, recovery is just a bit more difficult. In 2009, I gave up working night shifts in the ER and have not done one since—that was liberating, but I had to make a hard stop: the shifts were just too unpleasant to recover from. Maybe I need to stop getting out of bed for Crag Rats night missions as well? Or at least give them up when I have clinical duties the following day?

Clearly, I'm getting older.

I CHATTED WITH Bill Pattison before he died in 2023, at age ninety-four, in his seventh decade as a Crag Rat. He said the Crag Rats fell behind in the 1970s in terms of technology and skills. By the 1950s, founder Andy Anderson had moved to Cardiff-by-the-Sea, California. Dick Pooley, the MORESCO and MRA founder, had moved to Portland but was still active in social outings. Bill, a natural leader, was nearly continuously involved with Crag Rats until his death; he was a stalwart member and one of my chief mentors.

In the 1970s, the Crag Rats were a strong social group. To investigate this period, I went back to the hut basement archives. I had already combed through a half century of meeting minutes, financial reports, correspondence, Cloud Cap Inn logbooks, and newspaper clippings. A newsletter called *Rat Tales* was printed irregularly two to four times a year from around 1950 to 1982. As I mentioned earlier, the archives from 1974 to 1999 were missing—perhaps accidentally thrown out or moved to someone's basement or attic. I suspect that in 1973, the safe got full—as it's currently jam-packed—and documents were stored in boxes that then disappeared.

From scattered news clips, I surmise that the Crag Rats had about one alpine mission per year during the last three decades of the twentieth century. I found just ten missions in the alpine during the 1970s, almost all on the north side of Mount Hood and most on the Chisholm Trail—not a trail, you'll recall, but the route where people fall two thousand feet down to the Eliot Glacier after slipping on the upper Cooper Spur. On one mission Crag Rats searched for a boy lost in Dynamited Cave, a lava tube near Trout Lake, Washington. Crag Rats rappelled into the cave, found the boy huddled in the dark, and hauled him out. In another mission in 1972, Crag Rats brought the 1948 plane wreckage off Mount Adams. Even among this paltry number of missions, those that did occur often involved a relatively modern form of technology, the helicopter, most often a Huey from the Portland-based Air Force 304th Rescue Squadron or from the Salem-based Oregon National Guard.

One thing is for sure, rescues or naught, the Crag Rats spent a lot of time at Cloud Cap Inn. For example, on August 2, 1969, a party slid down

Cooper Spur, and the Crag Rats staged the mission at Cloud Cap Inn. When waiting to be deployed, the minutes said, they "had a good coffee session" on the porch.

On August 8, 1971, a family of four was downclimbing Cooper Spur after a successful summit. They slipped on the soft snow at the Chimney, fell down the Chisholm Trail, and landed on the Eliot Glacier at 9,600 feet. The mother had a broken leg and a pelvis injury, and one son was banged up; the father and the second son died. A small cadre of Crag Rats responded and assisted a helicopter crew to bring the injured off the mountain.

On August 18, 1974, Crag Rats responded to a fallen climber on the Coe Glacier. Two men were circumnavigating the mountain when one man fell into a crevasse and was crushed by an ice boulder. Crag Rats recovered the body. On August 3, 1978, Crag Rats, including new teenage members Bruce and Brian Hukari, were at Cloud Cap Inn when the call came in for a fall at the Eliot Glacier bergschrund between Anderson Rock and the summit. The 304th flew twenty rescuers from Cloud Cap Inn to the Eliot Glacier after spotting the climbers at the base of the Eliot headwall and then evacuated everyone via helicopter.

Occasionally, controversy over regulating mountain climbing continued to pop up. In January 1976, Randy Knapp (nineteen), Matt Meacham (sixteen), and Gary Schneider (sixteen) were stuck on the mountain for sixteen days in a snow cave and not only survived but also walked out on their own. The *Sunday Oregonian* on January 25, 1976, ran a story: "Mountain Climbing, Should It Be Regulated?" An anonymous rescuer wrote, "Not only yes, but hell yes. We have to risk our necks searching for too many irresponsible idiots who don't even have a map, much less know how to read one."

With the misplaced records and a drought of details to be found in the short newsclips, I start asking the generation of Crag Rats before me. I curbside Rick Ragan, veteran Crag Rat of five decades, at a business meeting. We're in the hut's crowded great room during the fifteen minutes of social time before the meeting starts. He remembers many of these missions as complex and danger-ous. The alpine missions, as ever, were on steep slopes, on crevassed glaciers,

TOP: *American Legion climbers approach the Mount Hood summit cabin. Crag Rats typically acted as guides for the Legion's annual climb, which took place annually from 1921 to 1953. Alpenstocks, the predecessor to ice axes, can be seen in the snow.* (Photo: Hood River Crag Rats Collection) **BOTTOM**: *Crag Rats circa 1950s, in signature black and white checks, use an akja to evacuate an injured patient from Mount Hood's north side. Hood River County Sheriff Rupert Gillmouthe observes.* (Photo: Hood River Crag Rats Collection)

TOP: *Crag Rats use snowcats to ski Ghost Ridge on the north side of Mount Hood. Circa 1950s.* (Photo: Hood River Crag Rats Collection) BOTTOM: *Crag Rats climb the Snowdome snowfield on the north side of Mount Hood, circa 1970s. Mount Adams and Mount St. Helens are visible in the background. Circa 1970s.* (Photo: Hood River Crag Rats Collection)

Crag Rats assisted with snow surveys from the 1950s to 1988 to gauge water for irrigation. Here, circa 1970s, volunteers use four-foot tubes to measure depth and calculate water content. (Photo: David Falconer)

TOP: *The author on an andesite cliff near Cloud Cap Inn. Crag Rats train in glacier, avalanche, and rock rescue.* (Photo: Corey Arnold) **BOTTOM**: *Crag Rats (left to right) Lisa Rust, Brian Hukari, the author, and John Rust search for a missing skier near Barlow Pass, Mount Hood.* (Photo: Walter Burkhardt)

TOP: *Crag Rats and Portland Mountain Rescue respond to trauma near the Hot Rock fumarole at the bottom of Mount Hood's Old Chute. The injured person was evacuated via Oregon National Guard helicopter.* **BOTTOM LEFT**: *Crag Rats, along with Pacific Northwest SAR and Cascade Locks Fire/EMS, complete a difficult extrication from a remote trail in the Columbia River Gorge National Scenic Area.* **BOTTOM RIGHT**: *Crag Rats Lisa Rust and Meredith Martin ski through the snowy forest on a night search near Bennett Pass.*

Crag Rats and Portland Mountain Rescue help a climber down Old Chute, near the top of Mount Hood's Coalman Glacier. Crag Rats Leif Bergstrom and Elliott Cramer in background; author in center foreground. (Photo: Theresa Silveyra)

TOP: *Crag Rats Ron Martin and Leif Bergstrom, in yellow shirts, assist with a helicopter evacuation from Cloud Cap Inn. A colleague from Pacific Northwest Search and Rescue assists.* BOTTOM: *Crag Rats Wes Baumann and Asa Mueller recover a body on the Eliot Glacier using the akja ski litter.* NEXT PAGE: *Brian Hukari, who joined the Crag Rats in 1973 at age eighteen, jumps a crevasse on the Eliot Glacier.* (Photo: Jerry Bryan)

and below cliffs with falling rocks and ice. I then get distracted by another conversation.

Later, I track down Jerry Bryan by phone at his house in Bellingham, Washington. He joined about the same time as Brian Hukari, and they frequently climbed together before they went off to college and careers. I want details about rescues mostly.

"We were a ragtag group that used mountain rescue for an excuse to play in the mountains," he says. "We were a bunch of guys who went out with whoever was available and went up the mountain to pick up people."

"Did you have any training?"

"Sometimes Brian [Hukari] and I went up on our own to practice yarding each other out of crevasses," he says. But essentially, Crag Rats had no organized team training and very little team equipment other than a few akja litters and a handful of radios.

One reason for the dearth of information about the rescues, says Jerry, is humbleness. "A lot of us just didn't talk much about our escapades." He called that generation of Crag Rats "naturally talented, exceptionally experienced, and extraordinarily courageous." Jerry recalls doing many missions and trainings with the 304th Rescue Squadron. He remembers the 1971 accident mentioned previously, as he and Crag Rat Bill Sheppard were on the scene. After evacuating the mother and one son, they watched the father die just before loading him into the helicopter. He remembers Bill saying to the father, "We're taking you home now," an attempt to instill peace in the man's last minutes.

Eventually, even the snow surveys—which provided most of the Crag Rats' operational income—began tapering. Back in the 1960s, the US Natural Resources Conservation Service began developing telemetry sites to measure snow water content, accumulated precipitation, and air temperature. Jerry explains to me that each site, comprising the SNOTEL system, had a pressure-sensing pillow, a storage precipitation gauge, and an air temperature sensor. Snow would accumulate, and the electronics would measure the snow weight and depth to calculate water content. This obviated the need for human-gathered measurements.

Cloud Cap Inn was still being cared for, but Jerry tells me it was often patched with hand tools and whatever logs they could find in the forest nearby, as if being held together with "Band-Aids."

The bottom line, says Jerry, is that in the 1970s and into the 1980s, the Crag Rats had "not much going on" for mountain rescues. But what missions they had in the alpine were big missions: technical, complex, and dangerous. "And we were always authentic." I don't have to ask him what he means, because it's clear from his enthusiasm during our conversation: the Crag Rats were devoted to Mount Hood, its culture, and its spectacular alpine environment and rescuing people.

I ask Jerry about missions beyond the alpine, in the foothills and lowlands. He reminds me about a distinct change in the community that occurred around 1980: the coming of windsurfers. Suddenly, Hood River wasn't just an orchard town with a small ski and mountaineering contingent. It became a multisport town, with the recreation economy challenging that of the fruit orchards. From what I can tell, this was a third surge of outdoor recreation, after the mountain boomed in 1925 with the construction of the Mount Hood Loop Highway and again in the postwar 1950s. In the 1980s, Crag Rats started responding more in the summer to the Columbia River Gorge trails, which burgeoned in popularity with the advent of outdoor pursuits and, in 1986, became part of a national scenic area (the second in the nation after Mono Basin, in 1984). Like today, many rescues back then centered on one of the region's most popular hiking trails: Eagle Creek. On July 25, 1971, Crag Rats responded to a body recovery for a twenty-one-year-old who fell off a 150-foot cliff into the pool below Punch Bowl Falls, reporting that "the routine task was made miserable by the brush and the moist, slick moss." Still, compared to the harshness and austerity of the alpine, yarding someone out of a forest canyon after a two-mile hike up a trail was fairly straightforward.

During this time, other regional teams flourished, but the Mountain Rescue and Safety Council of Oregon (MORESCO) began to "fall apart," according to Tom Stringfield, a forty-five-year veteran of Portland Mountain Rescue. MORESCO hibernated as a formal organization in 1973 to let the Crag Rats and teams from Portland, Eugene, Corvallis, Bend, and Medford run independently. The Air Force's 304th Rescue Squadron was called out on many missions. The Alpinees still responded to rescues, although began struggling with membership. And sheriff departments from Multnomah and Clackamas Counties developed ground SAR teams after the Oregon State Sheriffs' Association published their first SAR-qualification manifesto in 1973, outlining requirements for team members. Clubs that were traditionally not formed for SAR were occasionally helping also, like Eugene's Obsidians (a climbing club established in 1927), Bend's Skyliners Ski Club (established in 1927), Portland's Wy'east Climbers, and the Mazamas.

One of the last things MORESCO did before disbanding was discuss regulation again. Like today, they compared mountain rescue with other functions of public safety. "What about the fishermen who venture over the bar at the mouth of the Columbia River in foul weather?" someone was quoted as asking in MORESCO meeting minutes. Also like today, searches in Oregon back in the 1970s were, per the minutes, more often for "lost children, boating accidents, water skiers, fishermen, swimmers and divers, especially those who get no exercise all year long and suffer from heart attacks during hunting season." Whereas mountain-climbing accidents tend to get media attention, they were not the most common SAR callout. Motorists and hunters required more missions. John Olson, search coordinator for the state's relatively new (at the time) Division of Emergency Services, which governor Tom McCall opened in 1972, was quoted in a MORESCO meeting, "Last on the list are hikers and mountain climbers."

In addition to the trifecta of few missions, many other teams available to help, and Hood River's transformation to catholic outdoor-recreation hub, a fourth change also affected the Crag Rats. Technology began to grow and develop at a faster and more complex pace; we had fantastic changes in electronics, mountain clothing, and alpine equipment from the early 1970s into the 1980s. Skis transitioned from wood planks to metal-edged fiberglass. Ski boots metamorphosed almost overnight from leather with laces to plastic with buckles. Bindings went from straps to metal clamps. Plastics were formed into thread and then spun into cloth: I recall nylon jackets and polyester long under-wear appearing in my wardrobe in the 1970s, followed by Gore-Tex, Teflon, and polyester fleece. Joe Wampler, former Hood River County sheriff and current aviation deputy, told me that these advances in clothing revolutionized survival; the new clothing kept people so much warmer that they could more easily with-stand the unexpected night out. The Crag Rats still had aluminum litters, some that could be skied down the mountain like the akja and others that required a wheel. It took us years to upgrade to lighter fiberglass and eventually titanium and carbon litters, which is why, on the McGee Creek mission, we still had the old thirty-pound Russ Anderson wheel in our inventory.

Electronics followed ski technology. Radios went from heavy units the size of a shoebox to ones the size and weight of a brick. (Cell phones were invented in 1973 but wouldn't become common until the late 1990s. Despite having emergency position-indicating radio beacons for airplanes and ships, handheld GPS units wouldn't be available until after May 3, 2000, when the federal gov-ernment removed selective availability that limited accuracy to one hundred meters.)

Although records are missing and oral history is subject to the limitations of memory, it's clear that, during this time, changes in technology occurred more rapidly than in decades past. Technology boomed, development boomed, and the population soared. The community retained its orchards, but the coming of athletes, the thriving economy, and rapidly evolving technology changed Hood River and Mount Hood forever. And during this growth period, the Crag Rats' alpine rescue skills got rusty.

I am Gen X, born in 1966. As a young kid growing up in the 1970s, I rode my Schwinn Collegiate without a helmet, played outside, drank from the hose, and built tree forts using two-by-fours and nails. My heroes were athletes from the Olympics and ABCs *Wide World of Sports*, which featured mostly non-team Olympic sports like skiing, track, and swimming. I was enamored with Mark Spitz (nine gold medals in swimming), Greg LeMond (three Tour de France wins), Caitlyn Jenner (formerly Bruce, who wasn't even winded upon winning the 1976 Olympic decathlon), the 1980 USA

Olympic Hockey Team (underdog gold-medal winners), and Franz Klammer for his famous, on-the-edge-of-crashing 1976 Olympic downhill run in Innsbruck, Austria.

In addition to being sporty—skiing, hunting, fishing, basketball, and pole-vaulting—I was enamored with technology and have always been a digital pioneer. In the late 1970s, I had already been using an IBM computer with a 5.25-inch floppy disk at home; my dad had it for his home office. I remember in ninth grade when we got our first computers at high school, the Apple II. My friend and I taught the class because the typing instructor had little knowledge of the machines. Later, in college in the mid-1980s, I trudged to the basement of the Buckley Center computer lab at the University of Portland to write papers on an Apple Macintosh. During my first year of medical school, I bought a Zenith laptop with a ten-megabyte hard drive to use for my nascent writing career. I wrote my first two, still-unpublished novels on that machine. After medical school, during my internship in 1994, I used my first email address, which was assigned by the University of Utah and accessed either in the computer lab or by using a dial-up modem at home.

My daughters are Gen Z, first-generation digital natives. They grew up in the telecom-electronic communication age and had their first cell phones in middle school. Like me, they also grew up outdoors, learning to ski, playing school sports, and being patiently (or not so) instructed by me how to ride bikes, swim, and throw rocks in the Columbia River. They learned to balance the natural world with the digital one. When I call them simultaneously via FaceTime the evening after the McGee Creek rescue, they both are inquisitive, thoughtful, and retrospectively worried—but not so much, as they know I'm always careful. And, from years of hearing my stories, they know a summer trail rescue is much different than one in the alpine. We talk about this book: how it's hard to find time to write between doctoring, personal recreation, my international travel schedule, and all the rescues from this busiest year ever. Avrie offers to help me with research; Skylar offers to help me with marketing. I'm so grateful to my daughters for their offers, but even more so that I get to share with them the beauty of the alpine via hikes, ski days, and stories.

After I get off the phone, I turn back to this manuscript: my scrawled notes, the old photos, the books on Oregon climbing, the stacks of historic documents, and my outline, all neatly organized in my home office.

When crafting the original outline for this book, I thought I would focus on my chief mentors, the titans of Crag Rats past, who appear regularly in newsclips, meeting minutes, and *Rat Tales* newsletters. Andy Anderson started a mountain rescue team from scratch, a feat that had never been done before in North America. Dick Pooley helped create MORESCO and MRA, essential to coordinating life-saving teams. Bill Pattison participated into his tenth decile as a human and seventh as a Crag Rat. These guys were core leaders of the Crag Rats. They were not just leaders, but badass rescuers—for life.

The next morning after the McGee Creek mission, I'm bathed in the blue-light glow of my computer, hard at work before sunrise, when the veteran Crag Rat Kent Lambert pops into my brain. Kent joined the Crag Rats in the 1970s and still shows up to meetings, sits quietly in the back, observes, and occasionally speaks. When I interview him, he recounts stories of rescues but also informs me that he was one of only two Crag Rats who went through the six-year officer track twice: a twelve-year commitment to leadership. To be an officer, first you're voted in as Pip Squeak secretary. Then you're on a six-year track to advance to Little Squeak vice president, Big Squeak president, and three more years as a trustee.

"So, you committed twelve years?" I ask incredulously.

"Yes." He chuckles. "But things were simpler back then."

"Wow, we need to let everyone know!" I say.

At that moment, I realize that Anderson, Pooley, and Patterson aren't my only mentors; instead, it's the *entirety* of this group of men and women, who formed this club, kept it running in lean times, stayed true to the mission, and always held authentic mountain culture close to their hearts. They saved lives in the high alpine, reveled in mountain culture, and soaked in the deep beauty and solace of the wilderness. Every member of the Crag Rats is a vital piece of the team, a point I carry with me henceforth.

CHAPTER 8

AUGUST: HELI EVAC AT PERHAM CREEK

The downdraft from the helicopter hovering directly above us, invisible except for its lights in the night sky, is both terrific and terrifying. Leaves, dirt, and stones fly haphazardly in the whirlwind. Tree limbs and rocks ranging from golf ball to baseball size tumble down the embankment and pelt John Rust and me as we cower over our patient. I try not to look up for too long. Fortunately, I wear goggles and a helmet. Still, I wonder, *Should we call off this chopper?*

Everything started a few hours before at the Wygant Trail, whose trailhead is just a short drive from Hood River. A young married couple took the primitive, mostly unkempt trail starting at Mitchell Point, a small exit off Interstate 84. When they got to Perham Creek, they found the bridge washed out and the stream raging from summer snowmelt. They decided to scramble up the creek. At some point, the man slipped and careered into the woman, and then they both fell, bouncing down the jagged rocks and landing in the creek. They were both exhausted, cold, wet, injured, and stuck on the steep rocky slope. Fortuitously, they were able to get a call through to 911 (although cell coverage is often blocked by steep canyons, this one faces a cell tower in Stevenson, Washington).

The callout comes with minimal information like always: "Injured woman, needs evacuation, Perham Creek." The first thing that pops into my mind when the text message pings my cell phone is, *Where the hell is Perham Creek?*

When the text message comes in, I am just finishing a fourteen-mile run from Multnomah Falls—one of Oregon's most popular tourist attractions—to Sherrard Point on Larch Mountain and back. It's a solid run that starts at one hundred feet above sea level and climbs 7.5 miles and 4,602 feet to a hunk of volcanic rock, with a spectacular vista of Mounts Hood, Jefferson, Adams, Rainier, and St. Helens. Then it's all downhill on the return. I'm chilled, sweaty, tired, and hungry when I get back to my truck, but with urgency and fueled by adrenaline, I drive straight to the trailhead at Mitchell Point twenty minutes away, where I find HRCSO Deputy Eric Wahler.

He grins when he sees me. "You got here quick."

"I was running at Larch Mountain, so came straight here."

"Take a look at my laptop." He gestures to the computer perched on the hood of his HRCSO pickup. While he points out the woman's location on the screen, I strip off my running pants and shirt and change into dry SAR pants and a long-sleeve hoodie for sun, poison oak, and abrasion protection that I keep in a plastic storage bin in the back of my truck all summer.

"There are two firefighters from Cascade Locks and one sheriff's deputy up there," Eric says. "Plus the injured woman's husband. But they don't have any gear. Sounds like a head injury. We are trying to get a key to the gate," he says, referring to a gate that allows access to a power line road.

"Okay if I head up the trail? Crag Rats are not far behind."

"Yes," he says. "Two US Forest Service law enforcement officers will go up with you."

I jam my advanced life support kit into my SAR backpack along with a few blankets from the fire department. Then, the law enforcement officers and I set off at a fast clip, walking a half mile up the power line road, shimmying around a downed log, walking up the trail, and when we reach Perham Creek, clambering up the creek bed. In and out of the water and from one bank to the other, we make our way a quarter mile up the creek, where, up on a ledge, out of the water, two firefighters surround the woman lying on the cold, hard gray rock.

The story was that, as the pair fell, the woman tumbled down a scree apron into the cold creek bed, where she landed on a jagged basalt outcropping. The man, less hurt, was able to scramble to the woman and remove her from the water. The firefighters, who reached him a half hour before our arrival, wrapped her in a tarp, did a quick assessment, summoned the mountain rescue team, and waited.

I leave the woman bundled in a blanket as I complete a quick assessment—the firefighters did a good job at assessing and providing initial treatment. The man is awake and alert but quiet. When I question him, he says, "My leg hurts" and "I'm cold." He is filthy. I turn to the woman, who says, "I hurt all over." I don't find any head trauma. Neck and cervical spine are non-tender, and she can move her neck without pain. Lungs are clear as best I can tell listening with a stethoscope through her shirt, and she has no pain when I press on her ribs, clavicles, pelvis, and abdomen. She fell at least twenty feet, which could mean occult trauma—namely, a traumatic brain injury. And she, like her husband, is cold.

"We called for a helicopter," one of the firefighters says.

"We have a crew of Crag Rats coming," I say. "We can get these two down the creek in a litter."

"Impossible." The firefighter is incredulous.

"A helicopter hoist in this canyon will be nearly impossible," I say, surveying the tight box canyon. A hoist, if even possible with a Black Hawk's 250-foot cable, would be dangerous. Our team has done ground evacuations in worse conditions: we can get the subjects down the creek, but it will be rigorous and demanding. I hear on the radio strapped to my chest in a harness that a half-dozen Crag Rats have arrived, along with a dozen of our colleagues from Pacific Northwest Search and Rescue, an established team that is new to Hood River County. Lifting, carrying, dragging, and lowering the woman in a litter down the several hundred feet down the slippery boulders of the amphitheater will be like carrying a litter down a ten-flight staircase—if the stairs were slippery, uneven, unequal height, and periodically blocked by logs and boulders. Once we have our team here and ropes anchored, it will likely take a few hours. But it's two hours until dark. Maybe the firefighter has a point.

Herein lies a difficult decision in search and rescue, one that is made with experience, discussion, and bit of hope and guesswork. One that needs to be made quickly and definitively. Do we go down the trail or call a helicopter?

"Are you okay if I take command of this extrication?" I ask one of the firefighters. I represent the HRCSO mountain rescue team, but we also have the firefighters, the US Forest Service, and the HRCSO deputy on scene. Someone needs to take charge.

"Sure," the firefighter says.

I think for a minute and split the difference. "Okay, here's the plan," I say. "We'll start a ground evacuation while we're waiting to see if a helicopter can make it in here." Unfortunately, the Oregon Army National Guard helicopter is unavailable.

"We've got the Coast Guard helicopter coming," Deputy Wahler says over the radio. "ETA one hour. And we have a ground team coming to your location with rope and a litter." The Sikorsky HH-60 Jayhawk is on its way from the Coast Guard Air Station in Astoria, Oregon, one hundred miles away.

"Okay, we're going to prep for a ground evacuation," I reply.

"Do you want the helicopter to stand down?" Wahler asks.

"Stand by," I say. I talk it over with the firefighters, who are still skeptical about a ground evac, while I remain skeptical about a safe helicopter extrication. I look down-canyon at the large boulders in the creek, the gushing water, and the steep embankments. We will need to carry the woman down the creek using a series of rope lowers and passes while balancing ourselves on slippery rocks and roots and trying to keep her warm. Plus, we have the injured (but ambulatory) man.

"Keep the helicopter coming," I reply into the radio, knowing from my twenty years of volunteering in mountain rescue that it's better to have resources coming, even if we later have to call them off. This is advice from Wes that I'll never forget: I can hear his calm voice in my head. Plus, I know enough to listen to the firefighters and take all opinions into consideration.

A team of Crag Rats makes their way to the scene in a half hour. I'm instantly relieved when I see a stellar crew: Walter, Gary, Hugh, Lisa, Meredith, Ron, and John Rust. While getting sprayed by the mist, we gently roll the patient into the litter, place chemical heat packs on her chest, put her in a sleeping bag, cover her with spare jackets, wrap a tarp around her, put a helmet on her, and cover her face with a plastic shield to guard against falling rocks.

"How are you doing?" I ask the woman.

"Okay," she says softly and starts shivering.

After some discussion, we start the ground evacuation while we wait for the helicopter. We now have less than an hour until dark.

Once we strap the woman into the litter, it takes fifteen minutes to move her fifty feet. John, two firefighters, and I heave her off the basalt outcrop where she landed hours before, struggle a few feet, and then pass the woman hand-over-hand to Lisa, Hugh, Walter, and Gary, who are ten feet below the rock at creek level. They carry the injured woman across the creek and up a muddy embankment on the other side. From there, we take a break. By now it is dusk, with just a faint glow in the sky, and we hear on the radio that the helicopter is inbound, with a fifteen-minute ETA.

"Let's wait here for the helicopter to evaluate the scene," I say, knowing the extrication down the canyon will take at least another hour.

It's pitch-black save for our headlamps, so when the helicopter comes drifting slowly up the canyon, we hear it but can't see it. After a minute, we catch a glimpse of the Jayhawk's lights through the treetops, the underbelly lights blasting by like a spaceship in a science-fiction movie as the helicopter passes overhead. In an instant, we feel the tremendous downdraft, partly because of the normal rotor wash and partly because the narrow canyon walls accentuate the gusts. Rocks, sticks, dirt, and tree limbs zip past us in a blur. Hugh later tells me that because this canyon is so narrow and deep, it does not see much wind throughout the year, so it gets more loaded with debris. He works at the Bonneville Fish Hatchery nearby and has hiked so many of these trails that he knows them better than anyone. I worry about the personnel without helmets and eye protection, so I yell at everyone to seek shelter in the trees. It's difficult to send folks away from the scene because everyone wants to help. Meredith and Ron stay to hover over the patient and protect her from flying debris, while John and I hold the litter tightly.

The chopper lowers a Coast Guard rescuer into the creek. When he scrambles up to the patient, I yell the details of the patient's condition to him over the raucous noise. Then the helicopter lowers an empty litter, which starts its descent, begins spinning, and immediately gets tangled in a huge Douglas-fir about thirty feet above us. The chopper pulls the litter back up, flies away, and resets above us. I think momentarily about calling off the mission.

"We can take her down the trail," I holler to the medic.

"Let's try one more time," he yells back. The second time, the litter swings madly in a pendulum and spins around the cable. But it pierces the canopy through a tiny opening in the tree boughs and makes it to the canyon floor. We disconnect the litter, the helicopter flies away, and we quickly transfer the patient into the Coast Guard stretcher. The patient is cold and has stopped shivering, a bad sign. But at this point, I leave her bundled. We need to get her out as soon as possible, and if the helicopter hoist doesn't work, we've burned precious time we could have been evacuating by ground.

"Can we give her some water?" Meredith asks. I'm sure the woman is dehydrated. But since she possibly has a head injury and she's bundled in the litter, I don't want her to aspirate—to accidently suck water into her lungs.

"Hold off for now," I say.

"Do you need to go up in the helicopter?" the Coast Guard rescuer asks me. "I'm only basic life support. If she needs advance care, you'll have to go."

My adrenaline spikes. On one hand, yes, I want to go up into the helicopter on the cable, partly to help the patient and partly for the thrill. On the other hand, it will be really dangerous: the canyon is narrow, the trees are tight, and debris is flying everywhere. The risk of injury is great, but so is the reward of going up the cable with the patient into the helicopter. I have a sinking feeling: I want to go, but I'm scared for my safety.

The Jayhawk returns and creates a second fury of blowing rocks, sticks, and tree limbs. The empty cable comes down, and the Coast Guard rescuer connects the litter. I am still skeptical that this can be done safely. The rescuer holds a tag line, a rope connected to the litter to keep it from spinning while it is being hoisted. As the litter goes up, it starts spinning around the cable and then begins to pendulum. It careens into tree boughs about halfway up. I hope we don't lose the litter—and the patient. The weight of the patient and the tag line barely keep the litter from being sucked into the tree boughs. Finally, the litter makes it to the helicopter door, and I see the crew chief's hand reach out and pull the patient inside.

The medic looks at me for the first time in five minutes and says, "That was close."

I'm relieved. But I consider that the medic still needs to be hoisted and the patient still needs to get the hospital. I shake my head, point up, and yell over the helicopter noise, "I don't need to go." But I think: *I don't* want *to go. I don't* want *to get hurt.*

FOR MANY DECADES, summer was our busiest time. Roughly two-thirds of our missions were on the trails of the Mount Hood foothills and in the forests and canyons of the Columbia River Gorge National Scenic Area. Trail missions fall into one of four categories. First, hikers become lost without the navigational skills to reorient themselves. Second, hikers get injured, most often a sprained knee or ankle or fall, like this woman at Perham Creek with a head injury, or they have a medical condition such as heat illness or hypothermia. Third, hikers are neither lost nor injured nor ill, but just stuck somewhere: on a cliff, atop a waterfall, in a creek, in a canyon, down a mudslide, or in the deep black darkness of night in the forest. Or fourth, we have a fatality.

We tend to rescue people in the same popular, commonly visited spots. In spring, people climb Mount Defiance, a seven-mile, five-thousand-vertical-foot ascent. They encounter snow at the top and continue to the summit, often without winter gear. When they start down, they lose the trail, which is slightly off-camber; instead of following the path, they accidentally walk straight down-hill, into Warren Creek Canyon, and reach an impassible cliff. Often, we deploy to Herman Creek and the Pacific Crest Trail, where many hike the spectacular old-growth forest but get lost on Benson Plateau, a flat bench with thick trees and brush and a maze of trails in various states of unkemptness. And, most frequently, we answer calls for help in Eagle Creek, where we do more rescues than anywhere else; our rescues here often include forays into the nearby closed Ruckel Ridge Trail, the closed Ruckel Creek Trail, and the steep, narrow canyon between the two, bisected by a creek that is mostly impassible due to waterfalls, thick brush, downed timbers, and cliffs.

On a windless (no kitesurfing) afternoon (after my mountain-bike ride), I drive back to the hut to continue my research, open the cold building, and walk down to the basement. I again search for the missing records in the giant walk-in closet; the antique fireproof safe; the file cabinet; and an eerie, locked closet within the anteroom. The catacomb is so dusty that I immediately cease my search, walk out to my truck, and find an N95 mask, hoping the dust from the archives doesn't have hantavirus. After an hour of searching, I find a single manila folder from 1988.

I open the mysterious folder, which is labeled "Minutes & Trip Reports 1988 Jan–April." It gives me a tiny glimpse into this otherwise-obscure time period and loosely corroborates my conversations with the old-timers Jerry, Kent, and Rick. Crag Rats had many outings for recreational climbing, hut and Cloud Cap Inn maintenance, and social functions. I find a tiny blurb about first-aid training, which is followed by many paragraphs about maintaining and operating the Thiokol snowcat, a vehicle vital for commuting to Cloud Cap Inn. The membership grew to over one hundred. Votes were tallied for "Rat of Year," awarded to the member who does something memorably goofy or humiliating: forgetting boots at the Ice Follies (the fall ice-climbing social at Cloud Cap Inn), leaving beer behind at the Winter Outing (the February ski trip to Cloud Cap Inn), and denting a truck during a Mount St. Helens climb. "Hat of the Year" is an award that goes to someone exemplary. I find a reference to the Oregon Mountain Rescue Council, established in 1986 as a subunit of the national

Mountain Rescue Association. It gathered all five mountain rescue teams: the Crag Rats, Portland, Corvallis, Eugene, and Deschutes in Bend.

In the folder, just one rescue is briefly mentioned in the four-month span. By searching news clips, I find only five alpine missions that whole decade, three of which were on the Chisholm Trail. One involved fifty-one-year-old David Turple and seventeen-year old Bill Pilkenton, who died after a fall on June 6, 1981. Then, on June 21, 1981, ten Mazamas fell off the Chimney and down the Chisholm Trail. The five who survived were flown off with a 304th helicopter, and the five deceased were recovered the next day. At the time, this was the accident with the most fatalities on the mountain. And again, on June 23, 1982, several climbers from a twenty-member Mazamas team fell down the Chisholm Trail, one of whom died later in the hospital.

One key piece not mentioned in the 1988 folder that I am curious about because it was such an important part of Crag Rats' culture is snow surveys. What happened to them? I run into Brian Hukari all the time on missions, at trainings, and at meetings. I grab him at one Thursday meeting to ask him about this. He says that, by end of the 1980s, he was doing most of the snow surveys by himself. Jerry Bryan later confirms that the last snow survey was around 1988, and he completed it at Greenpoint Reservoir, at 3,500 feet just above Hood River, with his wife. At that time, telemetry had largely taken over, and Jerry said they were occasionally obtaining "ground truths," confirming the accuracy of the electronic system. Jerry sends me a fuzzy picture of him in a black-and-white-checked shirt, bending over the snow and taking the last sample, marking the end of an era.

I call Kent Lambert to corroborate the trends of the snow surveys petering out and the dearth of rescues. "These were lean years," he says, his voice tinged with nostalgia. The snow surveys, the Crag Rats' main source of income, had dried up, and they had not yet started renting out the hut for weddings—now a main source of income.

One issue stood out to me from 1988. As I mentioned, Crag Rats helped scout and consult on the Mt. Hood Meadows ski resort back in the 1960s. At the meeting on April 28, 1988, Crag Rats discussed the Cooper Spur Ski

Area's proposed expansion, which they opposed: "We would not like chair lifts to reach as high as the back side of Tilly Jane Campground." All of a sudden, environmental impact reached home and threatened the north side, the Crag Rats' playground for decades.

NOW IN PERHAM CREEK, the helicopter flies away, and the terrific whirlwind subsides. The two dozen rescuers plus firefighters and law enforcement officers scramble down the creek bed. I'm hugely relieved we got the patient extricated without wrapping her around a tree.

On the way down, the husband of the injured woman slips on the wet rocks in the dark, falls on an outstretched arm, and dislocates his right shoulder. *Fuck,* I think for a second. Then I click into doctor mode.

"It's dislocated," he says. "I'm sure of it. It has happened twice before."

"Let me have a look," I say. I sit him on a rock with John and Lisa helping me, while Hugh, Gary, and Walter all shine headlamps. The man holds his right arm against his chest. I slowly palpate the shoulder under his jacket. I find the empty shoulder socket and a bulge of the humerus bone in front of the collar bone. It's dislocated.

"I'm going to try once, slowly, to reduce it," I say. "Just sit here, try to relax your shoulder muscles, and don't fight me. I'll go slowly."

I ask John to bear-hug the man and Lisa to help with traction. I gently put traction on the right arm. Instantly, I feel a clunk as his shoulder pops back in.

"That's it," Lisa says.

At some point in my twenty-five-year career as a rescue mountaineer and doctor, I became cognizant of getting hurt. As I grow older, I realize, like all of us, that it takes me longer to heal from injuries and illness. I keep fit, eat well (except when I go to a rescue straight from a trail run), and sleep seven solid hours every night (except night missions). But still, injuries happen. So, at some point, on the heels of my near-death ski accident, which I wrote about in my second memoir, *Search and Rescue*, my brain made me back off a bit—it was not a cognizant decision nor one I could manipulate. Is this the beginning of the decline or demobilization that Anderson, Pooley, and Pattison experienced? I've begun to somewhat consciously and involuntarily try to protect myself. I think it's subtle, but I imagine my Crag Rat colleagues see it as overt. I start carrying the litter less. I take a supervisory role more often. I jam less gear in my pack compared to my young colleagues. I hand the heavy rope to Leif, Maurizio, Elliott, or Jon Gehrig. I announce at missions that I do these things to let young Crag Rats gain experience and pay their dues, but I suspect people see through my charade.

The Perham Creek mission will stay with me for a long time, mainly because of the personal risks to me, the Crag Rats, the Coast Guard pilot and medics, and the patients as the helicopter maneuvered in the narrow box canyon. In fact, I obsess about safety in the days following the helicopter mission. I discuss my concerns exhaustively with Heiko. We reconstruct the situation over lunch at the Hood River waterfront, sketching the mission layout on a napkin and looking at videos Heiko has collected from his King County helicopter rescue missions. I try to understand as Heiko educates me on helicopter procedure. He reassures me that I did the best I could during the situation. But deep down, I remain both frightened of the situation and grateful that it didn't turn out poorly. We can't foresee exactly what will come next, and no two missions are alike. We try to learn the lessons, assimilate them into our training and future missions, and keep them propagated at meetings. But still, we are human. We sometimes forget the lessons learned.

Later, at a business meeting, we discuss the Perham Creek rescue. There are nods throughout the room when I mention safety. Then, we move on to other topics, like the gargantuan project of replacing the roof at Cloud Cap Inn and Deno's ask for new $20,000 tracks for the snowcat. When a call comes to appoint a historian, despite my ongoing research into this book, I remain uncharacteristically silent. I do not want to be relegated to non-rescue tasks, not because I'm not interested, but because it seems that being appointed historian is too much of a step toward a life without rescues, and is a task best relegated to someone who is "old." I want to be too busy doing rescues to be the historian—I don't want to be old.

The woman from Perham Creek recovers. The man recovers too. Others will not be so lucky. While the pandemic and post-pandemic stress continues on an ever-busier Mount Hood, we will, in 2022, have other risky helicopter rescues. A head injury on the Eliot Glacier crossing on the Timberline Trail is worrisome: Heiko and I call Life Flight Network to pick him up at six thousand feet after we haul him out of Eliot Creek. The machine lands in the Cloud Cap Inn parking lot, spraying gravel and dust.

The years during and following the pandemic in fact turn out to be our busiest ever. For me—with a dearth of international trips, my two daughters off to their own adult lives, and no romantic partner—I fully absorb myself in mountain rescue. It becomes one way of satisfying my need for outdoor adventure without trying to skirt pandemic precautions. But I also see it as a bulwark against the future trauma of not being able to do rescues, when I'm finally too old. During the pandemic years, I participate in more missions per year than any other year so far, all somewhat centered on my intense yearning to fill my time, to be with my friends, and to be in motion outside. It's clear that, at some point, I'll have to start thinking about a way to transition into another role.

We also have something that will outlive me: this mountain we love. The wildness, clarity, and intimacy. The light, dry backcountry powder. The expansive glaciers that crunch underfoot at dawn. The trails replete with kaleidoscopic wildflowers and sumptuous huckleberries. The thick emerald forests with tall conifers and the family of pine martens that scurry under the lava-rock foundation of Cloud Cap Inn. The inherent value and meaning of this fragile alpine world, which, I hope, will outlive all of us.

CHAPTER 9

SEPTEMBER: MASS CASUALTY ON EAGLE CREEK

I'm driving home from a three-day trip to the Oregon Coast, where I just finished surfing and kitesurfing with friends for the weekend. We gathered at a rarely used parking area in Fort Stevens State Park, where we launched and then kitesurfed for an hour downwind, down the line of waves, for three miles to another beach, the Wreck of the Peter Iredale, where the rusted iron carcass of a ship that ran aground on October 25, 1906, stands out among the expansive beige sand, heaps of knotted driftwood, and windswept dunes. When we came into the beach from the crashing waves, one woman among the throngs of tourists asked, "Did you parachute from the sky?" and I realized how foreign my life of adventure sports must seem to some people.

A decade ago, when my daughters were launching into their high school and college years, I began spending more time away from Hood River and Mount Hood. I started working for a company to teach wilderness medicine around the world and spending three to four weeks overseas every year, which expanded to twelve weeks annually, on various work-play expeditions. I was fortunate to work in spectacular mountain locales: Kilimanjaro, Everest Base Camp, Bhutan, Italy's Dolomites, the Tour du Mont Blanc in the Alps, Machu Picchu, and Patagonia. I even signed up for some non-mountain adventures: Galapagos, Cuba, Fiji, and Costa Rica. And I kitesurfed and surfed in Mexico, Morocco, Tarifa, the Canary Islands, and Chile. Often, I brought my daughters along. To make this work financially—I'm not that wealthy, considering my lifelong penchant for part-time work—I paired work trips with pleasure, sought grants, tapered my living expenses at home, postponed buying a new truck for years, and forewent amenities like a lifestyle van or hot tub. I do not collect bikes or skis, but when I'm due for a new steed or planks, I sell the outgoing ones. Some might call it frugal living. But I call it focusing intently on what makes me most happy—human-powered adventures with friends and family.

On this trip to the coast on Labor Day Weekend 2017, late in the evening on Monday, after packing up kitesurfing gear and saluting my friends, I'm driving home through the quaint, cute town of Astoria when my phone pings: Callout. I ignore it for a second to see if Meredith or Cully will pick up the coordinator text. Cully likes to coordinate when he's on surgery call since he can't go on rescues. Meredith takes the coordinator duties instantly when she is available and can't go on the rescue. And we've recently added Wes, Walter, John and Lisa Rust, and Won Kim, a longtime Crag Rat and financial whiz, as coordinators, to share the load. But my phone pings again after five minutes, so I pull over and call dispatch. Unbeknownst to me, this will be the greatest number of people Crag Rats have to date on a mountain rescue mission, in a context that is slightly out of our scope as alpine rescue mountaineers: wildland fire.

A fire, I learn, has trapped 144 people on Eagle Creek, one of Oregon's most popular trails, where Crag Rats have been rescuing people at least as far back as the 1950s. The trail is rugged, steep, rocky, and thickly treed. In just a mile up the trail from the parking lot, the path ascends a cliff so exposed that cables were placed in 1910 to serve as handrails. In two miles, many hikers congregate at Punch Bowl Falls, a swimming hole. In six miles, the trail ducks behind Tunnel Falls through an opening in the basalt, 175 feet above the creek, where another set of cable handrails helps protect hikers from falling. At 7.5 miles, the trail turns away from Eagle Creek and climbs to Wahtum Lake, an additional 6.5 miles.

In Eagle Creek, the single most common trail for rescues, if we don't go after someone with a sprained ankle or knee, it's more often an injury from a cliff jumper at Punch Bowl or someone lost on Benson Plateau. We've also hauled out a woman actively seizing with new-onset epilepsy and another with hypothermia and hypoglycemia for new-onset insulinoma, a benign pancreatic tumor that causes too much insulin to be released and thus drops blood sugar to a critical nadir. Today, though, the call is for wildfire rescue. Apparently, a fire has moved to a point just a mile from the parking lot, choking off the trail near the first set of cables. Several scores of people—an exact number is not possible, but it might be as many as 160—are trapped at Punch Bowl Falls, many wearing flip-flops, T-shirts, and shorts or swimwear.

My first thought: *Let's get a crew.*

My second thought: *We're not prepared for fire.*

My third thought: *If the one-mile downhill hike to their car is blocked by fire, they'll all need to walk thirteen miles uphill to Wahtum Lake, where they can be picked up via a dilapidated, potholed road that leads down to Hood River.*

The hikers are instructed to head uphill, away from the fire. As darkness nears, a sole Forest Service ranger runs down the trail from Wahtum Lake, finds the group, and shepherds them to a flat spot near Tunnel Falls, where they hunker in for the night. The youngest is three, the oldest a septuagenarian.

At eight p.m., I pull into incident command at the Eagle Creek National Fish Hatchery, direct from the coast, to coordinate the Crag Rats callout. The parking lot smells like campfire and is encapsulated by thick, acrid smoke and backlit by bright orange flames flickering behind towering Douglas-fir. Trucks are parked haphazardly, having brought in personnel from the Crag Rats, US Forest Service, Hood River County Sheriff's Office, and Oregon National Guard. Our mission is paramount: to save the trapped people. Despite the pungent, smoky sky and dancing flames, Brian, Gary, and Tom bolt up Ruckel Ridge to reach three hikers who will eventually be airlifted. Another Crag Rats crew, led by Wes, drives an hour to Wahtum Lake and starts hiking downhill at midnight with three Forest Service firefighters. They skirt the Indian Creek Fire, which has been burning since July 4, and eventually find a group of 144 trapped people plus the forest ranger.

It's still the middle of the night, so they distribute snacks and water and wait for morning. John Rust has the brilliant idea of writing a number on each person's hand with a marker to keep track of them all. At dawn, they begin the long hike out to Wahtum Lake, seven miles from the makeshift camp. At the top, the rescued hikers are loaded onto buses for the ride back to their cars. By early afternoon, all are safe. "Mission complete. Stand Down. Not one death or major injury."

At a debrief weeks later, Wes sounds calm and deliberate about the hike down the trail to Tunnel Falls, into the fire. "I was scared. We could hear the fire crackling and see the flames just a few hundred yards away." I don't tell him, but at that moment I have a great awe and respect for him just getting the mission completed.

Two days after the rescue, the fire will travel west to within a few miles of Portland, grow to over thirty thousand acres, and start spot fires across the Columbia River in Washington. In the following week, one thousand personnel, a dozen aircraft, and at least a gross of vehicles will battle the blaze. It will burn full-on for three weeks, smolder for months, and pop up a year later from a subterranean festering stump.

Months later, Deno leads a basic wildland-fire training, and we discuss getting fire-resistant Nomex shirts, a notion that's tabled to address other, more pressing issues.

The Eagle Creek Fire was not a routine mission for the Crag Rats. But then, nothing has ever been "routine" for us. Consider that in our history we've had a broad range of volunteer duties beyond the alpine: assisting the US Forest Service to fight wildland fires in the 1920s; helping the sheriff with law enforcement and lifeguarding in the 1950s; and up until the late 1980s, helping the Soil and Water Conservation District with snow surveys. Basically, if someone asks us for help, we're likely to assist. A few members have considered joining the

HRCSO marine patrol to assist with boating safety on the Columbia River. In recent years, Hood River County has accounted for around ten percent of the state's one thousand annual SAR missions; we are in the top five counties, the other four being more than ten times our population. Crag Rats get called on about half of these missions. And after the Eagle Creek Fire, we have no break. Just three days later, our phones pop to life again: "Injured hiker, Timberline Trail, needs evacuation."

BASED ON MY review of the archives, the Eagle Creek Fire involved the largest number of people rescued in a Crag Rats SAR operation ever, and we were fortunate it was not a mass casualty incident (MCI) with fatalities.

Another tragic MCI, one that occurred many years ago much closer to home—the Oregon Episcopal School (OES) tragedy on Mount Hood—was the second-worst climbing accident in the United States based on fatalities. (The most fatalities in a single US mountaineering accident was on June 21, 1981, on Mount Rainier. Eleven people died when a serac collapsed on the Disappointment Cleaver route. Ice blocks the size of cars fell, sweeping fifteen people roped together in groups of four to six 800 feet down the mountain, to land 100 feet deep in a crevasse.)

On Sunday, May 11, 1986, fifteen students and five adults set off at midnight for the summit of Mount Hood via the South Side Routes on a school trip. A forecasted storm brought freezing temperatures, 103-mile-per-hour winds, and deep snowdrifts. A few turned back early, and by two p.m. at 11,000 feet, in a whiteout, the entire team finally turned back, descended to 8,200 feet on the White River Glacier, and got lost. They dug a snow cave and huddled in—wet, cold, hungry, and thirsty—for three brutal nights. This led to the largest SAR mission in Oregon at the time.

Crews searched ineffectively for three days in tempestuous weather until the storm broke. Finally, the snow cave was found on Thursday at 5:32 p.m., almost four days after the group departed Timberline Lodge and after three days of searching. Nine of the climbers would die by freezing to death. For information about this mission, I have nothing from the Crag Rats archives. So I scour news reports, Jack Grauer's book, and Ric Conrad's self-published *Code 1244: The 1986 Mount Hood Tragedy*. I find little in these historical accounts regarding the Crag Rats other than a list of participants in the front matter of Conrad's book and a mention in Grauer's book.

I revert to oral history.

I talk to Dwayne Troxell, who joined Crag Rats in the 1970s as a lifelong Hood River resident; he was also a member of the US Air Force 304th Rescue Squadron and eventually became the chief deputy for the HRCSO. During the OES search, he served as a helicopter pilot for the 304th, shuttling rescuers and evacuating students. The first two days the weather was nasty; the third day was the first real search day.

Then I talk to Kent Lambert, who says, "I was there with several Crag Rats. Troxell shuttled us up in the helicopter. We were working with the PJs [pararescue jumpers trained in combat SAR] from the 304th and members of PMR." As Kent's team was walking on a snow bridge on the White River Glacier, close to where the snow cave was eventually found, the snow bridge collapsed. "The crack split between my legs, and I dropped ten to fifteen feet," he recalls. The air blast from the collapse was so loud it was noticed down at the incident command post at Timberline Lodge. Luckily, Kent landed on a "rubble heap" of snow blocks. "I trained in high school by climbing rope without my feet, so I was able to use my ice axe and climb out of the hole," he tells me.

Three interesting things developed after the nine deaths and many permanent injuries. First, the subject came up about charging for or regulating rescues, but the Oregon legislature failed to pass a bill.

Second, members of the alpine community developed an emergency beacon specific to Mount Hood: the Mountain Locator Unit, or MLU. It was an emergency transmitter like those used for tracking wildlife that you could rent from mountain shops from about 1987 through 2017, until phones and GPS units made MLUs obsolete. Climbers carried the beacon and could activate the transmitter in an emergency. But once activated, nothing happened automatically, because the signal wasn't monitored. So a rescue team would need to know you were in trouble, know you had an MLU, and have access to a receiver to find it. Once a rescue was afoot and someone got the MLU receiver, which was the size of a car battery, it worked through triangulation. Rescuers would search for the signal with an antenna, find the compass bearing that produced the loudest signal, and call the bearing into command, where it would be plotted on a map. Distance was unknown, so a second bearing from a second location would need to be found, recorded, and plotted on the map. The MLU was located where the two bearings intersected.

Both Crag Rats and PMR had MLUs and receivers. I remember using the technology once only, back in 2007, when climbers were caught in a storm in White River. We had never used the transceiver and the battery was dead, so we used a spare car battery from then Sheriff Joe Wampler's truck. That stormy night, Jeff Pricher and I got a snowmobile ride with Mt. Hood Meadows ski patroller Paul Klein (now a Crag Rat) up the mountain and found a signal emanating from the east moraine of White River Glacier, in the ski resort itself. Jeff wore the headphones and moved the antenna. When he found the loudest signal, I took a compass bearing and called it into command. Meanwhile, another team from PMR climbed up the west moraine, got the signal, and plotted a second bearing. Where the bearings bisected was the location of the party. Another team that skied up White River found them the next morning in that exact spot.

The third interesting thing that came about in the wake of the OES tragedy was an acknowledgment that coordination and communication could have been better, just like the debrief after the 1956 mission to aid the nineteen hostelers who fell into the fumarole concluded (see chapter 6). Thus the Mt. Hood SAR Council was created around 1987, forming a group designed to meet periodically and address issues among the various teams that respond around the mountain. The council is still a functioning group today, meeting monthly. (I attend the meetings to lend a medical perspective.)

I think back to this time just prior to my involvement with the Crag Rats, the last three decades of the twentieth century when the group had very few missions. Crag Rats, PMR, and the 304th Rescue Squadron collaborated on most missions. I found four alpine missions of significance in the years after the OES disaster.

On September 18, 1989, Gerald Kennedy, a twenty-four-year-old dental student, fell on the north face, broke a tooth, and spent the night on the Newton Clark Glacier after his climbing partner, Mike Connell, walked down for help. A helicopter came to Kennedy's rescue.

On September 24, 1995, the Nike executive Ken Budlong went missing on Cathedral Ridge, and a search was launched two days later. His tent was found near the McNeil Point shelter, with backpack, sleeping bag, climbing book, and bible. Freezing and high winds impacted the search, and the helicopters had trouble flying. Budlong was never found. Troxell remembers this mission for its foul weather, lack of success, and controversy because the 304th Rescue Squadron was reluctant to fly a helicopter in bad weather.

On September 6, 1997, the Hood River resident and purveyor of an outdoor-clothing company Mark Frass died climbing Cooper Spur, falling down the Chisholm Trail. And again, on May 23, 1999, Carey Cardon, thirty-one, and his wife, Tena, twenty-nine, fell to their deaths down the Chisholm Trail. Warm temperatures and the direct sun causing soft snow were the likely culprits of the latter accident, according to a *Hood River News* article on May 26, 1999.

To fill in gaps about the missing decades, I email members requesting help. John Arens, a second-generation Crag Rat, writes back, saying he has "some info" for me pertaining to the missing documents and would prefer to meet in person. *What is this?* I wonder. We meet for lunch at the Hood River waterfront. John surprises me with three files from the mid-1990s, when he was president—three files from one of the missing three decades! I am elated!

John explains that during the last two decades of the twentieth century, the Crag Rats had, as I surmised, fewer than ten missions per year, but were very busy with Cloud Cap Inn and social functions. The inn went through nearly a full remodel at the end of the 1990s, spilling into the first few years of the twenty-first century. The shutters were encased in aluminum to withstand the weather, and the windows were rebuilt after hardware was specially ordered. The foundation was reconstructed with cement instead of glacier-tumbled andesite stones. The interior of the east wing was refurbished with new flooring, walls, and ceilings.

Meanwhile, social functions like the fall Ice Follies and the Winter Outing were going strong. John mentions an event I'd never heard of, the Cooper Spur Breakfast, which involved hauling propane grills, beer, champagne, and such up the snow to seven thousand feet and serving breakfast on the spur. "At five thirty we started serving, and by ten the food was gone," he recalls.

And John confirms what Kent, Jerry, Dwayne, and Rick have already told me: rescues were infrequent, training was sparse, and no team gear was maintained save maybe some radios, a few ropes, basic rope rescue hardware, and the aluminum akja. But when the callout came, Crag Rats mustered both numbers and expertise, born from their near-constant alpine climbing adventures. In the folders from John, I find several interesting documents. One is the 1989 "Operations Manual," which outlines Crag Rats' rescue procedures in four type-written pages. I find a membership list of ninety-two people: ten are Hukaris, seven are Sheppards, six are Wellses, and a dozen more families have at least two members. This testifies to the multigenerational vibe of the group.

Finally, in the last of the three folders, John pulls out a gem. It's a spiral-bound, four-by-four-inch *Mountain Rescue Council Team Leaders Handbook* from the 1950s. I pull open the pages carefully, thinking I should be wearing white gloves like an archivist in a Dan Brown novel. Amazingly, one of the first mountain rescue manuals ever made has diagrams of things we still do, like the basic mechanical-advantage system for crevasse rescue, which involves a rope, two pulleys, two prusik cords, and three carabiners. It also has things that are completely outdated, like Morse code. The pamphlet is dedicated to William A. Degenhardt. I have no idea who this is, so after a quick internet search, I find out he's a Washington climber who was president of The Mountaineers from 1952 to 1954 and a vice chair of the Washington Mountain Rescue Council around the same time. Part of his lifework was to create this handbook, which he did before he died in 1956. This is a powerful reminder for me: while the Crag Rats were the dominant force on Mount Hood, during the second half of the twentieth century, many other mountain rescuers and rescue teams saved lives across the West, as outlined in Dee Molenar's 2009 historical *Mountains Don't Care, But We Do: An Early History of Mountain Rescue in the Pacific North-west and the Founding of the Mountain Rescue Association.*

I vaguely remember the OES accident. At the time, I was in a college study-abroad program in Salzburg, Austria, so I was keener on riding my bike to Berchtesgaden and skiing in the Alps with my friends than following the news. After college, I took a gap year traveling around the world and then landed for the summer in the Columbia River Gorge prior to starting medical school. While attending medical school from 1989 to 1994, I spent my summers in the gorge working at a brewpub, windsurfing, and writing two novels. I continued to spend summers in Hood River during residency, balancing work with play by augmenting school with adventure. One clinical rotation, I helped PMR with winter-survival and avalanche classes. Another rotation, I worked in a clinic in White Salmon, Washington, for six weeks and windsurfed on my time off. A third rotation, I shadowed a ski-patrol doc in Whitefish, Montana. A fourth, I worked at a clinic in Boise, Idaho, that did research on rattlesnakes.

I tried to join the Crag Rats in 1999 after I was finished with residency but got declined because I lived across the river in White Salmon. Crag Rats had a strict rule in the bylaws: only Hood River County residents could join. I smiled when I found the Crag Rats meeting minutes from October 12, 2000, that originally discussed my request to join: "Jay asked about a prospective member who lives in White Salmon. He can come to functions or move to Hood River." When I moved to Hood River in late 2000, I finally joined the team. But I struggled with getting to know people because there was no formal orientation program, training, or rescue procedures to follow. I also struggled with traditions that I didn't understand and that seemed hurtful to our organization.

For example, it wasn't until 1990, and only with much consternation, that the Crag Rats admitted the first women. Interestingly, Brian's cousin Beth Hukari, a would-be second-generation Crag Rat, tried to be a member in 1989—she came up for a vote twice. But the rules state that just two no votes can block a membership, and you get only three attempts total. Beth had two attempts in 1989, and then her application was delayed. By going through a folder with membership applications and talking to Crag Rats present at those meetings, I learn that, in 1990, Beth, Karen McCurdy, and Mary Edmundson were voted in as the first women members, the latter voted in posthumously as a long-time mountaineer with many summits of Mount Hood and the wife of Doc Edmundson, a stalwart member. Beth remains very active with the Crag Rats today: she runs the hut committee, orders our T-shirts and hats, comes to meetings, and even showed up on a rescue in recent years.

Jerry Bryan and I talk about these times as well. He remembers much spirited, heated, and emotional discussion. I'm sure the debate was agonizing. We once had a fiery twenty-minute discussion about whether we should move the couches from the first floor to the basement of the hut, so I can only imagine the debate over allowing women. And I'd also seen these intra-club dynamics at play firsthand in 2018, when I proposed a change to the bylaws, to allow non–Hood River County residents to join. I wanted to get my friend Heiko Stopsack in, but like me, during my first attempt to join, he lived in White Salmon. It was a long process that entailed many discussions with members, understanding traditions, and fielding questions and concerns. The bylaw change was eventually approved, allowing members from neighboring counties: Wasco County in Oregon to our immediate east, and Klickitat and Skamania Counties across the river in Washington. The following year, Heiko would be voted in. To this day, he's one of the most active among us and a regular participant in our Crag Rats ski group.

When I am well into many drafts of this book, completely done with research, Paul Crowley calls me. "I found them," he says. "I'm coming by your house." Paul joined the Crag Rats around the same time I did and has, like me, been active in many aspects. A former accountant, a former judge, and now part-time mediator, he brings logic and calm to the sometimes-emotional discussions at Crag Rats business meetings. He's our go-to for interpreting the bylaws. Once on a search of Herman Creek on a sunny summer day, Paul and I were paired to hike a two-mile section of the Pacific Crest Trail. It was an easy hike, and the lost person was found uninjured later that day by another team. I don't remember the topic as Paul and I hiked the easy trail, just that the conversation was rich and meaningful.

Now, Paul shows up at my house. A day prior, he was digging through an armoire that holds his retired judge's robes. In the dark recesses of the cabinet, he found four grocery bags: the missing records. He plops reams of documents on my kitchen table, smiles, and says, "Good luck." I'm elated to find the records but also agonized by the time it will take to read them at the height of rescue season—and when the manuscript is nearly finished.

"I'll bring them back in a few weeks," I say to Paul.

"Nope, they are yours now," he smiles.

As I read through the notebooks, including a scrapbook from member Les Hukari, I confirm what I know already: few missions. Before 2000, the Crag Rats had only around ten missions annually, most in the Columbia River Gorge and most described in just one or two sentences. One thing stands out in nearly every rescue: the teenager who joined in 1973 and is still one of the most active members. I make a note to myself: *Find time to talk with Brian Hukari.*

When I joined back in 2001, I had no idea how much the Crag Rats had to grow. However, I quickly recognized, compared to other teams, that we were not keeping up with the times. I had medical training and a bit of wilderness medicine experience, so I could see that our technology, rope systems, and medical training all lagged. We had little training and few rescues. No radios, no team jackets, no vehicle other than the Logan Machine Company snowcat and Cushman Trackster in various states of being repaired. Our black-and-white buffalo-checked wool shirts were not readily available from any vendor, and the heavy wool was not exactly suitable for high-effort, foul-weather missions. Many folks were outdated with their CPR certification. Now, reading through the missing records, I understand this was a deep issue.

This road to rebuilding was long and slow, and it took the efforts of many people. As 2000 rolled us into the new century, the Crag Rats had some work to do. First, we had to recognize our deficits and try to make changes while we were busy running our nonprofit, going on rescues, and training. Second, we had to retain some traditions, let others lapse, and create new ones. And third, we had to modernize.

I didn't know it at the time, but something else was also beginning to lapse: the health of the mountain, with the crowds on its slopes swelling thanks to advances in technology and outdoor equipment. And it wasn't just crowds on our volcano, but rather crowds coupled with consumption the world-around. All humans can probably agree on certain things that need to be preserved: clean air, clean water, healthy food, an equitable economy, and good health. But when change happens on a global scale and negatively impacts people's ability to meet these basic needs, it's unfathomable how we might catch up. Climate change was not on the Crag Rats' radar at the turn of the century, nor was the slow demise of the mountain's glaciers. But on Mount Hood—as everywhere—we are dealing with the effects of human consumption and climate change today, whether we're ready for them or not.

PART IV
FALL

CONFEDERACY OF THE HIGH ALPINE, 2000 TO PRESENT

CHAPTER 10

OCTOBER: LOST BEYOND WY'EAST

"We've been searching for the missing man for three days," the Olympic National Park ranger says. "We could use a technical rope team, as we have none for the weekend. In fact, we will take anyone you can send."

"Stand by. I think I can round up a team," I reply on the phone.

It's a Thursday afternoon in autumn. I have the weekend free, and my wont is adventure. As you know by now, I'm on a constant quest for new experiences, and I have an unremitting urge to help. Take a beautiful fall weekend—colorific leaves, dry trails, cool temps, clear weather—and then add in best friends, a few days of tramping through the forest, and the overarching purpose of trying to help someone. This is my, and likely all the Crag Rats'—Ron, Lisa, John Rust, Heiko, Hugh, Cully, Brian, Gary, and the rest of the squad's—idea of a perfect life experience.

Washington State has a strong contingent of mountain rescue teams—nine total—plus many ground SAR teams and rangers from Mount Rainier, Olympic, and North Cascades National Parks. But they are tapped out from searching for the missing man for three days in Olympic National Park. Many need to go back to work, family, and the other commitments of daily life. Plus, the search is expanding geographically.

I am optimistic that we can rally a crew. But several tedious steps will need to happen for an out-of-county, out-of-state mutual-aid request. First, I need to find at least one other Crag Rat who's willing to go, so I send out an email. To my delight, within an hour, Lisa, Joe McCulloch (a longtime member and frequent responder who's fit from near-daily cycling), and Ron are in, and we plan to make the five-hour drive on Friday afternoon to help search. Then, I call SAR Deputy Chris Guertin for permission: we don't deploy without the sheriff's approval, both for insurance reasons and, perhaps more importantly, to respect this symbiotic and deferential relationship. Approval comes in less than an hour. I book two nights at the historic, rustic Lake Quinault Lodge, where the rescue teams are staying. We plan on taking SAR 2, the dilapidated but serviceable secondhand truck, with its manual transmission and manual windows. John Rust and Walter took SAR 2 this past summer to Mount Jefferson to search for a missing man. After two days' bivouacking on Jefferson—as in, sleeping outside without a tent, sleeping bag, or stove—they drove home for three hours in 90-degree weather with no air-conditioning and grumbled about it for months, good-naturedly of course. Luckily, the battery didn't die on them, which has been known to happen. But Deputy Guertin doesn't trust the truck to take us to the Olympic Peninsula.

"Take the SAR 1," he says. *Sweet!* I think. Later, John and Walter will grumble and laugh about our cush ride to the Olympics compared to their crappy ride to Mount Jefferson.

On Friday, we start the trek in SAR 1, with its shiny black body, sleek rooftop box, front-grill guard and winch, and Hood River County Sheriff and Crag Rats logos. We banter cheerfully—especially at the expense of John and Walter—as we take turns driving. Then we turn to more important issues.

"We need more Crag Rats. It's a weekend, so I'm surprised we didn't get more people," Lisa says candidly and with a hint of disquiet.

I share this sentiment: "I'm glad we got a foursome."

"And look around the truck," Lisa says with a sudden revelation. "We're all over fifty!"

"We're all old," Joe says in an even tone from behind the wheel.

"Who's the oldest?" I ask.

"Me," Ron replies in his quiet, hardened tone. He's listening to NPR on his old-school wired headphones per usual, with one earbud in so he can participate in the conversation. "We need some young people," he adds. In a few hours, we check into Lake Quinault Lodge and have dinner in the dining room. Ron doesn't want to pay for dinner, so I pick up the tab to later submit for reimbursement.

"I'm fine sleeping on my cot," Lisa says when we squeeze into the two-bed lakeside room. "I brought one." Considering that we all spend many days per year sleeping in tents, mountain cabins, and our cars, the fact that we have to cram into a small room is a minor inconvenience. Ron volunteers for the pull-out couch. Between sleeping arrangements, our rescue backpacks, and duffel bags of extra clothes and gear, we have almost no extra floor space. The room is packed.

My biggest challenge is to ensure I keep track of my stuff. When I pull something out of my duffel, I run the risk of misplacing it in the jumble of gear. We quickly arrange our packs for the morning. I stuff in foam earplugs and go to sleep.

The next morning at seven o'clock we report to the South Shore Quinault Ranger Station. The story is that a seventy-eight-year-old collector of antler sheds has been missing for several days. We are assigned to the Graves Creek Trail, a river trail that meanders through old-growth forest about fifteen miles from the ranger station. Our job is to hike up the trail and rappel over all the trailside cliffs, which rise fifty feet above the creek.

Joe is fit and strong; he sets a brisk pace in the lead. As we hike up Graves Creek, I feel like I am walking back in time. The giant old-growth forest is intact. Huge cedar trees drip with moss and old man's beard lichen in hundreds of shades of green. The off-trail understory is so thick that we must bushwhack through brush and clamber over boulders and logs in a several spots just to get a dozen feet off-trail to the cliff. Even signs of humans—established trails, trail signs, and bridges—are antique. This reminds me of skiing with my family in the 1970s. The ski areas back then sported trapezoid brown-and-cream US Forest Service wooden signs with cursive lettering, while the National Park signs were arrowhead shaped—both designs are still used today. This pristine old growth is a good, positive reminder that we, as humans, *can* protect the things we value, like wilderness areas (Mount Hood) and national parks (Mount Rainier and Olympic). But then, a greater issues looms: whatever we preserve locally is still impacted by what happens globally. I consciously, unabashedly suppress thoughts of geopolitics and climate change because this ancient forest is absolutely picturesque, serene, and sparkly—and unlike anywhere else in the world. At this moment, I want to revel in its loveliness.

The forest is cold and shaded in the morning, since the sun is blocked by big mountains and tall trees to the east. The canopy is thick with the overarching limbs of ancient cedar and hemlock—long, tentacle-like boughs that seemingly start in the sky and dip to the ground. An eerie understory fog lingers in the damp, cool ravines and creek drainages. By midmorning, the fog lifts and the sun comes out. But because the trees are so monstrous, the limbs filter the sunlight, which streams through the canopy like refracted light off a mirror ball, never becoming bright and full. We tie webbing around a tree, throw a rope down, and take turns being lowered twenty to thirty feet to inspect the creek before being hauled back up. By late afternoon, the forest is warm and sunny. After the all-day hike and half-dozen rappels, all fruitless for finding the man but fruitful for being alive in the forest and having fun in nature, we call it a day and head back to the lodge.

The next day, we hike again along Graves Creek to the confluence of Graves and Success Creeks, to make sure we clear the entire trail. The morning is warmer: the sun streams through the canopy and steam rises. We quickly shed our outer layers of clothing. The creek bubbles noisily, and birds flit through the woods. The meandering trail is blockaded occasionally by a gigantic, downed cedar as thick as a car. We scramble over, paying more attention to the beauty of the forest than the charcoal-colored duff that rubs off onto our hiking clothes and turns them brown. The exposed innards of the recently fallen logs are bright orange, while the old, decayed logs are covered in moss and have saplings growing from them; chunks of decay and moss flake off these nurse logs. We don't talk much. Eventually, we make a few more rappels and clear the trail, but there's still no sign of the missing hiker.

Back at the ranger station, we sign out in the late afternoon and start the drive home. As of this writing, the man has not been found.

OLYMPIC NATIONAL PARK is not the only place we've responded to for mutual aid. Because of growing crowds everywhere—and not just on Mount Hood—we are called more frequently out of county. Amid our busiest year ever, we get a mutual-aid request from Skamania County, Washington, for a missing climber on Mount St. Helens. It's another Thursday evening at eight o'clock. The local Volcano Rescue Team (VRT) and ground SAR team have been searching for a couple of days. They need more help. A text pops when I'm in bed reading William Finnegan's *Barbarian Days: A Surfing Life* for the second time. Earlier that day, Ron and I made a plan to ski Friday. So when the callout comes, he shifts gears and promptly texts me: "Want to go to St. Helens tomorrow?" Certainly, Ron is up for an adventure, and he knows I am too. Lisa, Heiko, and John Rust all want to come per a group chat, but they all have to work. Ron and I talk on the phone to solidify plans, and we check in with Deputy Guertin, who gives us approval. I go to sleep at ten, wake up at my usual five a.m., drink a cup of strong coffee, grab my ski gear and some food, jump in my truck, and head to the county yard.

Ron and I depart Hood River at six a.m. in SAR 1, drive two hours, and check in with incident command, which is a Skamania County SAR deputy sitting in an SUV on a Forest Road pullout in Mount St. Helens National Volcanic Monument. The sky is obscured by the gray, monotone cloud cover that's typical for the Pacific Northwest. Fortunately, the outlook forecasts midday clearing. The road and the roadside trees are damp with dew, so the whole morning feels dank—opposite the crisp and clear invigoration that I oft associate with the alpine. The deputy asks us to drive to the Swift Creek trailhead at Marble Mountain Sno-Park. There, we find the VRT team unloading snowmobiles.

Jared Smith, a senior rescuer from the VRT, introduces himself. He's a quintessential mountain rescuer who would be the exact representation if AI generated one: bearded and fit, smiling and affable, focused and motivated, dressed in a once-bright-red mountain rescue parka bedecked with team patches, mismatched repair tape, and stains and grime. "We searched the last two days. I'm glad you showed up," he says, smiling as he shakes our hands. "No one has cleared the summit: it's been too stormy, and we're out of people. We're going to pull you on snowmobiles as far as Chocolate Falls." The falls, named for the glacier melt tainted cacao brown by pulverized volcanic pumice, flanks the two-mile Swift Creek Trail, which meanders through the woods to timberline.

"After we drop you off," Jared continues, "we want you to ski to the summit. But first check the radio-relay station at seven thousand feet. That's where the last phone ping shows the subject."

"Sounds good," I say.

Ron studiously asks several questions about snow conditions and the route; Jared astutely and succinctly replies. Then Ron and I grab our skis and backpacks, walk over to the snow-covered trail, click into our ski bindings, and grab a rope behind snowmobiles. We are then pulled, yanked, and yo-yoed up the Swift Creek Trail, covering in fifteen minutes what would otherwise take an hour.

"I'm glad Wes and Asa ran that training last week," Ron says as we regroup at tree line after the roller-coaster ride.

"Me too," I say. Fortuitously, Wes and Asa, two of our professional ski-patrol contingent within Crag Rats, showed us how to properly ski while being towed behind a snowmobile, which often involves wearing a backpack and careering along a cross-country-ski trail in the woods, navigating turns, dips, ruts, troughs, dirt patches, icy spots, puddles, and snowbanks, all while trying not to let the abrupt jerks of the rope burn your hands and yank your shoulders.

We salute goodbye to Jared and his partner and continue uphill on skis. The outing is familiar, unintimidating, and routine. Ron and I ski together regularly, and I've skied this trail and summited this volcano two dozen times. I first climbed Mount St. Helens solo in 1989, during my first summer in Hood River, taking the summer rock and sand route. Just last August, I ran to the summit also when the terrain was just snowless boulders and fine pumice. Today, it's all snow. Ron starts out leading and puts the skin track straight up. Ron and I have routine disagreements about our uphill track. When we are skiing for fun, Ron prefers a straight-up skin track, since it's the most direct. I purport that this expends more energy and prefer a more meandering skin track, because while it's longer, you can ski at a faster pace and with less energy expenditure. Once in a while, we each make our own track and race—we're nearly always at the top at the same time. If Meredith is along, she laughs at us debating and, depending on her energy level, will occasionally follow me but mostly follows Ron. Today, we are climbing a mountain on a rescue mission, not backcountry skiing for fun: time is more critical. So I agree with Ron, and we go straight up.

Early morning fog cocoons the summit of Mount St. Helens in ping-pong-ball white. But by midmorning, the fog burns off and the sky pops to cobalt blue, a stark contrast against the bright white snowfields, refreshed by a storm earlier in the week. The air heats up, and the snow begins to soften, then turns gloppy and sticky. The sodden feeling of the early morning mist is replaced by the clammy feeling of sweating. In an hour, the route steepens and the snow hardens, so we affix ski crampons for better traction. About halfway along the two-hour climb, we reach the radio-relay and weather station at seven thousand feet, the point of the missing man's last cell phone transmission. We are about to start a circumferential grid search of the area when the radio pops to life.

"Crag Rats from command," the deputy says.

"Crag Rats here," Ron says.

"The subject has been spotted. On the summit. Deceased."

The climber was spotted by other climbers, who called 911. Ron and I make short work of the one-thousand-foot climb to the summit and quickly locate the deceased. Up top, we can see miles in either direction in the clear skies; there are thirty other climbers on the summit ridge, one hundred feet to the west of us. We wait and chitchat until the radio crackles. "We've got a helicopter coming, one hour," radios the deputy. "Do you want a ride down?"

"No, we'll ski down," Ron replies automatically. We just skied uphill all the way to the summit, so why not enjoy the ski down? But as we wait for the helicopter, I consider the snowpack conditions.

"It's late in the day and will be four p.m. by the time we're ready to descend. It's going to suck skiing down, and it will be dangerous. It's already manky," I say, referring to the deep, sticky-soft slush that's almost impossible to ski through.

"Yea," Ron muses. "You're right." Ron's levelheaded and safe, which is why I like skiing with him. He adds, "Let's get a ride. I'll call them back."

In less than an hour, a helicopter lands on the summit. Jared and another rescuer jump out.

"Hey, Jared, good to see you. Thanks for coming," I say. The helicopter drops a net sling on a cable, we load the body, and Ron and I climb into the cabin for the seven-minute ride back to the Marble Mountain Sno-Park, getting a scenic tour of the climbing route on the way down.

After the mission, Ron drives home but hasn't brought any food. So, while riding shotgun, I hand him string cheese, crackers, apple slices, and carrot sticks from the lunch I'd hurriedly packed that morning. We pull into the county yard at eight p.m., a good day's adventure.

When I drop Ron off at home, we tell Meredith about the helicopter ride, and she's bummed.

"Why do I go on the boring missions and miss all the exciting ones?" she pouts. The last few missions have been straightforward, relatively uneventful trail rescues, often involving individuals who were able to walk out on their own.

"It was basically reverse heliskiing: we skied uphill, then got a heli ride downhill," I smile, and then add, "We will have more."

UNFORTUNATELY, WHEN WE get a call for mutual aid, the rescues are often large, with multiple agencies responding, multiple days invested, and poor outcomes, like the Olympic National Park search in which the man was never found or the Mount St. Helens climber who was found dead. In 2018, Brian and Walter pulled a deceased climber off Mount Adams. The missing climber Walter and

John Rust searched for on Mount Jefferson was found dead a week later by helicopter.

But it's not all doom and gloom, not all *deceased* and *lost forever*. More often, we help people and have a good outcome, like a rescue on Mount Rainier, in which we happened to be in the right place at the right time.

Annually the last few years, Cully, Eric, Heiko, and I book a weekend on Mount Rainier to patrol. In exchange for using the refurbished 1941-built ranger cabin #123 at the Longmire headquarters of Mount Rainier National Park, we are on call for rescues. We arrive at the cabin one Thursday afternoon in January. The weather is unseasonably warm, and the sky is clear—the heating of the earth is clearly showing in the great volcanoes. We check in with the rangers who live and work out of Longmire, and we plan our ski days. In the forest around the cabin, the trees are giant one-thousand-year-old evergreen conifers: western redcedar, western hemlock, Douglas-fir. The lowland understory is densely packed with broadleaf ferns, huckleberry, and salal. Old man's beard lichen drips from the trees.

After a quick check-in, we ski for three days in the surrounds. The first day, we park at Narada Falls, a popular waterfall near Longmire, and skin uphill on the north-facing slopes of the Tatoosh Range, the east-west peaks and spires just south of Mount Rainier. These slopes offer hard, firm snow thanks to the all-day shade. But when we reach the saddle and drop down the south-facing side, we find smooth, silky, untracked snow.

At one point, after looking south at the beautiful view into an expansive, heavily wooded, roadless area, I look to Eric and say, "We should be careful."

"Yep, we're far from everywhere," he says. The farther we descend, the deeper we get into wilderness, far from any road. Eric and I have skied together in Japan, the Alps, and Norway. We know enough to recognize that this remoteness runs as deep as the beauty: we need to exercise caution.

On the second day, we zip up to Paradise, the hub of Mount Rainier climbing and the site of the gigantic Paradise Inn, where the forests of Alaskan yellow cedar, noble fir, western white pine, and Pacific silver fir give way to scattered subalpine fir and mountain hemlock, sparingly spaced on slopes perfect for us to ski. We carry a radio and check in with dispatch. The airwaves teem with the nonstop chatter of park rangers encountering tourists to give directions, haul them out of snowbanks, or help them navigate the parking lot. We don our backpacks and ski uphill. We make many laps in Edith Basin, relatively close to the Paradise visitor center, ranger station, lodge, and parking-lot complex.

The snow isn't great—a few inches of dense, untracked snow on top of rain runnels—but the weather is glorious and feels like spring. So, the third day, we decide just to pick a destination for something to do: Camp Muir, a climbers' bivouac at ten thousand feet on the most popular route to the summit, Disappointment Cleaver. The camp has a shelter for climbers, a ranger shack, a solar composting toilet, and a cook cabin. From the Paradise parking lot, it's a three-mile, 4,800-foot climb. We ascend the drainage to Panorama Point, a rocky outcrop at 7,000 feet, and then continue up to McClure Rock, a large rock outcrop on the Muir snowfield just above Panorama Point. At 8,000 feet around noon, we encounter bulletproof ice. The wind is blasting, but it's oddly warm, well above freezing. We watch around fifty people continue upward. We see several who are ill-prepared, with little clothing, small packs, and no crampons or ice axes.

"I don't get it," I say. "Why are people continuing uphill in these horrible conditions? Am I missing something?"

Heiko shrugs.

"It's not good skiing," Eric says matter-of-factly with a chuckle. Eric, like me, skis one hundred days annually, so when conditions are lousy, he knows there's no reason to continue. "I don't need to keep going," he adds.

"Me neither," I say.

"Let's find better snow, down low," Cully suggests.

We bail on our Camp Muir objective and ski down into Edith Basin near the inn. We find soft snow lower on the mountain, make a few laps, and call it an early day. We are back in the cabin at four p.m., thinking about starting dinner. The refurbished two-bedroom structure has wood floors, a small kitchen, a wall-mounted electric heater, a tankless water heater, and mountain rescue pictures adorning the walls.

"I'm making chili," Heiko announces as he walks into the kitchen. Then he returns, holding the SAR radio and asks, "Should we turn this on?"

I shrug and say, "I suppose so."

Heiko clicks on the radio and sets it on the table. In a matter of minutes, the radio pops to life: "Any available mountain rescue team?" We stare in disbelief.

"I guess we're on duty," I say. It's four thirty, and we pull our ski clothes back on. Two snowshoers are stuck somewhere past Reflection Lakes, just above Narada Falls in the Tatoosh Range. We meet up with the rangers at the emergency operations center in Longmire and then get dispatched to Narada Falls at dusk. Initially, they want us to be the backup team behind three rangers on foot. But when we unload our skis from my truck, the tune changes.

"You are on skis?"

"Yes," I say. "And if it matters, we are two doctors, a flight nurse, and a paramedic."

"Okay," says the lead ranger. "I have skis, so you guys will be the first team with me. I'll send the other two rangers up on foot with backup gear."

At dark, the four of us, led by a park ranger, ski uphill. It's windy, but the wind is still oddly warm, and the air temperature is 40 degrees. In an hour, we climb up the north-facing side of the Tatoosh Range all the way to the Castle Peak saddle, where we find two snowshoers uninjured. They are dressed in damp cotton clothing and wearing soft hiking boots; one has a broken snowshoe strap. They are cold, hungry, and thirsty. After a short assessment, we give them food and fluids and spare clothes. We start down quickly.

Our headlamps pierce the night, and the only way I can see with the wind is to put on goggles. Once we reach the top of a steep section, we are met by two additional rangers, who unload extra harnesses, helmets, and crampons for the two snowshoers, as well as a two-hundred-foot rope. We make three consecutive descents down the slope with the rope. Each subject climbs down, escorted by one of us and tied into the rope. We fashion belay anchors by using either two vertical skis jammed tail-first into the snow or an ice axe buried to the hilt.

When we get to Reflection Lakes, we walk out, just before midnight—all is well. We later hear that a small kerfuffle ensued over getting us dispatched because we're an Oregon team operating in Washington. At first, when the ranger called Washington Emergency Management, they had no idea who we Crag Rats were—they thought we were some dirtbag climbing group. Then it dawned on someone: "Oh, *those* Crag Rats!" Someone called the Oregon Department of Emergency Management, who called the Hood River County Sheriff Office, who approved us to get dispatched—after we'd already started the mission.

Back at the cabin, we scarf Heiko's chili and catch a few hours of sleep. In the morning, we decide to pack up and drive home. We could ski one more day, but we've been up half the night, and home life, as always, is calling. Cully needs to get home to his wife and kids. I have loads to do, as always, like writing this book and finishing a final draft of a paper on the medical aspects of avalanche accidents, and, like Eric, a slew of upcoming trips in various stages of planning.

When I get home, I look up the last documented Crag Rats mission in Mount Rainier National Park, best recounted in *Death, Daring, and Disaster: Search and Rescue in the National Parks* by Charles R "Butch" Farabee Jr. On July 2, 1929, a climbing party led by Leon H. Brigham, two apprentice guides, and three clients summited Mount Rainier in a storm so fierce and the wind blowing so hard "they had to crouch low and crawl the remaining distance" to the summit. On the descent, one apprentice guide, Ray Strobel, fell and pulled the whole team down the Ingraham Glacier into a crevasse. One client, Edwin Wetzel, and the other apprentice guide, Forrest Greathouse, died. The other four were rescued within a day, and Wetzel's body was recovered on July 3—but the storm was too great to recover Greathouse.

After the storm abated, with resources exhausted, the Crag Rats were called. Led by Andy Anderson, eleven Crag Rats drove from Hood River on July 6, four days into the search. They left at three p.m. and arrived at Paradise at one thirty a.m. The men slept an hour at Paradise, climbed to Camp Muir with a toboggan, then traversed to the Ingraham Glacier in fog and snow. After scouring the glacier, the Crag Rats found Greathouse fifty feet deep in a crevasse, dead, frozen into a "mass of snow and ice." They hauled Greathouse out, then hauled the body down the mountain to Paradise Inn. Round-trip, including the rescue, the Crag Rats traveled 480 miles in thirty-five hours.

AT THE END of the twentieth century on Mount Hood, Crag Rats annually deployed on one mission in the alpine plus a handful in the lowlands. After I joined in 2001, we bumped to a dozen total rescues per year for a decade, two-thirds of them on the trails of the Columbia River Gorge National Scenic Area and one-third in the foothills of Mount Hood, plus the occasional alpine mission. We were very much that ragtag group that John Arens, Jerry Bryan, Dwayne Troxell, and Kent Lambert spoke of; we had a strong social component and our long-standing, quirky, sometimes-annoying traditions. Our equipment was rudimentary: no radios, no trucks, a few ropes, some climbing hardware, one stretcher with a wheel, oxygen bottles, and a snowcat—something we seem to have always had over the last at least seven decades. The rescue gear was stored in the barn of Craig McCurdy, a longtime Crag Rat and local orchardist. Cell phones were just becoming popular, so callouts came mostly via a land-line. When a mission occurred and we needed the gear, someone had to go to McCurdy's barn, where I found it on my second mission, piled in the corner, covered in dust.

Then, sometime around 2010, we saw a fourth surge of outdoor recreation. It was around this time that rescues began increasing and never slowed. We jacked up rather suddenly to thirty missions per year (or forty days per year, because many missions last multiple days). And callouts today continue at a pace of around three dozen per year, in part because there's simply more people in the world (including in the nearby Portland metro area) and in part because the outdoor-recreation industry is booming. With increasing rescues, and more complex ones, Crag Rats have had to marshal ourselves, modernize our gear, upskill our techniques, and organize. It took several years. And it took our whole membership.

The first change I remember came from Devon Wells, who broke a seven-decade tradition. Devon is a second-generation Crag Rat and former Hood

River city fire chief. When he was Big Squeak in 2002, he abruptly truncated the twice-monthly business meetings: he consolidated all business into one meeting per month and then earmarked the second meeting for orchestrated training. This was a fantastic change because not only did we have training on ropework, patient packaging, and patient care, but we also had fun, a huge break from gathering to sit on metal chairs and talk business for two hours. For the first time in the Crag Rats' history, we had a formal, regular, monthly training program.

The second change came when I realized we needed better equipment, namely radios. Prior to the widespread use of cell phones, when I'd participated in a mission to carry out a woman with an injured knee across the Eliot Glacier, I'd had to use a radio borrowed from a deputy because the Crag Rats had none. I'd realized the value of communication. In 2003, I asked the Providence Hood River Memorial Hospital Foundation for funding for a dozen radios.

Then improvement began snowballing. Many people helped instigate this revitalization, including an important new cohort of Crag Rats who joined in the aughts and teens. These were professionals whose day jobs involved at least some component of patient care or rescue: ski patrollers, firefighters, mountain guides, EMTs, and medical professionals. This high-caliber crew infused new energy into our club's SAR component, rather than solely focusing on the social elements. Adding members who possessed working knowledge of rescues and medicine, in addition to high-alpine passion and mountaincraft skills, was a monumental, albeit unhurried, step up for the Crag Rats. Now we had pros who were not only reliable at pulling off simple tasks like communicating clearly via radio but who could also execute complex tasks like rigging ropes and skiing toboggans.

As just one example, Gary took on revamping our technical-rescue capability. He formed the Ropes Committee along with Lisa, John Rust, Asa, and Walter. He took our equipment from a mismatched set of gear to two *systems*. One system uses lightweight ropes and minimal hardware to lower a litter and rescuer to a patient and then haul them back up. The other is a more heavy-duty system with thick ropes. He cataloged, standardized, and duplicated gear for three separate complete kits for SAR 1, SAR 2, and Cloud Cap Inn. We had regular training on skills like anchors, haul systems, and mock rescues.

Wes and Asa organized training with the Mt. Hood Meadows ski patrol. They taught us how to use the akja, a skill no other rescue team on Mount Hood would possess outside of ski patrol, and obviated the need for a rope lower: Crag Rats could ski a patient down from ten thousand feet on the South Side Routes in forty-five minutes, whereas a rope lower took several hours. We worked on avalanche rescue, crevasse extrication, cliff recovery, and snowmobile towing.

Tim Mortenson, a retired pararescue jumper from the 304th Rescue Squadron and firefighter, rejuvenated our relationship with the squadron, which had been somewhat dormant, by rekindling joint trainings at Cloud Cap Inn. This arrangement traded use of the inn in exchange for the opportunity to attend their training sessions.

Tom Rousseau, although not a professional rescuer, took our communications to a professional level. He programmed our radios and then installed a solar-powered light and radio system for Cloud Cap Inn. He even hand-built a portable radio repeater that we can take up the trail to use as a relay in deep canyons.

Similarly, Paul Crowley, the accountant turned lawyer turned judge, helped us craft better documents and provided expertise at meetings all the while going on missions. Jay Sherrerd, longtime Crag Rat, my initial sponsor for membership back in 2001, and an attorney, spent time reorganizing our nonprofit and, for the better part of two decades, served as our representative with the Oregon Mountain Rescue Council, which credentials the state's mountain rescue teams.

Heiko, Cully, and Eric came aboard and, along with me, formed the solid Medical Committee. We got defibrillators, heat blankets, splints, and medical kits and hosted trainings on how to use it all. We trained on not just CPR and first aid but also advanced wilderness topics like heat illness, hypothermia, patient packaging, splinting, triage, and mass-casualty-incident management.

Early on, I watched and learned, to see what teaching styles were well received. I had nowhere near the alpine rescue skills that some of the ski patrollers and mountain guides had. I learned from Wes and Asa how to take a calm view of the global picture in an incident. Tim taught no-nonsense practical skills, not from a book but from his years as a parajumper. Cully taught a patient-assessment class that somehow walked the precarious line of giving detailed advanced information on patient care without making things too complicated. Heiko taught many courses—mostly based on thousands of patient-care hours in his job as a paramedic—and infused direct patient-care anecdotes into his lectures.

At some point, I realized leadership needs to change hands to infuse new ideas and dynamics, so I turned over chair of the Crag Rats Medical Committee to Heiko. I know I'll have to turn over medical director duties someday too, but I suppress that thought.

Our club, meanwhile, has so many crucial background tasks that fall to our membership, in addition to jumping in on rescues. Take Beth, for example, the first among a cohort of women admitted nearly four decades ago. She runs the Hut Committee and maintains our team clothing. Deno maintains our 1976 Logan snowcat. Joel Piersall, Bernie Wells, and the late Todd Wells repair and maintain our two buildings; the trio has done this for decades with passion and devotion. Mark Flaming, Won Kim, and Gavin Vanderpool run the financial aspects—a monumental task. And I should mention, if you haven't figured this out, that none of us get paid or reimbursed in any way.

We also had Jenn, as in past tense. Jenn Donnelly, an urban planner and outdoor athlete, was soft-spoken and smart. She spent her free time hiking, running, cycling, and competing in triathlons. We met in 2008, dated for a couple of years, and then remained deep and true friends. She wanted to join the Crag Rats, though a few members were suspect of her mountaineering skills. I had climbed Mount Hood and Mount St. Helens with her, taught her to backcountry ski in the Wallowa Mountains, and cycled at least two 100-mile bike rides with her around Oregon's Elkhorn Mountains and the Blue Mountain Scenic Byway. I knew she was fit but not necessarily an alpinist with a catholic cadre of rope skills. But she brought something rare that few could have pulled off in our two decades of building back: business organization. She reorganized the hut as a rental venue, shored up our finances, got a new bookkeeper, acquired better insurance, and started regular meetings of the officers, which had never occurred. Then, midway through her six-year officer track, she was diagnosed with advanced terminal cancer and died in six months. This great loss is a stark and vivid reminder that even the best-intentioned, kindest, can-do people are at the whims of natural diseases.

Notwithstanding this tragic loss, the Crag Rats were back. Andy Anderson and Dick Pooley would have been proud. I know Bill Pattison was. Before he died, he told me, "Crag Rats have never been stronger. We are at the top of our game." He was proud of this crew. And Jerry Bryan is too: he reminisced fondly about the "ragtag" years and said admiringly, "You all have turned the group into a real mountain rescue team." None of it, I realize deep into this project, is without the solid foundation built by past Crag Rats.

Now, a recent project, spearheaded by Lisa soon after the Olympic National Park search, is aimed directly at recruiting. We need more members. We also need, as Lisa and I discussed several times, younger members. We've never had a recruiting campaign as long as anyone can remember. I found just one reference in the 1950s regarding wanting more members, but no action taken. We generally have a dozen inquiries a year; these often come to a group email and get just cursory attention, as we're too busy seeing to the club's aforementioned tasks. Occasionally, if someone is persistent, we'll invite a potential member to trainings, social functions, and ski outings. If their personality seems like a good fit and they are determined to join, we may sign them up, to the tune of two or three new members each year. But we still need more members, those who are willing to leave a family birthday party, miss a day of work, and crawl out of bed in the middle of the night in the middle of a storm to hike up the middle of a glacier. Gary said it best: "We need alpinists. We can teach them the rescue skills." In other words, we need members who have a passion for the mountains.

When the Crag Rats formed in 1926, the world had fewer than two billion people. Sixty years later, when I graduated from high school, the earth's population had doubled to four billion. When I completed my first mission for the

Crag Rats in 2000, the world had six billion. Now, as the Crag Rats near one hundred years, we have eight billion people in the world, and the population still growing at around 2 percent per year. So if you're shocked by all the rescues and crowds, or shocked by all the car traffic and development in your local neighborhood, or shocked by too many students in classrooms, consider that humankind's numbers have quadrupled in the past one hundred years.

A growing population means more consumers who need more houses, more roads, more food, more factories, more cars, more chairlifts, and more restaurants. We need more energy, whether it's fossil fuels such as oil, coal, and gas, and less-polluting energy such as wind, solar, and hydro—none of which are completely harmless to the environment, since clean energies still need smelted steel, fabricated aluminum, assembled electronics, mined metals, plastic parts, batteries, and real estate for solar arrays, wind farms, and hydroelectric dams. And more people generate more garbage and more waste, both biologic and synthetic.

Locally on Mount Hood, the impact has been subtle, since the upper mountain is protected as a wilderness area. But in the lowlands, mostly encompassed by the Mount Hood National Forest, every spring cycling season I'll see a newly carved logging road and more clear-cut slopes—more immediate, visible markers than the glaciers that are melting at a rate of one meter per year.

I love seeing all the folks enjoying the mountains and utilizing backcountry skis, climbing gear, running shoes, mountain bikes, and hiking boots to enjoy this land. Crowds on Mount Hood mean that these people hopefully love the mountain as much as we Crag Rats do. But the impact at some point becomes unsustainable, as the needs of greater numbers of people outstrip the resources available. The glaciers melt, the forests fall, the slopes erode, the cliffs crumble, and the streams dry up.

More people also bring the need for more rescues. In my first memoir, *Mountain Rescue Doctor*, I chronicled nearly all the missions in a five-year period starting in 2000. I had just enough missions to fill a book. In my second memoir, *Search and Rescue*, I covered a set of rescues over a decade and left many rescues out. Now, after our busiest year ever in 2022, I could easily fill a tome with missions from just this single year (although in this book, I chose to present missions covering several years).

What I see on Mount Hood—crowding, overuse, environmental degradation—occurs round the world in many capacities. Unfortunately, it's more pronounced in under-resourced countries with high concentrations of people. As the population grows, disparate groups become more separated in culture, religion, resources, income, and other factors. Disparity leads to inequal and inequitable resource allocation, especially for meeting basic needs like food, water, and shelter. Often, under-resourced people need to take the least expensive way because they simply need to survive. In other words, it might be great that many of us in America are affluent enough to buy an electric vehicle or shampoo that comes as a solid bar without a single-use plastic bottle. But for those just trying to feed their family and get their kids to school in Port-au-Prince, Bengaluru, Bangkok, or Mexico City, the cheapest alternative is going to be the only choice. And that choice may be the costliest to the environment, driving climate change. And what happens across the planet happens to Mount Hood's high mountain glaciers.

In a Crag Rats meeting, we gather around and socialize before our pre-meeting training on avalanche rescue or splinting. I feel somewhat frustrated and apathetic as we discuss the same issues that recur year after year as a result of poor decision-making: too many people on a rope, climbers roped on a steep slope without anchors, or communication problems between rescue teams. When we sit down for the business meeting—which seems unchanged in terms of tone and tenor from meetings across the last one hundred years—good-natured teasing and fond recollections of a goofy fall skiing or forgetting to lock a window at Cloud Cap Inn are juxtaposed with serious business. John Rust and Paul Crowley are working on funding for a new roof for the inn, the hut cleanup weekend is scheduled, and we have finances to discuss. The solid triad of Bernie Wells, his son Todd, and Todd's son Joel Piersall report on their maintenance efforts on both Cloud Cap Inn and the hut. These three are skilled craftsmen and can shore up a foundation, repair a broken pipe, or shingle the roof in a hot minute. Their love of Cloud Cap Inn and the hut is unrivaled. Gary brings up the communication issue and begins to organize a National Incident Management System training for all nine Mount Hood SAR teams. I admire this proactive streak in Gary and applaud his verve and tenacity.

Despite the effects of climate change, population growth, and the recent surge in recreation impacting Mount Hood and the world, there's little we Crag Rats can do other than watch from the sidelines and help in the same ways we always have. Anyway, we have another, more tangible issue to address, one that's only accelerated after the widespread use of cell phones in the late 1990s: the exploding and turbulent world of electronic telecommunications, with its complex, intertwined pros and cons.

CHAPTER 11

NOVEMBER: TELECOMMUNICATION ON THE ICE

In November, we are summoned for overdue climbers on the north side of Mount Hood. *North side? In November? What the hell?*

Mount Hood used to have a principal alpine climbing season, which ran from April through July. Now, however, people climb it year-round, during any open weather window. During November, few people hike and climb the upper mountain. The snow has yet to coat Mount Hood, the warm summer weather has passed, and the clear fall skies are often replaced by a monochromatic gray with a chance of rain, drizzle, showers, and other forms of non-snow precipitation. Wildflowers have gone dormant. Leaves and fruit have come and gone on the thinleaf huckleberries. And most of the upper-mountain routes present long ascents up crumbly rock and sand, without snow to glue the landscape into a walkable surface.

On a Tuesday, two climbers are reported missing. Their car is located at the Tilly Jane trailhead, so HRCSO Deputy Sheriff Joe Wampler fires up the Piper

Super Cub and scours the rugged and remote north slopes. He spots a backpack at nine thousand feet elevation on the Coe Glacier.

Thus, late in the day, we get the callout: go to the backpack. We can't wait until morning.

We rally five people in two groups that evening and drive up to Cloud Cap Inn. Due to the lack of snowfall, the road is clear, so we're able to open the locked US Forest Service gate and drive up. John Rust and Heiko arrive first, at eight p.m., and set off up the east moraine of the Eliot Glacier. After hiking up the sandy and rocky primitive trail on the moraine, they hike down onto the Eliot Glacier at 7,500 feet on the even rockier, sandier, and more primitive Pooley Trail. Brian, Gary, and I arrive a half hour behind them in SAR 1. We decide it's quicker to take the Timberline Trail west down to Eliot Creek, cross the stream, then climb up the gut of the old glacier bed. A few decades ago, we'd have been on glacier ice year-round. But now, because of the melted glacier, we're hiking on rocks—well, actually, a mix of boulders, rocks, pebbles, scree, and sand that shifts with every step. These rocks range from car-sized boulders of abrasive andesite that we have to scramble over, all the way down to tiny pebbles that weasel into our boots and socks. A few of the rocks are smooth from being tumbled for years by the glacier. Most are jagged and irregular from trundling off the moraines. The andesite is so sandpapery it shreds my brand-new leather gloves like a cheese grater.

As they scramble up the boulder field, John and Heiko are halted abruptly by a steep section of water ice that is too dangerous to ascend in the dark. So they traverse, and our paths convene at the bottom of the Snowdome snowfield just before midnight. By headlamp, we don crampons. Brian only brought soft hiking boots and traction spikes, which he straps over his boots.

"I'll make them work," he says with confidence and a smile. He is so strong and skilled, he cruises up the hard ice and walks more gracefully than me, despite my full-frame, ten-point steel crampons.

"I'm tracking," Gary says, perhaps the most skilled of us at using GPS. Utilizing his phone to follow the coordinates that Wampler recorded earlier that day, Gary gives clear directions: "Up to nine thousand feet, then traverse to the west." We climb in the cold November dark, our crampons gripping the ice with crunching sounds and our thoughts flittering quietly in the night. As we reach nine thousand feet, we traverse to the west edge of the Snowdome snowfield, where the terrain rolls dramatically and drops one hundred feet into the crevasses and seracs of the upper Coe Glacier. We stop for a second, waiting for Gary's instruction. Sometime around two a.m., amid a light wind and cold temperatures, we spy the backpack precisely where Gary said it would be.

"Wampler's good," Gary says. "Coordinates are right on."

"Yeah, much quicker than the old days," Brian says matter-of-factly. He's been doing this for fifty years.

We find a tent nestled in a rock outcrop of the glacier. Heiko and I cautiously approach, yell "Hello" a few times, and unzip the front panel. I'm prepared for either dead bodies or sleeping ones. We peer inside, lighting it with our headlamps: the tent is empty save for two sleeping bags, two pairs of hiking shoes, and two camping pads. Nothing more.

"Empty," I say loud enough so Brian, Gary, and John can hear me over the deafening flutter of the nylon.

"Nothing?"

"Just sleeping gear and shoes."

"They must be out climbing."

"Or dead. Missing since yesterday or the day before."

We consider searching the area, but it's late, still windy, and the seracs of the upper Coe are too dangerous at night. John radios Deputy Bob Stewart, who is running the mission from Cloud Cap Inn.

"Nothing here, tent empty. It's too dark to see much."

"And too dangerous with crevasses," Gary says. "We don't need to be scrambling around at dark. We've accomplished our task."

"Agree. This is all we can do tonight," I say and check my watch. Then a wave of agony hits me: now that the night's goal has been accomplished, I realize, we face a long, awful downhill scramble in the dark over the stones, scree, and sand.

"Okay, head back; we have teams coming at first light," Deputy Stewart says over the radio.

"Going to take a lot of people to search," John muses. "I have to work tomorrow."

"Me too," Brian says.

"Me too," I say. The thought of trying to concentrate on emails, patient charts, and procedural protocols gives me a sinking feeling. I know I'll be exhausted from the horrible hike down and the lack of sleep. We walk down the ice, shuck our crampons, and then scramble over the rocks of the west moraine. The old glacier bed is loose, slippery, and steep. Again, our shoes fill with sand and tiny pebbles. Once we make it down to the trees and to the Timberline Trail, we pop out two miles west of Cloud Cap Inn. So we still need to traverse the trail, which is blocked by a dozen big logs. Once we reach Eliot Creek, we find it raging and about four feet deep—falling in would be bad. We cross the torrent by bounding across semi-submerged boulders. Once across, we climb five hundred feet back up to Cloud Cap Inn. All this takes well into the morning. We don't reach the inn until around eight a.m., when we encounter fifty people: teams from the Crag Rats, Portland Mountain Rescue, and Pacific Northwest Search and Rescue are assembling to deploy and search for the missing climbers.

Deputy Stewart asks us for a briefing. We are so tired that we don't really say much.

"Be careful—the mountain this time of year is crumbling," I say. "The rocks, sand, and scree are loose. Every step is a potential sprained ankle."

As teams scatter onto Mount Hood searching the Eliot and Coe Glaciers, the five of us from the hasty team go straight home.

Had this been a mission from the mid-twentieth century, the two climbers would likely never have been recovered, unless a plane happened to fly directly overhead and the pilot spotted the bodies. But as a sign of the times, we have technology, or more specifically, telecom. Deputy Wahler, who takes over for Deputy Stewart, speaks with the family of one of the missing climbers in Portland, far from this giant inselberg. A sister of one of the climbers recalls that her brother, on his phone, has a social media app that tracks users' activities. The account is private and locked, but Deputy Wahler is able to contact the company, locate the track, and see where the signal stopped moving—on Tuesday, two full days before the search started—near the backpack on the Coe Glacier. This information comes midday; two rescuers from Portland Mountain Rescue (PMR) are in proximity, so they beeline it to the coordinates by climbing the Snowdome, precariously traversing down the Coe access gully to the glacier just below the spot where the backpack and tent were found. There, the two men are located right where the coordinates said they would be. Unfortunately, they are both dead in a crevasse. Two more lives claimed by this mountain, with about 140 since records started being kept over a century ago. The first documented fatality, in 1883, was a US soldier identified as Bernard, who disappeared as a member of a supply party camping near Government Camp.

Recovery of the bodies is delayed several days due to weather, glacier conditions, and rockfall, but we start planning. As a sign of the times, we orchestrate planning via videoconferencing. Rescuers from the Crag Rats and PMR as well as sheriff's deputies gather online to study pictures and maps, listen to two rescuers from PMR explain the scene, and hear Brian give a brief overview of the route, based on his half century of knowledge of Mount Hood. We wait a day for a better weather window. And then we wait another day. Unlike rescues, the nonurgency of recovery missions gives us more discretion to organize, plan the route, gather equipment and personnel, clear our schedules, notify family, and most importantly, look for a clear weather window that is free from not only storms, wind, and rain but also soaring temperatures that can melt the ice and cause rockfall or serac collapses.

A helicopter is out of the question because "mechanical transport" is not allowed in wilderness areas based on the 1964 Wilderness Act unless life, limb, or eyesight are threatened. "Mechanical" is ill-defined in the act but, based on a 1966 interpretation, generally means motor vehicles, motorized equipment, aircraft, and "any contrivance which travels over ground, snow, or water on wheels, tracks, skids or by flotation and is propelled by a nonliving power source contained or carried on or within the device." (It's an incomprehensible quirk of humanity that mountain bikes are also not allowed despite being nonmotorized.)

Drones, meanwhile, are also out of the question. Not only are they currently not allowed in wilderness areas, but the technology isn't there yet to zip in and pick up a body. Although we are discussing using drones, we'll probably leave that for now to another team in the region. Once we had a mission in Dry Creek in the Columbia River Gorge National Scenic Area during which we used a drone from a local off-duty firefighter to confirm a fatality of a canyoneer. I wrote about the rescue in a medical journal article titled "First Report of Using Portable Unmanned Aircraft Systems (Drones) for Search and Rescue." For now, HRCSO still uses the old-school Piper Super Cub to fly over the mountain and is experimenting with a camera mounted below the belly.

For patient packaging for live rescues, we utilize one of several litters. There's the akja, of course. There's our Cascade 200 litter, a fiberglass toboggan that, when used with a wheel, is our standard device for trail rescues. And we have a titanium cage litter, which we have rigged with a harness for technical rope rescues when a subject is down a sheer cliff.

For body recoveries—and rarely for a live rescue—we most often use the lightweight Skedco litter, a vinyl sheet, originally designed for the military, that wraps the body up like a burrito and can be slid, carried, or pulled down the mountain. For this mission, we'll take two Skedcos.

Our nylon ropes are lighter and stronger than back in the days of hemp rope. But still, the ropes are heavy. PMR pioneered the use of the Hogsback kit, mentioned in chapter 2. After this mission, Gary will dub the same rope-rescue system the "Snowdome kit," in spirit of the friendly rivalry with our kindred spirits from the city. This is the rope we will use for the mission. Our rope-rescue hardware consists of modern-day incarnations of time-tested equipment. Our carabiners are made from aluminum, not steel, and have sliding and twisting locks instead of screw gates. For hauling, we still use the classic 3:1 mechanical-advantage system with carabiners, pulleys, and prusik cords. For this mission, we plan to use the simplest form of lowering the bodies: a Munter hitch on a carabiner.

Next, we go through a brief discussion of personal equipment—namely, the biggest question for Crag Rats: *Do we take skis?* Being that it's late in the year with little snow, we have to walk on dirt and rocks for 2,500 vertical feet up the Eliot Glacier and two miles. Then we climb the 500-foot Snowdome and walk down to the Coe Glacier. So we all decide not to take skis, which will later seem weird, as we Crag Rats are so used to wearing ski boots on snow. In fact, many of us don't have any boots for mountain climbing other than hard-shell ski boots and lightweight summer hikers.

I get frustrated from needing so many different boots for so many different conditions of terrain. (It's a sentiment I feel about all my mountain sports, and I've recently become disenchanted with a garage full of sports equipment and sought to pare things down to the most-used essentials.) So, in 2019, I asked Danner Boots, a Portland-based company founded in 1932, if I could design a better boot—a single boot to do every mountain rescue mission for which I didn't need ski boots. A boot that could summit Mount Hood in the summer-to-fall season, climb light snow or glacier travel with crampons, and tackle the canyons and forests of the Columbia River Gorge in spring through fall. I designed this three-season alpine boot based on the best European alpine boots with American flair. The Crag Rat Evo was built for the varied terrain of non-ski mountain rescue and for the current conditions found on Mount Hood, since we are more frequently not on snow in the summer and fall, but instead navigating looser soil, more scree, longer approaches, and remoter areas. It has a crampon-compatible lugged sole, a full rand (a strip of rubber around the boot, just above the sole, to protect from rocks and water), lacing to the toe for a precise fit, and fully synthetic uppers, which make it lightweight. This shoe is a far cry from Crag Rats' first climbing boots, improvised, you'll recall, by taking orchard boots, cutting the back away to allow more space for calf muscles when walking uphill, and pounding hobnails into the soles for traction on glaciers.

Similarly, our clothing has changed dramatically. Crag Rats went from waxed-cotton coats and black-and-white buffalo-plaid wool shirts to garments made from petroleum: nylon, polyester, polyurethane, and various other synthetic polymers that are light, durable, and warm. Although natural fibers like wool and silk don't use fossil fuels for raw materials, they are not as durable as petroleum products. I'm still using the bright orange and magenta nylon wind shirt I bought during medical school at a Patagonia store in Seattle in 1991, and I still pull on the polyester long underwear I bought during my medical internship at the Salt Lake City Patagonia outlet in 1994.

Although upgrading equipment, clothing, and boots is necessary as time progresses, I try to be cognizant whether the changes are actually beneficial to performance or are just me succumbing to consumerism. New equipment is often lighter, more compact, stronger, and better performing, but it can also be less durable, expensive, and overdesigned, with accessories that aren't useful or needed. New equipment can also have the side effect of eclipsing prior equipment, rendering old gear to the garage shelf forever, into the landfill, or hopefully gifted. Similarly, sometimes technology changes before we master or fully utilize a piece of equipment it replaces.

On the video call, we also have a truncated discussion regarding avalanche safety equipment. Since the Snowdome snowfield and the Coe access gully are both around 25 degrees, they are barely steep enough to avalanche (avalanches most often occur on slopes between 25 and 40 degrees), and this is autumn, with hard, compacted ice, so the risk of avalanches is extremely low—close to negligible. In winter, we all carry a shovel to dig someone out, a three-meter probe to poke the snow to locate a buried person, and a transceiver to broadcast an emergency signal to be detected by partners. A few of us carry airbags, a backpack with a fan or canister of compressed air that, when activated, fills a 170-liter balloon attached to the backpack, hopefully preventing burial. But we decide that, for this recovery mission, no avalanche-safety gear is needed.

By far the single most important change in mountain rescue technology has been in electronics, specifically telecommunications. Ideally, if someone calls 911, the best option is for the caller to read the GPS coordinates off their phone compass app. This gives the dispatcher the most accurate location in coordinates that are usually latitude and longitude (in SAR, we often use another coordinate system, Universal Transverse Mercator, or UTM, and we can easily convert between the two systems). However, GPS data from satellites can be inaccurate because sometimes phones cannot receive satellite signals in thick forests or under heavy cloud cover, or the signal gets reflected off steep canyon walls. In some situations, a text message can be sent to 911 dispatch when a phone call cannot go through.

Alternatively, if someone carries an emergency position-indicating locator beacon, they can send a distress call via satellite to the Search and Rescue Satellite-Aided Tracking system, run in the United States by the National Oceanic and Atmospheric Administration (NOAA). Once a distress call is received, NOAA (or its equivalent in other countries) relays coordinates to the local sheriff. Instead of receiving GPS data, the beacon can *send* GPS data. This is similar to what happened with the mission described above, except instead of sending a distress call, the phone was continuously sending his location to the hiking app.

For another method, the sheriff's office can utilize Enhanced 911 (previously called "reverse 911"), in which data from the closest cell towers are sent to dispatch. This can occur automatically when the subject in distress calls 911, or can be obtained after the 911 call if the subject's phone number is known. This information displays which tower the phone pinged and the approximate distance from the tower. Combined with other facts, such as location of parked car, these details can help rescuers determine an approximate location. But this method isn't as precise as getting the exact coordinates from the phone or a GPS locator. More recently, an iPhone 14 or newer can send a text via satellite to 911 when the phone has no cell reception.

If neither the phone nor the tower data help, one can try to extract data from a third-party app, such as a hiking or a fitness tracking app. Similarly, data can be extracted from images and videos sent via text or to social media and which have location and time data embedded in the file metadata. GPS location data can also be obtained by the sheriff from the phone carrier—AT&T, Verizon, T-Mobile, and such—but this information is stored on the carrier's server and takes more time and effort to obtain because of privacy laws.

Finally, if a cell phone, tower, or app doesn't work out, there are some newer devices that can locate a cell phone that's broadcasting a signal. The cell phone location device acts as a portable cell tower (also called "small cell"); these range from aircraft-mounted to handheld devices that can pick up a cell phone that's transmitting a signal. However, we're not using these yet in Hood River County.

All of this is more complicated than I've explained: I'm a doctor, not a tele-communications engineer. But regardless, we get so much more information now than when I first started with the Crag Rats—and for sure than when the Crag Rats themselves first started. On the plus side, we have more ways than ever to search for lost or injured people, including their coordinates, whether approximate or precise. On the minus side, our searches and rescues are more complex with regard to electronic telecommunication and require a fair degree of digital sophistication. Plus, there is a tendency for people to rely on this technology when they either don't need to or otherwise could help themselves.

In addition to extracting data about a subject, we use phones extensively now as rescuers to communicate. When radios don't work, cell phones often do. We also use phone mapping apps, which have nearly fully replaced old-school paper maps and compasses: they work without cell service as long as we download the maps to our phone and can get a GPS signal. What's more, we can track an entire mission as it's happening. Rescuers log in to the mission file, and then as long as we have cell reception, everyone appears in real time on the map on our phones, just like Harry Potter's Marauder's Map.

For completeness, I need to mention that cell phones are not perfect tools and have their downfalls. They are dependent on batteries, a lack of obstacles such as buildings and deep canyons and thick clouds, the availability of cell towers, a lack of physical damage, and user skill. Meanwhile, one of the biggest personal problems I have as a rescuer today that I didn't have back in 2001 is servicing batteries. On a typical mission, I have many devices requiring power: watch, phone, SAR radio, avalanche transceiver, fan-powered avalanche airbag, and headlamp. And my medical equipment consists of battery-operated devices including a laryngoscope with a fiberoptic light for placing an advance breathing tube, a pulse oximeter for measuring heart rate and blood-oxygen level, and an automatic external defibrillator (AED). All this stuff makes preparing for missions and repacking after a mission more complicated, as I hunt down all the power cords to recharge the many devices. (For this reason, I keep my road and mountain bikes pure analog: I do not utilize a heart rate monitor, a bike computer, a power meter, or electronic shifters.)

Another modern-day issue: electromagnetic interference can block some devices from operating properly. So the very electronic equipment that is designed to save a life—heated gloves, cell phones, smartwatches, SAR radios—can all interfere with, block, or scramble the signal from another device like an avalanche transceiver.

But, much to my dismay, there is a more global issue with all this technology. The massive amount of electronic data from all devices worldwide is stored in terms of petabytes (a petabyte is one quadrillion—1,000,000,000,000,000—bytes). I have trouble grasping this. I bought my first laptop as I entered medical school specifically to write my first novel. It had a 10-megabyte hard drive. Now my cell phone has 256 gigabytes, or 26,000 times more memory than my first laptop. If you drive east of Hood River toward Idaho, you'll pass by Google and Amazon server centers near the dams in the Columbia River; they are placed here for the inexpensive hydroelectricity (and backed up with both batteries and diesel generators). Data storage, data transmission, and electronic communication create the need for a massive amount of energy, one of the hidden costs of telecom. So as we consume and generate data via telecommunication, we generate the need for more phones, batteries, antennae, towers, computers, server centers, and fiberoptic cables. And this requires more electricity, generated by any way—coal, oil, gas, hydro, wind, solar, nuclear, or some combination thereof, and none of which are completely environmentally damage-free. Too bad we can't or don't generate more electricity from garbage. Or simply reduce our need for electricity by being more efficient with its use.

This reliance on telecommunication can be frustrating and eerily unsettling. In the middle of finishing this manuscript, my new cell phone dies. Luckily, I have a work cell. Even so, without my personal cell, I am nearly paralyzed. I can't communicate via text or phone call, unless I use my work cell, and then I have only a few numbers memorized, mostly family. I can't log in to anything at the hospital or the health department because nearly all these websites require secondary authentication with my phone. And to try to get my cell fixed—we've all been here—it takes the better part of two days, hours spent on the phone and computer with customer service. When that doesn't work, I drive to the city to the phone store (after first meeting my buddies on the mountain to ski). When I finally get the phone replaced, I then need to talk with the carrier to get service restored. As a rescuer, I have AT&T FirstNet, a specific cell phone service for first responders, so if cell towers get jammed or limited in a disaster, mine will work. The lesson: make sure you have a backup way to communicate, and make sure you have some analog survival skills, be they urban, rural, frontier, or wilderness.

WE HAVE A SECOND video meeting on Friday and decide to hold the recovery for better weather. Cody Taylor, ski patroller and avalanche expert, and Leif head up the mountain that morning to check the best approach route and scout conditions. They report back that the mountain looks stable, if we have good weather. "We need to be off the mountain before the sun starts the melt midday," Cody says. "But we didn't see much rockfall."

Then, on Saturday, Brian takes a day off his orchard work and bucks out (chainsaws) the blowdown from the approach trail, clearing it for a recovery team, both to speed up the mission and make it safer. Brian knows this: he's been on a few hundred missions. I feel like I'm one of the old guys until I'm on a mission with Brian. A decade older than me and a longtime mentor, he's fit, strong, skilled, and authentic—as well as quiet and reserved. Once, when we were on our fifth mission together in a month, I looked at him and said, "I think we're out of stuff to talk about."

Now, we wait.

I remember my first Crag Rats meetings, in the early 2000s. I listened to the older guys talk, not really knowing who they were or what badasses they had been in their day. I was young, fresh, and wanted to save everyone. I knew little about rope rescue, patient packaging, radio use, and even how a mission worked. Now, I'm one who has been here for decades, so I step up to lead this body-recovery mission. This aging thing just kind of snuck up on me, like it does to us all.

I like to speculate where the next step is in technology for mountain rescue. A tram from Government Camp to Timberline Lodge is in the works.

However, this will create a car problem in "Govy," and a parking structure is being discussed—which, to me, will negatively affect the ambiance of this micro alpine town. Someday we'll likely have 24/7 tracking via GPS chips in our phones and even better battery life and data storage. Someday, satellite phones will replace cell phones, or a newer, yet unknown technology will be developed. We might have even better clothing—we already have jackets, socks, and gloves heated by batteries. We may someday use drones for delivery of SAR gear, electronic litter wheels, and electronic winches for recovery—this technology is already available. Electronics are likely to get smaller: I'm waiting for the day when we have an AED the size of a cell phone so I don't have to carry the clunky, two-pound device in my pack.

Wherever the technology takes us, the Crag Rats will, as always, adapt—perhaps with some growing pains. As a group, we still want the traditional experience of alpine climbing and hold fervently to many traditions. We still revel in human-powered ascents of big mountains and gliding down on analog skis. But we upgrade our technology with better boots and clothing, lighter and stronger ropes, lighter and faster skis—and new electronics for forecasting, communication, navigation, and safety.

Finally, five days after we found the climbers' bodies, we're a go. We assemble a recovery team and have a window of good weather. Rescuers from the Crag Rats and PMR climb to the 9,500-foot elevation on the Snowdome snowfield and climb down into the Coe Glacier seracs. Being that it's a no-fall zone, we build anchors with pickets and ice screws several hundred feet above the icefall. Two rescuers hike into the crevasse, tie the rope to the first dead man's harness, and haul out the body.

Yank, pull, drag.

Then we repeat the process with the second body.

Once we drag the bodies out of the crevasse, out of the serac field, and up to Snowdome, it is eleven a.m., much earlier than we expected, as the warm temperatures kept the bodies from being frozen into the ice. Gary and I quickly package the bodies into black body bags and then into the Skedco litters.

I radio command. Stage one completed.

"So, command said we should bring the bodies down to Snowdome and leave them for another day," I say, recounting the radio traffic that others have overheard.

"It's pretty early," Gary says.

"How long will it take to get them down Snowdome? It's about two thousand feet, so maybe five lowers with the six-hundred-foot rope?"

"Maybe an hour or so?" Gary says optimistically. "We have lots of people."

"Should we try to do the haul-out all in one day?" I ask the team. "If so, I'm going to ask command for more people for the carryout on the lower mountain."

"It's only eleven—let's get it done so we don't have to come back," Gary says.

"We don't want to have to come back," someone else says, and everyone agrees. Leaving something undone is not in our nature—it's awkward and unnerving.

I radio command: "We are bringing the packages down the Snowdome. Probably be at the bottom at one p.m. We'll need help getting down to Cloud Cap. Requesting more ground resources."

Utilizing the strong, light, thin Snowdome rope, we complete six consecutive lowers. For anchors, we use low tech: pickets and ice axes. To add friction, we brake with a low-tech Munter hitch on a carabiner. The lowering goes quickly, as the Skedco-packaged bodies slide easily over the snow. When the bodies get bogged down on a suncup, a deep depression in the snow caused by solar radiation and heating, someone grabs them and yanks, and the sliding continues. We take turns building anchors, running the belay rope, and serving as litter attendants. As the eight of us on the recovery team make our way down Snowdome, we gather more people who hiked partway up to help.

Once we're back on rocks, we still have two thousand feet to descend, over boulders for several hours, until we reach the Timberline Trail. Hugh and Cody walk up from the trail to meet us on the west moraine. The west moraine has three or four microdrainages between Compass and Eliot Creeks. With the receding glacier, the snow and ice are gone, so we drag the bodies over rocks.

"Hey, I've got the best route down for you," Hugh says when we encounter him hiking up.

"Great," I say. As I've burned through two radio batteries, Hugh passes me his radio. "Lead us."

We follow Hugh to the bottom of the Compass Creek drainage; around three p.m., we hit the Timberline Trail. There, we run into Clackamas County and Pacific Northwest SAR trail teams in bright orange shirts. We drop the two heavy Skedcos on the trail at the foot of the fresh rescuers, say a quick, "Thanks, guys," and walk off down the trail, exhausted, with barely a handoff. The ground teams bring the bodies the last mile across the Timberline Trail, over Eliot Creek, and back up to Cloud Cap Inn. The fifteen-hour operation concluded at seven p.m.

I scarf a grocery-store turkey sandwich that someone from the sheriff's office brought up and sit on the inn's porch with Gary, Cully, Lisa, and Leif. There are fifty people coming in and out of the building, sitting on the deck, going to and from cars. People are hanging out for a debrief, mingling but also half getting ready to leave. We pack up and head home, letting Rick stay behind to close up.

Months later, when I'm skiing with Cully, we have our typical robust conversation about ski technology, parenting, the latest financial instruments, and maximizing our retirements via our common employer, the local hospital. Then I turn to a discussion about Crag Rats. "At some point, you'll have to take over as medical director," I tell Cully, who's ten years my junior.

"Yeah, some day," he says.

I have another conversation with Lisa and her husband, John, many days later on a similar topic, probably when we are riding a chairlift on a mission or hiking up Eagle Creek on a mission or eating raclette at their house. By now the Crag Rats have brought our skills, our technology, and our training up to speed. We are hailed to Mount Jefferson, Mount Rainier, the Olympics, Mount St. Helens, and Mount Adams to help. Clackamas and Multnomah call us frequently. But we've got one other problem that technology can't solve: we still need more members so that we have enough people to respond to increasing numbers of rescues.

"We need more rescuers—younger, skilled, motivated," Lisa says. It's easier to get people in their fifties, as their careers are solid and maybe even moving to flexible hours, their kids are grown up, and their finances are secure. Plus, fifty-year-olds are often smart and fit: smart because of life lessons learned, and fit because they have the time to exercise. But we need young people, people like Brian Hukari, who joined at age eighteen, fifty years ago, along with his brother, Bruce, and his climbing buddies Jerry and Jim Bryan.

"We've never recruited before," I say. "This might be a hard sell to the membership."

"We need more people," Lisa repeats.

"It's dangerous when we do rescues with too few," John chimes in. "Any litter carryout should be a minimum of six people."

"Agree."

Recruiting is a big transition and a major break from one hundred years of culture: we've never, ever done this. Then I realize we have another reason beyond just the need for more people for rescues. In the past, we had second-, third-, and even fourth-generation Crag Rats, the so-called legacy members. But this has become less common nowadays. We need to bring new people into the culture, to carry on our customs and traditions. This task may not be easy, given our fairly eclectic and protective group (euphemisms perhaps for *surly* and *stodgy*). How do we find these people? After the ski-patrol/firefighter/guide cohort, we got a few members per year, of great quality. With the first young cohort in several years, Leif came first, soon followed by Elliott, Jon Gehrig, and Maurizio.

I have a conversation with Gary when we are out on a bike ride, and he has a brilliant synopsis: "We need alpinists who can ski. The rescue stuff, we can teach them. But the basic mountain skills need to be solid." This resonates with me, and I agree. We can't teach people to love the mountains; they have to come to the Crag Rats with the fire, the passion, and the skills of uphill skiing, cramponing, and climbing all night in a storm.

Meanwhile, Lisa develops a good filtering system in which prospective members need to take certain mandatory steps: come to trainings, social outings, and work parties; take the online basic incident command courses; and get CPR certified. Similarly, we institute a one-year probation period under the guidance of Paul Crowley: if a new member doesn't complete the components in a year, they are dropped.

On another ski day, the topic comes up again. "We have a good crew," I say to Meredith. "We still need more people."

"No, we need more Lisas," she says with a smile, referring to Lisa's enthusiasm, expertise, and commitment.

"Yeah, we need more Lisas," I repeat.

Upon drafting this manuscript, I decide that I can be one of two people: I can be the guy who wants to hold on to techniques and equipment because this is the way we've always done them. Institutional knowledge is important in an all-volunteer club where the people change over the decades but the landscape remains static. But that's never been my modus operandi. I've always embraced new technology and techniques. Alternatively, I can be the wise, old guy in the surf lineup, present and giving advice periodically, but letting the young guys take over the wave and push the boundaries to better, stronger, faster. As a parent, I know that sometimes it's important to provide advice and oversight, but that other times it's just as important to let my daughters roll with their program, even if they have snafus. But I think there may be a third option: utilize what I've learned for the greater good *and* find another capacity and role in the Crag Rats that fosters mountain safety, mountain rescue, and possibly even positive global change.

I felt like I was at the top of my game during the Coe Glacier mission: able to lead forty people, high on the glacier, teamed up with my best friends, doing a huge community service. But for the first time ever, I started counting years. Is this what people do? I'd long joked with friends that I'd scuba dive or fly-fish or river-raft some day when I'm not able to rip on a mountain bike or kitesurf ocean waves or ski off the summit of Mount Hood. That someday was always a mythical, far-off date. But for the first time, closing in on sixty, I wondered, how many years do I have? How many years before I'll no longer be able to head to the legendary mountains and be a Crag Rat?

I decide Brian will be my yardstick. He's still one of the strongest, most skilled, and most knowledgeable as he approaches seventy. In fact, New Year's

Day 2024 we'll stand atop Mount Hood on a climb with Leif, Elliott, and Asa. So I decide I'll stop at the same age he eventually stops. But the next mission, the final of 2022, shows Brian's dedication and passion—he'll likely never stop. Which means I probably won't either.

CHAPTER 12

DECEMBER: FITNESS IS NOT ENOUGH

My phone buzzes in my pocket, and I ignore it for a second. It's late in the year, the end of the rescue season. Autumn transitions to winter. Warm fall days turn cold, symbolized by the bright bigleaf maple leaves that turn a spectrum of colors from green to yellow to deep red, and the lemony larch needles. When the sun is out, we hit the trails to mountain bike and run. Despite clear days, we bundle up in full sleeves and leggings. Every day could be our last of good weather. When the rain arrives, we anxiously check the freezing level, wind, precipitation amounts, webcams, forecasts, and telemetry data, all courtesy of a collection of modern-day websites and apps: the National Weather Service, the Northwest Avalanche Center, the Oregon Department of Transportation, and ski resorts.

When it does snow on the mountain, we track temperatures, snow depth, and snow level obsessively. Ron and I know which locations are skiable with a just foot of snow—or less if the snow is dense with a high water content—because they are grassy and sans rocks. When snow is followed by rain and cold to create a firm, icy surface, we know which south-facing slopes are first to soften in the midmorning sun. When it's windy up high in early season, we know which runs to avoid because the wind is likely to expose rocks, and which gullies to ski because they are likely filled in by wind-deposited granules. Part of this is science, much is years of experience, and a skosh is trial and error, as in, "Let's give it a try—it might be good!" Or, "Remember when we tried that last December and it was horrible?"

I've spent most of my life in the Pacific Northwest and have learned to live the seasons—that is to say, to take advantage of what each has to offer. Winter is for powder skiing and occasional trips abroad to warm, sunny beaches or foreign mountains, waves, and trails. Spring is the time for invigorating bike rides and sunny, high-alpine volcano skiing. Summer is full-on: mountain biking, surfing, kitesurfing, trail running, and cycling; occasional summits of Mount Hood; and frequent trips to the coast. Fall is the time for beautiful mountain-bike rides and trail runs . . . until it rains. Now, it's pouring rain, so it's a good time to get much-neglected house chores checked off the list. When I say "house chores," I really mean outdoor-gear maintenance. I wax skis, replace bike tires, order new kitesurfing gear, and wash ski-boot liners that have become stinky after many long days of ski-touring.

Phone buzz. I ignore it again to finish this paragraph, since Crag Rats rescues and adventures have interrupted the writing of this manuscript so many times already.

This month, Crag Rats also have another tradition: the December business meeting, during which we'll elect a new Pip Squeak, a.k.a. secretary, to start a six-year stint as an officer. It's a long meeting because we also approve next year's budget and have many lively conversations about a new vehicle, new uniforms, a work party at Deno's to help with snowcat repairs, more deets on the new roof for Cloud Cap Inn, and the upcoming banquet. We also vote in new members; this year, as we have in others, we agree to accept just a handful. We are excited to usher in strong, capable, high-caliber members, including Justin McBride (Air Force 304th Rescue Squadron parajumper), Mick King (Navy SEAL and ski patroller), and Dillon Mosnot (a transfer from PMR with a decade of mountain rescue experience). Nate Gebhard (ophthalmologist), Kirra Paulus (Hood River native and emergency medicine resident doctor), and Will Bibbo all jumped in and joined rescues as soon as they signed up.

Phone buzz. Ping. Hold on; here we go again. Now, another mission, hopefully the final one of the year. Unfortunately, it's in the middle of a storm. Rain down in the valley, snow above five thousand feet.

"Missing person, Timberline Trail, need hasty team." It's rainy, dank, and cold. I wait a few minutes to see if another coordinator picks up the call: Meredith grabs it. Then I wait a few more minutes to see if Meredith can get a crew together, because I really don't want to go.

"Did you get a crew?" I text her. If I call, I fret that she may talk me into going.

"Yup. John Rust and Heiko." Two is enough for a hasty team. I put my phone on "Do Not Disturb" so I can get interrupted sleep. But in the morning, I wake up as usual at five o'clock to a slew of texts. John and Heiko hiked all night in the rain and wet snow. No luck. Need more responders. Here we go again. I meet the Crag Rats at the county yard at seven. While we're deploying, some behind-the-scenes folks are working the technology. Cully needs to stay home because he's on call for general surgery at the hospital, yet he still participates. He pores over data from the subject's cell phone. Meanwhile, Meredith finds a video of the missing person on Facebook and uses a phone app to decrypt the metadata: the time, date, and location of the video put the person on the Elk Cove Trail—way up in the alpine on the north side, near the trail's intersection with the round-the-mountain Timberline Trail—midafternoon the day before, just a few miles from where the car is found at the same trailhead.

The sheriff's office asks the FBI for a cell phone ping. It's significantly imprecise, as I explained in the last chapter: the data show distance and a swath of probability that's about two miles wide and spans two steep, rocky trails separated by a one-thousand-foot-high ridge that is thickly forested with sky-reaching Douglas-fir and hemlock. The deep, narrow canyons and thick gray cloud cover likely impact the accuracy of the signal. In the arc of probability, a most likely point has been determined—how they got that is a mystery to me.

Hugh, Meredith, and I scurry a mile up the Elk Cove Trail and then bush-whack uphill to the base of a cliff to the most likely coordinates we've been provided. Our pants get soaked with dew. I put on a plastic emergency poncho, but it gets shredded in minutes. Meredith looks at me and laughs. Hugh shakes his head and smiles. Once we reach the cliff, we need to scale the twenty-foot rock face, which is wet and covered in moss. Hugh, being the best climber, ascends with ease by clinging to the wet rock, bracing off a tree, and using me as a spotter in case he slips. For the first few feet, I hold his boot against the rock. Then he crests the cliff and anchors a rope by looping it around a wiry white oak. Meredith and I follow, self-belaying with a prusik hitched onto the rope in case we fall. Once atop the cliff, we leave the rope set up and clamber two hundred feet up a steep hillside that's covered with thick brush. In twenty minutes, we reach the provided cell phone coordinates.

Meanwhile, Brian and Gary have hiked up the Pinnacle Ridge Trail to the top of the ridge above the coordinates, then clambered and bushwhacked down-hill toward us. Two hours after we left the truck, our two teams converge at the coordinates. The slope is steep, with downed logs, large boulders, and a thick understory of salal, vine maple, and poison oak, which I mostly unsuccessfully try to avoid. We attempt a grid search, but straight lines are impossible with the thick foliage and downed logs. We inspect high-probability areas like ravines, cliffs, clusters of white oak, and rocky outcrops.

We find nothing, which is disheartening. We are now sixteen hours past the time the hiker was reported missing—things are not looking good. Additionally, as highly focused, highly motivated rescuers, we are accustomed to completing a task, finding a missing person, rendering medical care, and hauling some-one from a crevasse or canyon. Now: we find nothing. Moreover, it's a feeling that's more common with a greater number of rescues. At one time, when we had fewer than ten missions a year, the occasional sad situation was manage-able. Now, though, these sad outcomes are more common, and their cumula-tive effects wear on us. That said, I'm with all my friends, tromping through a secluded part of the foothills where no one would ever go, on a beautiful, sunny fall day. I focus on the positive.

After a while, we decide that we have adequately cleared the area. We are drenched from the wet foliage, cold from the brisk autumn air, and tired. The sun steams the moisture from our clothes, making the day seem more mystical.

"Let's go home," I say.

"Okay. Let's rap the last pitch. Hugh can come last and pull the rope," Gary says.

"Sure," Hugh says.

The search will continue the next day.

I get home by three thirty p.m., dump my clothes in the washer, and scrub my body with soap and a loofah to rid myself of any urushiol oil from poison oak. Then Deputy Chris Guertin calls and asks me to help plan tomorrow's search.

"Do you want me to come back up?" I ask, nonplussed.

"Sure, if you don't mind," he says. So I drive back to the staging area at the Elk Meadows trailhead and pore over maps with a crew of sheriff's deputies to plan the next day's mission.

Then I head home again.

Sometime around nine p.m., I get another call from Guertin. "I need another crew," he says. "We got another set of coordinates we need to check out."

"More accurate this time?" I really want to go to bed.

"Her family was able to get into her computer, open a hiking app, and find her track. So we've got good coordinates. Not too far from where we were searching, all the way to the Timberline Trail. I want to check this out tonight."

This time, instead of Meredith, it's me who sends out the group text to call for rescuers. Leif and Brian deploy, even though Brian was out hiking all day with us. I go back to bed.

The phone rings again after midnight: "We found her," Guertin says. "She's alive," he adds. "At the bottom of a cliff. We'll need a rope team."

We get out of bed again.

Many days later, I read an article from Colorado about missing trail runners. The gist of the story: "Fitness is not enough to stay safe in remote mountains where risks are amplified." The story discusses trail runners who achieve monumental feats of athleticism, running long distances in difficult terrain; however, they do so with minimal packs that have little food, water, and spare clothing, and if they go missing or get into trouble, there's very little margin for error.

In addition to growing crowds and exploding communication technology, as discussed in the prior two chapters, this is a third trend that has impacted our mountain: the way people interact with wilderness. They go farther, faster, deeper, lighter. Bigger adventures with less gear. Greater distances in less time. The landscape zooms by. This is not a new trait of humans: Feyerabend and Brownlee, from chapter 3, wanted to be the first to summit Mount Hood on New Year's Day in 1927, an outing that led to Brownlee's tragic disappearance. But it is a growing and expanding trend with the growing and expanding population. This push toward fast and light is as admirable as it is risky. The woman we went to look for was doing just that: trail running the Timberline Trail, solo, with minimal gear, in chancy weather.

As I wrote about in the prologue, there was the man I met in the Timberline Lodge parking lot during the pandemic who was heading for the summit wearing nothing but tights, running shoes, traction spikes, and a ten-liter running vest. While he turned back at the Pearly Gates, had he continued, his story might have had a very different outcome. And you may also recall, back in chapter 6, the controversy in the *Oregonian* about the climber who was criticized for climbing Mount Hood without crampons in the 1950s. But the difference today is the speed of transmission of information and the greater number of people looking to be the "first" or the "fastest."

Similarly, on another pandemic ski on the south side one June, I finished my ski-tour and saw a man in the parking lot wearing shorts, ski boots, and no shirt. *Odd*, I thought. Then I packed up and went home. Later I found out he was a climber and skier who set an FKT for climbing and skiing Mount Hood. Sporting a tiny pack, skinny skis, shorts, and a T-shirt, Jack Kuenzle bolted up the mountain and skied down in one hour, thirty-one minutes, thirty-one seconds; the previous FKT for a self-supported trip was Jason Dorais in 2014 at one hour, forty-four minutes, three seconds. Not just light and fast, but rocket speed, wearing nearly nothing, carrying nearly nothing. With essentially no margin for safety.

FKTs became popular during the pandemic when formal competitions in outdoor sports like trail running and ultrarunning were canceled. As way to keep competing, folks attempted to complete routes faster than anyone before. In fact, a de facto competition recently ensued for two pairs of climbers attempting to put the first American woman on the summit of all fourteen peaks eight thousand meters or higher. They were on Shishapangma, a Himalayan giant, when an avalanche struck in October 2023. The American Anna Gutu and her Nepalese guide Mingmar Sherpa and the American Gina Marie Rzucidlo and her guide Tenjen Sherpa were all killed by an avalanche.

If FKTs are not enough, people also look for new and different ways of being the first when the "first summit" or the "first climb" up a route have already been claimed. Routes are combined to create new FKTs. For example, a trend on the Cascade volcanoes is to complete an "infinity loop": climbing to the summit one way, descending another way, running halfway around the mountain back to the starting point, climbing again, descending again, and running halfway back around the mountain in the other direction to regain the starting point. On Mount Hood, for example, an infinity-loop climber starts at Timberline Lodge, ascends the south side to the summit, descends the north side to Cloud Cap Inn, runs half of the round-the-mountain trail back to Timberline Lodge, climbs back up the south side again, descends back down the north side again, and runs the other half of the round-the-mountain trail back to Timberline Lodge. On Mount Hood, the men's FKT self-supported infinity loop took eighteen hours, fifty-three minutes, fifty seconds. There's no women's time. On Mount Rainier, the infinity loop is burlier, almost double the elevation and distance as Mount Hood: ten thousand feet up and down twice, and around the ninety-three-mile Wonderland Trail. The men's self-supported FKT is two days, six hours, seventeen minutes, forty-five seconds; the women's self-supported FKT is three days, twenty-two hours, nineteen minutes, thirty-eight seconds.

And if the infinity loops are not enough for you, you can always invent another route and another FKT. The Portland-based ultrarunner Christof

Teuscher posted a Mount Adams summit, walk to Mount Hood, and Mount Hood summit—158 miles and 40,000 feet of climbing—in two days, sixteen hours, forty-eight minutes. He posted a Triple Wonderland Trail run—three times around Mount Rainier for 279 miles—in five days, eleven hours, forty-nine minutes.

Aside from inventing new feats, the internet transmits more information faster, which can be both wildly beneficial and wildly consequential. Firsthand reports arrive instantly—sometimes people make social media posts from the summit of Mount Hood. This can be helpful when planning a summit bid. On the other hand, you have to make sure you're getting accurate information, which can be difficult. One person's "safe and fun route," may be too challenging for a novice climber. People can post inaccurate information. The speed and volume have magnified the situation, though boasting, exaggerating, and not telling the full story have not necessarily changed over the course of one hundred years.

PMR has addressed this issue with a robust social media program for mountain conditions and safety on Facebook, Instagram, YouTube, and a podcast. They partner with the Mountain Shop in Portland for lectures. They lend not just an authoritative, informative voice but also disseminate objective data—"The fumarole crack is open at Devils Kitchen"—coupled with expert advice—"We recommend you go to climber's right to get around it." But, for now, we Crag Rats have neither time for nor a stake in social media. For one, we've traditionally not embraced social media or public outreach—it's just not part of our culture. But more importantly, we're just too busy. We have to run the club, train, maintain gear, maintain fitness, keep up with our personal lives of work, family, and recreation, and attend to missions. We simply don't have time to have a big internet presence.

I, too, joined in the trend of going farther and faster. During the pandemic years, I ran the volcano circumnavigation circuit. I ran the Timberline Trail in a day (forty-five miles), the Mount St. Helens Loowit Trail in a day (thirty-two miles), the Timberline Trail in a day a second time, the Three Sisters circumnavigation in a day (a physically ghastly but visually spectacular forty-nine miles), and rounded out my quest with the Rim-to-Rim-to-Rim on the Grand

Canyon (forty-five miles). That last one was hard. But going light and fast, completing routes that usually take backpackers several days, was an exhilarating achievement.

With my safety brain, I know the margin for error is less and the probability and consequence of injury and illness are higher. I found the volcano-circumnavigation summer to be exhilarating, humbling, physically and spiritually rewarding, and physically and mentally draining. It was a different connection to the mountains, with the trees, rocks, and snow zipping by in a blur and my eyes constantly scanning the trail for the next foot placement; the human-versus-mountain challenge was accentuated. If I wanted to look at the views, I had to stop. If I stopped, I prolonged the run. If I'd gotten into even a minor predicament—a sprained ankle, for example—I would have needed outside help. Knowing this, I was doubly cautious. This seemingly ridiculousness is still a connection with the wilderness, but one that's less about the solace of skiing and the experience of traveling over snow, rocks, dirt and more about being in motion in the wilderness, skillfully navigating the terrain on foot, the physical triumph, and the goal attainment.

AS YOU KNOW by now, the search for the missing trail runner on Mount Hood can end one of four ways: injured, ill, lost, or deceased. Fortunately, this story ends with survival. The woman is stuck in the early season snow: cold, hungry, thirsty, alive. She got off-trail slightly, slid down an embankment, and got stuck in a ravine. Then she was resourceful: she made a shelter under a tree, donned all her clothing, and hunkered in to wait for help—she did most things right. The whole crew—Cully, Heiko, John and Lisa, Jon Gehrig, Hugh, Gary, Ron, Meredith, Leif, Maurizio, and Elliott—empties their beds to save her, a group of good friends and skilled alpinists just doing what we do best. And the woman is so grateful and pleasant—constantly thanking us as we give her dry puffy jackets, food, water, and assistance in getting down the trail.

The Crag Rats have come a long way since I joined in 2001, and longer since 1926. We've managed to shuck some traditions intentionally. We let women join. We let out-of-county folks join. We have only one business meeting per month instead of two, swapping the second meeting for field training. And we got rid of the no-recruiting vibe, swapping in Lisa's less prescriptive, more orderly vetting procedure, which went through several spirited discussions to fine-tune.

Some traditions we retain with fervor, as these form the core of the Crag Rats: black-and-white buffalo-plaid itchy wool shirts; voting in a Pip Squeak in December; holding the socials like Steak Fry (November social at the hut), Ice Follies (September ice climbing at Cloud Cap Inn), Winter Outing (annual February ski outing at the inn), and Wood Party (October outing to restock the inn's firewood for winter); and voting for "Rat of the Year" and "Hat of the Year" at the annual banquet.

Some traditions get waylaid by lack of interest, like life membership or the rule that every member must summit Mount Hood once a year (per the minutes, this was enforced back in the 1940s and 1950s). Some functions, like the Cooper Spur Brunch, just fizzle or simply vanish. But we remain steadfast in maintaining the deep sense of purpose and what Jerry Bryan called "authenticity," most poignantly exemplified by two short anecdotes about Lisa and Gary.

One day, Lisa was hunting mushrooms after work in the forest above Parkdale when a call came in for an injured hiker on the Tamanawas Falls Trail, a popular waterfall hike on the remote east side of Mount Hood. She responded immediately, and as the first on the scene, she ran up the trail with the gear she had in her car: a canvas tote bag and a blanket that looked like it had come from her kid's bed. She was wearing sweatpants, a dirty hoodie, and running shoes. Nonetheless, she expertly orchestrated a technical rope rescue, all without any formal rescue gear.

Similarly, one summer day, Gary was riding his bike to Cooper Spur; he was midway through the one-hundred-mile ride when the callout came for an injured hiker on the Tilly Jane Trail. Since Gary was just a few miles away, he rode his bike to the trailhead, borrowed boots from a HRCSO deputy, and hiked up the trail to help carry the litter—all while wearing full cycling spandex and his bike helmet.

I have many more of these heartwarming stories. Once, a full year after a mission, Heiko, Cully, and I led the spouse of a deceased man back up to the accident site on a clear, sunny, fall day, the forest glowing in sunlight, to help her process and grieve.

And in autumn 2022, John Harlin III would do something I remain ecstatic about: organize a team climb for the Ice Follies, what used to be an ice-climbing weekend but had mostly fizzled in recent decades. John is a longtime Crag Rat, climber, and author. He left for a decade to live in Mexico and teach in Switzerland. When he came back, he jumped right back into rescues as if he'd never left and signed up as Pip Squeak. For the Ice Follies, he led a team climb of the Sunshine Route in September. I liked this idea so much that I followed John's lead, and on New Year's Day 2024, just before turning in the final first draft of this manuscript, I organized a team climb to summit Mount Hood via the Old Chute. Our team spanned the deciles: Leif and Elliott in their second, me and Asa midway, and Brian closing in on his seventh.

I try to put this in perspective: the journey of the Crag Rats, the journey of me, the journey of the mountain. And there's a final piece that's important to me: the piece about risk. Not so much risk in the moment, which I wrote about in my prior memoirs, but the risk that pertains across a life of rescues, the life of an organization, and the life of a mountain. An emerging field in first responders is called Psychological First Aid (PFA). It addresses the human side of a mission, looking at the stress both to the patient and to the rescuers. When addressing the lost, injured, or ill subject, there are five components to PFA used to help minimize stress and anguish: (1) safety, for the group and the individual; (2) calm, as people function better without calamity; (3) efficacy, working toward a group goal; (4) connection, establishing a human bond; and (5) hope, not of false promises but of finding something that's going right.

PFA is helpful during a mission, but once the mission is over and the patient is taken home or to the hospital, it's important to address the residual effects on the rescuers—the stress of the rescue on them, especially the cumulative stress of a lifetime of rescue. The military developed a stress-continuum for rescuers based on four colors: green, yellow, orange, and red.

Green is ready. This means someone is functioning optimally and is feeling mentally and physically fit and well, a.k.a. having fun. Yellow is reacting. This means someone is experiencing minor stress from the rescue: perhaps a mild feeling of anxiety or irritability, a loss of motivation and focus, or difficulty sleeping, or they're just plain tired, a.k.a. not having fun. Orange is injured. This means someone has more significant and persistent problems: depression, anxiety, sleep difficulty, guilt or shame, and a lack of sense of purpose, meaning, or hope. And finally, red is ill. The person is experiencing life impairment, symptoms so severe that they're unable to function without help, or full-on depression or anxiety with social and occupational impairment.

This stress continuum strikes a chord with me. I always hope my patients are okay, but I also hope my team is too: my daughters, my friends, the Crag Rats, and me. I begin to pay attention to this and start calling people after tough missions, bringing up difficult situations at meetings, trying to prevent anyone from reaching yellow, orange, or red by adding more medical—and, specifically, medical leadership—training. And I seek this support for myself. On the cusp of sixty at the end of writing this book, I feel that I am green (ready): feeling secure and healthy, living a full life complete with time with best friends, thrilling missions, success outshining tragedy, and opportunities to mentor and educate. And I am searching for new meaning and perhaps a new role on this team that I will never abandon.

Similarly, the Crag Rats are green: good to go, having fun, saving lives with dedication, expertise, and passion. We are, as Bill Pattison said, at the top of our game, with the skills, experience, and sense of camaraderie that put us on par with the nation's top teams.

Unfortunately, Mount Hood—if not the world itself—is not green, but probably somewhere between reacting (yellow) and injured (orange), considering the roads, buildings, dams, and clear-cuts directly impacting the land. And the pollution and climate change altering, among other things, the glaciers. And the overuse and ever-more-reckless, social-media-fueled recreation taking place on Mount Hood's trails, glaciers, canyons, and forests. I don't know the future of this mountain. I don't know the fate of the glaciers, forests, streams, and moraines. But in my tenure as a Crag Rat, we've already seen changes. The mountain will outlive me, but in what form, I cannot speculate.

In this book, I don't talk much about the volunteer life's effect on family and close friends. Like any vocation and avocation, our personal need to gravitate toward mountain rescue impacts others. Perhaps that's why most of my best friends are Crag Rats. Unlike other avocations, mountain rescue is marked by two extraordinary challenges: the unpredictable nature of rescue calls and the omnipresent duel of a deep love of the alpine with high-stakes risk.

When I ask Maureen, Cully's wife, about this, she acknowledged Cully's devotion to the Crag Rats for the selflessness of helping strangers, the draw of adventure, the deep friendships, and the opportunity to hone mountaincraft and even improve parenting skills by becoming more thoughtful. But she also vividly recalls specific rescues or accidents that had caused her consternation, worry, and frustration: the Eagle Creek fire from chapter 9, during which Cully returned from an all-nighter just hours before Maureen went into labor with their first child; the mid-pandemic body recoveries on the Coe Glacier from chapter 11; a middle-of-the-night fumarole rescue in which Cully dropped into the hole in the mountain; and the death of our mutual friend, Cory Johnston, an athlete, surgeon, and father, who died in 2019 on his forty-seventh birthday while skiing Mount Hood. Maureen says, amid the worry, that it comes down to trust. Trust in Cully. Trust in the Crag Rats.

I call Tami Hukari, Brian's wife of forty years.

"Do you worry about Brian?"

"No—not as long as he's had enough to eat and sleep," she says with confidence. I recalled a mission on which Tami had brought Brian food and dry clothes as he responded directly from the ski resort. "I figure you guys take care of each other. Although the general public sees risky behavior, you guys take calculated risks," she adds.

When I mention Brian will turn seventy just before I turn sixty, Tami says, "I tell him to let someone else drive after a mission."

Indeed, getting old has not been something I want to think about.

A few months after our record year, I sit for a podcast with a local Hood River engineer my daughters' age to discuss, among other things, the Crag Rats. At the end of the podcast, he asks me a difficult question: "What do young people of the future want?" My first answer would usually be, "Do we have another hour?" as the heady topic is complex. But off the cuff, I say, "We all as humans want clean air, healthy food to eat, and some sort of security in [our] basic needs. [The young people of the future] will want some sort of financial security: health care that doesn't cost a huge amount that's good quality, a transportation system that gets them to cool places that doesn't cost a lot of money or destroy the places they are trying to get to. How that exactly looks, no one exactly knows, because there's probably technology that's yet to be invented. Somehow, we'll have to set up future generations so they have that opportunity."

Now, after some time to reflect, I think I can give a more complete answer. In my opinion, the young people of the future will want what we all want now (though, because of greed, human fallibility, and short-sightedness, so often fail to attain): clean air and water; security with finances, lodging, food, and health care; transportation that's inexpensive, efficient, and clean; a good place to make a living—nice bosses, a pleasant environment, meaningful work; nice people as friends; fun activities and entertainment; and a world that is safe and secure, as free as possible from both natural disasters and human-caused ones.

As a doctor—whether it's in the emergency room, the clinic, the health department, or on the side of a mountain—I'm programmed to diagnose and treat. Identify problem, find solution. So, with all the troubles on Mount Hood, in our country, and in our world, I'm just going to continue to solve problems because it's what I do as a mountain rescue doctor. I can see the solutions—they are as clear as the cerulean morning sky above the stark Eliot Glacier from the vantage at Cloud Cap Inn.

In the end, the mountain will continue. The Crag Rats will continue. I will someday not, but I will use the rest of my life to help, to be part of this team, to revel in the high alpine, and, along with my best friends, to save people's lives.

CODA

As this book closes, you might breathe a sigh of relief at the conclusion of the busiest rescue season ever in the one hundred years of Crag Rats. But it doesn't really stop for us. Doesn't even slow down. At the opening day of 2023, nearly a century after the missions for Jack Strong, Calvin White, and Leslie Brownlee, and Al Feyerabend, we have another mission.

That January 1, beneath a cold, clear sky and traveling on snowy roads, we respond to a backcountry snowboarder with a blown knee. He's nearly in the East Fork of the Hood River, at the bottom of a popular backcountry-ski run called Gunsight. We know exactly where this is but log the GPS coordinates into the mapping app anyway. Hugh is at the resort skiing, and Wes and Elliott are working at the resort: they all respond immediately. Leif, Eric, Cully, and I are at home, with our ski gear already poised for a powder day, so we jump into SAR 1 within ten minutes and speed up the mountain. At the staging area, Bennett Pass Sno-Park, Eric and I ski up Bennett Pass Road to the top of the clear-cut, then ski downhill to the creek. The skiing is worse than awful: hard, firm snow with breakable crust. The clear-cut is no longer really a meadow, since it has been a couple of decades since the harvest. Rather, it's a swath with monochromatic, twenty-foot-tall Douglas-fir scattered like Christmas trees across the slope.

We reach the man, who is solo on a snowboard, and soon thereafter Hugh and Jon Gehrig come in hot with the carbon akja, along with two AMR paramedics on snowshoes. Lisa has arrived too. It's early afternoon, the sun is high, the sky remains clear, and the wind is minimal. The snow is dry and crunchy from the crust.

I inject some pain medicines in the injured man's arm. Eric and I splint his knee, bundle him in warm clothing, wrap a chemical heat blanket around him, and gently place him in the akja. Then we start the long pack out. Wes is knowledgeable about the area and takes command of the extrication: we'll be skiing uphill on a hiking trail that goes unused in the winter. I volunteer to take the first round on the back handles of the akja because I want more experience and proficiency. We cautiously make our way out of the creek, navigating the bumpy slope and awful snow that's littered with obstacles like buried logs and snow-covered creeks. Then, strenuously, we drag the litter up the slightly uphill trail. In a few minutes, I hand off so that someone else can have a go. It takes an hour to go a half mile. Quickly, we are back at Bennett Pass.

We must wait another fifteen minutes for Lisa. She has the task of skiing out with a medic on snowshoes; they have fallen behind, but Lisa won't leave her post.

And then it's over. A fast, efficient rescue. I'm really proud of this crew and thankful that I have this rare chance in life to be part of such a close-knit group and of the Crag Rats' one-hundred-year history. And I'm much less grumpy about our quirky traditions. We finished the 2022 season with sixty days of missions—more than one per week. And now well into the subsequent years, the rescues keep coming. In this book, I left out many rescue stories that were duplicative but equally thrilling. There were simply too many tales to tell here, and the tales keep on coming.

I would be remiss not to mention that as I edit this coda midway through 2024, we're likely pushing another record year. We have had seven missions in ten days, which came smack in the middle of my review of this manuscript's copyedit.

Friday morning just after July Fourth, a woman was hiking the Wahclella Falls Trail and was hit by a boulder, which knocked her fifty feet down a steep embankment. The Cascade Locks Fire Department is first on the scene and provides stabilizing medical care. Hugh, Jon Gehrig, Joe, Jay, and I race to the trailhead. We rig two ropes, I'm lowered with the litter, and then we haul the patient up to the trail and carry her to the awaiting ambulance.

Then, early the next day, a man falls in "the Pocket" swimming hole on Mosier Creek. Although some twenty people are on the scene from Hood River Fire, Mid-Columbia Fire and Rescue, Mosier Fire, Life Flight Network, and the Wasco County Sheriff's Office, they need us—Heiko, Hugh, Jon Gehrig, Tim, Walter, and me—to haul him fifty feet up the trail with our ropes.

Just as I walk in the door after the Mosier Creek mission, my phone pops again. A climber tumbled seven hundred feet down Old Chute, landed in the Hot Rocks fumarole, and sustained trauma to his head, chest, and ankle. Brian, Gary, Cody, Mick, and I speed up to Timberline Lodge in SAR 1, check in with Deputy Scott Meyers, jump on the chairlift, and climb in near record time—a little over an hour—to Hogsback. Gary takes lead over the Crag Rats, the Forest Service climbing rangers, the AMR RAT team, PMR, and bystanders. I take medical. A helicopter from the 189th Aviation Regiment lands on the Hogsback, and we load the patient directly into the chopper. Once the machine flies away, we collect our packs and ski back to SAR 1, just three and a half hours after we left.

But we have little time to rejoice, as the rescues keep stacking up in the subsequent days. A man suffers from dehydration and heat exhaustion on Eagle Creek and needs to be walked out. A person is lost near Panorama Point and is found alive. A hiker on the Timberline Trail is injured and needs to be carried out in a litter. A hiker falls two hundred feet off the Triple Falls Trail, and we have to conduct a complicated rope rescue at night, deep in a canyon. A family of five on a trail near Indian Mountain are out of water and suffering from heat exhaustion.

In addition to missions, other duties compound the time commitment. We need to write reports, debrief, retrieve our vacuum mattress from the Portland trauma center, locate the AED that was left in someone's pack, clean the ropes, and replace chemical heat blankets.

UPON FINISHING THIS book and reflecting on the busiest year of rescues, one century of Crag Rats history, and the one mountain that's the backdrop to all this,

I hope to leave a reader with a final thought. Not one of hanging off the cliff or skiing up Mount Hood in the middle of the night in the middle of a storm. Not one of utilizing high-tech ropework and cell phone coordinates to save a life. Not one of the paramount values of tradition, mentorship, change, and growth. Not another story about Gary, Hugh, Cully, Lisa, John, Meredith, Ron, Brian, or Heiko—although any one of those myriad stories would be riveting.

No, the final sentiment I want to leave you with is one of gratitude for that which Crag Rats and Mount Hood have given me. It's not just the thrilling adventure. Not just the lives saved and the lives lost. Not just the deep, high-value, lifelong friendships and camaraderie. But rather, it's the tastes in our mouths and the fires in our guts that are bred from pure passion, intermixed with grit, determination, and enthusiasm, from the tedious, lackluster rescues in the lowlands to the awe and beauty we feel when saving lives amid the high-alpine glaciers, cliffs, crevasses, arêtes, and seracs.

We—all human beings—exercise the ability to make the small changes that create a better world. For us Crag Rats, it's saving a life, but for others, the passion for creating something good could be directed toward anything that makes our world safer, kinder, and healthier. Whereas the health of the mountain is most poignant in these pages, it's really the health of all the high mountains, vast oceans, expansive deserts, thick forests, deep canyons, and even the urban greenspaces of cities that is paramount. It's the health of humanity and of our home, Planet Earth. Hopefully you will take the lessons and tales on these pages to heart, to somewhat understand the risks and rewards, passions and pitfalls, and struggles and triumphs of mountain rescue, but also gain insight into why we love this singular place. And possibly take some steps, however small, to help people be safer, to help the Crag Rats be safer, to help the mountain survive, and to help humanity survive.

Indeed, I have experienced loss, more deeply than I describe in these pages. During the years spent crafting this project, a dear friend, Jennifer Donnelly, died, and I lost my mother. Lifelong, devoted Crag Rat Todd Wells passed away from cancer, nonagenarian and seventy-year veteran Crag Rat Bill Pattison died, I lost my friend and the Hood River surgeon Cory Johnston to a fall on Mount

Hood, and Kent Lambert died at age eighty-nine, just a few months after I interviewed him for this book and honored him at the banquet for serving two stints as a Crag Rats officer for twelve years total.

Readers of my second memoir will recall the near-death ski accident I had more than a decade ago. During the crafting of this book mid-pandemic, I was nearly caught in an avalanche while on a backcountry ski trip to the Wallowa Mountains. And later, I was impaled by an Atlantic needlefish on a kitesurfing trip to the Outer Banks, North Carolina, and required emergency surgery. And after that, a ski binding failed when I was skiing the Old Chute and I took a short ride in a small avalanche (I self-arrested quickly and efficiently). It's not that I'm prone to accidents; it's that I'm so often outside, in the world's glaciers, powder snow, ocean waves, forest trails, canyons, and rivers, because of my deep passion—call it an obsession—with being in motion in nature.

But these personal stories of love, loss, and injury are best saved for another time. At this very moment, I'm trying to tidy up a draft of this book; my ski boots are on the dryer, my climbing skins are on the rack, and my radio is on the charger. It's six thirty a.m., and I've already received a half-dozen text messages from Heiko, Cully, Eric, and Leif about heading to the mountain. Ron and I have already traded a few texts about the weather and snow conditions. Meredith grumbles about getting up early, which makes me smile. It's a powder day today. We are going skiing.

ACKNOWLEDGMENTS

Although many colleagues in mountain rescue contributed directly and indirectly to these stories, I have a few specific people to acknowledge.

My daughters, Skylar Van Tilburg and Avrie Van Tilburg, have supported me in myriad ways.

Joelle Delbourgo, my agent, has been a longtime believer in my passion.

Emily White at Mountaineers Books acquired the manuscript and gave excellent input early on. Beth Jusino was a superb project editor. Hannah Wallace edited the initial drafts. Matt Samet completed a comprehensive developmental edit. Jenn Kepler completed a detailed copyedit. Jen Grable did the layout and design, and Erin Greb drew the maps.

A number of Crag Rats reviewed a draft of the manuscript, particularly Tom Rousseau, Gary Szalay, Eric Peterson, Cully Wiseman, Don Pattison, Meredith Martin, and Jerry Bryan.

Arthur Babitz and Lisa Commander at the History Museum of Hood River County assisted with historical images. Jerry Bryan, Corey Arnold, Daniel O'Neil, Peg Falconer, and Theresa Silveyra also provided images.

The Hood River County Sheriff's Office and the Clackamas County Sheriff's Office gave me approval to write these stories.

Daniel O'Neil

ABOUT THE AUTHOR

Christopher Van Tilburg is an American physician and author specializing in emergency and wilderness medicine. He is the author of twelve books on outdoor recreation, wilderness medicine, and international travel, including two previous memoirs on mountain rescue, *Mountain Rescue Doctor: Wilderness Medicine in the Extremes of Nature* and *Search and Rescue: A Wilderness Doctor's Life-and-Death Tales of Risk and Reward*.

Van Tilburg earned a BS magna cum laude in science communication from the University of Portland and an MD from the University of Washington School of Medicine.

He is on staff at Providence Hood River Memorial Hospital in Hood River, Oregon, where he works in occupational and travel medicine, in the emergency department, and at the Mountain Clinic at the Mt. Hood Meadows ski resort. In addition, he has worked around the world as an expedition doctor, an educator, a cruise ship doctor, and a team leader for humanitarian medical-relief programs. He is also a mountain rescue doctor and medical director with Portland Mountain Rescue and the Hood River Crag Rats, and medical director for Pacific Northwest Search and Rescue and Clackamas County Search and Rescue. He currently serves as public health officer and medical examiner for Hood River County.

More information is available at christophervantilburg.com, linktr.ee /christophervantilburg, and at cragrats.org.

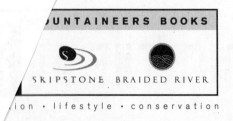

UNTAINEERS BOOKS

SKIPSTONE BRAIDED RIVER

...ion · lifestyle · conservation

lg

n

...**S BOOKS,** including its two imprints, Skipstone and Braided ...ublisher of quality outdoor recreation, sustainability, and conservation ...(3) nonprofit, we are committed to supporting the environmental and ...s of our organization by providing expert information on human-powered ...tainable practices at home and on the trail, and preservation of wilderness.

...ations are made possible through the generosity of donors, and through sales ...les on outdoor recreation, sustainable lifestyle, and conservation. To donate, ...e books, or learn more, visit us online:

MOUNTAINEERS BOOKS

1001 SW Klickitat Way, Suite 201 • Seattle, WA 98134
800-553-4453 • mbooks@mountaineersbooks.org • www.mountaineersbooks.org

An independent nonprofit publisher since 1960

YOU MAY ALSO LIKE:

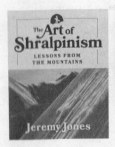

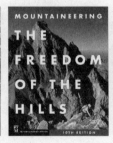